The Social Impact of the Asian Financial Crisis

The Social Impact of the Asian Financial Crisis

Edited by

Yun-Peng Chu

Research Fellow and former Director, Sun Yat-Sen Institute for Social Sciences and Philosophy, Academia Sinica and Adjunct Professor of Economics, National Taiwan University, Taiwan

Hal Hill

H.W. Arndt Professor of Southeast Asian Economies, Division of Economics, Research School of Pacific and Asian Studies, Australian National University, Australia

Edward Elgar

Cheltenham, UK • Northampton, MA, USA

Published by
Edward Elgar Publishing Limited
Glensanda House
Montpellier Parade
Cheltenham
Glos GL50 1UA
UK

Edward Elgar Publishing, Inc.
136 West Street
Suite 202
Northampton
Massachusetts 01060
USA

A catalogue record for this book
is available from the British Library

Library of Congress Cataloguing in Publication Data

The social impact of the Asian financial crisis / edited by Yun-Peng Chu, Hal Hill.
       p. cm.
    Includes index.
    1. Financial crises—Asia—Case studies. 2. Asia—Social conditions—Case studies.
    I. Chu, Yun-Peng. II. Hill, Hal, 1948–

HB3808 .S63 2001
306'.095—dc21

2001018970

ISBN 978 1 84064 546 0

Printed and bound by CPI Group (UK) Ltd, Croydon, CR0 4YY

Contents

Figures

Tables

Contributors

Yun-Peng Chu

Dr Chu is a research fellow and former director of the Sun Yat-Sen Institute for Social Sciences and Philosophy (ISSP) at Academia Sinica, Taiwan, Professor of Industrial Economics, National Central University (joint appointment), and Adjunct Professor, Department of Economics, National Taiwan University. He also served as the commissioner of the Taiwan Fair Trade Commission of the Executive Yuan. His published papers are found in such journals as *The American Economic Review*, *Journal of Development Economics*, and *Asian Economic Journal*, and co-edited books published by Routledge and Edward Elgar.

Hal Hill

Dr Hill is the H.W. Arndt Professor of Southeast Asian Economies at the Australian National University. His main research interests are the economies of ASEAN, especially Indonesia and The Philippines; industrialization and foreign investment in East Asia; and Australia's economic relations with the Asia-Pacific region.

He has authored/edited 12 books on these subjects, in addition to about 110 academic papers and book chapters. He is also an occasional invited contributor to several Australian and Asian newspapers and magazines, and has worked as a consultant for the Australian Government, the Indonesian Government, the World Bank, the Asian Development Bank, and several United Nations agencies. He has held visiting appointments at Gadjah Mada University, the University of the Philippines, the Institute of Southeast Asian Studies, the University of Oxford, and Columbia University.

Arsenio M. Balisacan

Dr Balisacan is a professor at the School of Economics, University of the Philippines Diliman. He is currently under-secretary at the Philippine Department of Agriculture. His research interests include poverty, income distribution, food security, and agricultural and rural development.

Rosemarie G. Edillon

Ms Edillon is a lecturer and doctoral student at the School of Economics,

University of the Philippines Diliman. Her research interests include poverty, mechanism design, and program monitoring and evaluation.

Medhi Krongkaew

Dr Krongkaew presently holds the positions of director in the Institute of East Asian Studies, Thammasat University, Thailand, director of Thai APEC Study Centre, Thammasat University, Associate Professor, Faculty of Economics, Thammasat University, Member, Board of Directors, East Asian Economic Association (EAEA). He served as the President of the Economic Society of Thailand from 1985 to 1989. He is the former Dean of the Faculty of Economics (1980–82) and former director of the Thai Khadi Research Institute at Thammasat University (1985–88).

Ishak Shari

Ishak Shari, a Professor of Development Studies, is the Director of the Institute of Malaysian and International Studies (IKMAS) at Universiti Kebangsaan Malaysia. He continues to conduct research on poverty and income distribution, particularly on the impact of globalization on these problems. Some of his published works include: *Development Policies and Income Inequality in Peninsular Malaysia* (1986; with Jomo, K.S.); *Development and Underdevelopment in Rural Kelantan* (1989; in Bahasa Malaysia); *The Fishermen Economy: Capital Accumulation, Technological Change and Economic Differentiation* (1990; in Bahasa Malaysia); *Technology and Social Change: Impact of Technological Change on Fishing Communities* (1993; with Chang Yi Tan). Professor Ishak Shari has also served as the President of the Malaysian Social Science Association.

Suk Bum Yoon

Dr Yoon is currently a professor in the Department of Economics at Yonsei University in Seoul, South Korea. Yoon's main research interests are in econometrics and comparative economic systems, particularly focusing on measuring income and wealth inequality, relative poverty income levels, and regional income distribution patterns. Yoon was president of the Korean Statistical Society and the Korean Econometric Society, and served as a member of the Monetary Board, Republic of Korea. He has extensively published books, journal articles and chapters in books published by the University of California, University of Hawaii, Scandinavian University Press, UNESCAP, the Asian and Pacific Development Centre, Kuala Lumpur, Griffith University, Australia, and Yonsei University, Seoul.

Preface

This book is the outcome of a research project supported by the Program for Southeast Asian Area Studies (PROSEA) and the Sun Yat-Sen Institute for Social Sciences and Philosophy (ISSP), both at Academia Sinica.

When the project was first initiated in 1996, there was little anticipation of the impending major crisis, and the focus was set on the social implications of rapid economic growth in the East and Southeast Asian region. The advent of the crisis gave the principal investigators a new angle, a new challenge, and a new responsibility. It also gave them an opportunity to apply their long-accumulated knowledge of the economies in question to the analysis of this new phenomenon. The result is this book, which explains how the crises began, how the economies were affected, how they coped, and what the social impacts have been.

The experiences in these various countries are important sources of knowledge. The crisis was a rare experience in which a sudden disturbance pierced through various economies at different stages of development and with assorted sociopolitical structures and institutions. Not unlike a major celestial event in astrology, the crisis gave us a precious glimpse of how economy and society interacted, as unveiled by the ripples of the impact.

The overview chapter will provide an overall observation of each country's experiences. Here I will only note some of the simplest regularities that seem to have emerged from these experiences.

In Thailand, where the crisis struck first, there appeared to be three important vulnerabilities. The first was excessive investment in real estate and other sectors of the economy. The non-performing loan ratio rose prior to the summer of 1997, and the situation was particularly bad among the finance companies which mushroomed in the 1990s. Many investors initiated investment projects in their efforts to jump on the bandwagon of 'fast-growing emerging markets'. Many of these projects were related to real-estate development. Commercial floor space in Bangkok already saw excess supply many months prior to 1997. Many large 'white-elephant' projects in other sectors and in other geographical areas of the economy suffered the same fate.

The second vulnerability was the excessive presence of short-term foreign capital in the foreign debt portfolio amidst a relatively freely mobile capital environment. Obviously, there would be a liquidity problem if for some reason such short-term foreign capital all decided to leave.

The third vulnerability was the handicap in collective decision-making that was associated with various institutional failures. The government is said to have suffered from weak leadership. The bureaucracy probably also suffered from an ill-prepared liberalization (inadequate supervision and monitoring), from its incapability to deal effectively with the above-mentioned flaws early on, and from behavioral improprieties by some of its members. So the third institutional vulnerability is actually an assortment of several weaknesses, all related to the behavior and politics of the collective decision-makers.

The above three vulnerabilities were connected and interrelated in Thailand. But this does not necessarily mean that they were both sufficient and necessary conditions of each other. The first vulnerability, which was associated with an overheated economy (or overheated sectors), could emerge quite independently of the other weaknesses, and has been one of the most frequently observed phenomena in all market economies. After all, isn't it what business cycles are all about? When overheating, often described as a 'bubble', develops, a vulnerability is present because it is not sustainable. There would definitely be a downturn, often called a 'landing'. The only question is whether the landing will be soft or hard, managed or unmanaged.

The bubble phenomenon was also present in Japan, whereas the second vulnerability did not exist. The boom-and-bust story of the real-estate sector in that country in the past decade did not have a happy ending, dragging the economy down for many years to the present day. In Taiwan, where the second vulnerability was also non-existent, the same sector experienced a similar downturn in the early 1990s, following a boom that began in the second half of the 1980s. The real-estate developers jumped on the bandwagon, both because of their optimistic prospects of the duration of the boom, and because there was an anticipated change in building regulations that would reduce the value of the land, if it were not developed quickly. The result was the presence of the boom-and-bust vulnerability, at least in the real-estate sector. This had much to do with the rising unemployment rate in recent years.

These cases reveal the importance of the management of landing in an overheated economy or in an economy with important overheated sectors. Here one begins to realize the significance of the US Federal Reserve Bank's determination in managing a soft landing in the first half of 2000.

The second vulnerability no doubt added to the difficulty of a managed landing in Thailand, but it is probably premature to point to the reliance on foreign capital as the origin of all sins. Developing countries do not have to be apologetic about their current account deficits, if domestic savings are not sufficient for worthwhile investments. However, the authorities should be very cautious about the misalignment of maturities, and should be prepared for the difficulties in exchange rate management that would arise in an environment of liberalized capital accounts, which the authorities themselves created. Neither aspect received enough attention from the relevant government agencies in Thailand, unfortunately.

The third vulnerability is more 'basic', in the sense that its presence would adversely affect the performance of an economy repeatedly and continuously. To the extent that market economies are bound to experience disturbances from within ('bubbles') and from without ('contagion'), it is very important that their collective decision-making is adequate to deal with such disturbances. The weaker, or less ineffective, or more corrupt the government is, the more likely it will make mistakes (by actions or the lack of them) in dealing with disturbances which would definitely be present somewhere down the line.

So the core of the issue seems to be the ability to manage disturbances in market-oriented economies. When the frequency and magnitudes of disturbances rise as a result of economic liberalization, the demand for capable management rises. Vulnerabilities developed into crises when the effective supply of capable management falls short of demand.

What happened after the crises struck? There were economic, social and political impacts, all of which were related to each other. These impacts could have led to ever worse scenarios — when crises hit, the demand for capable management would have been even higher than pre-crisis, so excess demand for capable management would have become ever larger. The economy could have slipped into long-term depression.

The alternative scenario is that institutions in the societies impacted by the crisis evolved in such a way that the capabilities of the authorities were strengthened (often involving changes in government, in institutions, in policies, or all of these). The twilight of recovery emerged, and, more importantly, the gap between demand for and supply of capable management was narrowed. It seems that most, if not all, Asian economies that suffered from the financial crises were able to manage a route that has been closer to this second, virtuous scenario.

It is not easy to understand why and how this has been so. But it is hoped that the following chapters will give us important clues. It is also hoped that this will be a harbinger of efforts that do not focus attention on the economic aspect of the crisis alone, but also on the aspect of the social and political institutions of the crisis.   Only by such an integrated approach can the process of economic changes be truly understood.

I previously mentioned the supporting institutions of this project. Here I would like to thank specifically the PROSEA at Academia Sinica, which under the leadership of Professor Hsin-Huang Michael Hsiao made this research effort possible.   I would also like to thank the Institute for Social Sciences and Philosophy at Academia Sinica, which included this research as one of its mid- to long-term research projects and helped to make possible the publication of research results.   Many thanks also to the participants at the two workshops held in Taipei, who gave valuable comments and suggestions.   Last but not least, I would like to thank Professor Hal Hill, who generously agreed to be the co-editor, Professor Medhi Krongkaew, who throughout the years gave us much guidance and support, as well as all the other principal investigators in this project.   I would like to extend my appreciation, too, to Marcia Pope for her assistance with this project. It has been a privilege working with everyone and learning from their insights.

Yun-Peng Chu
June 2000, Taipei

1. An overview of the key issues*

Hal Hill and Yun-Peng Chu

1. INTRODUCTION

The economic and financial crisis which erupted in East Asia in 1997 is one of the defining events of our time. It was largely unforeseen and unexpected. It affected countries which had experienced 30 years or more of almost continuously rapid economic growth. It caused much social dislocation and hardship. It was also instrumental in removing from office the seemingly impregnable leader of Southeast Asia's largest country.

Just as the unexpected ferocity of the crisis was unanticipated, so too has the recovery been surprisingly rapid. In the first year of the crisis, there was a general expectation that, in contrast to Mexico in 1994–95, recovery would be a slow process. According to this view, Mexico was pulled out of its crisis by the buoyant North American economy, and by a Washington-orchestrated bailout organized by the major international financial institutions. East Asia in 1997–98 appeared different, owing to its economic interdependence, the absence of economic dynamism in the region's major economy, Japan, for most of the 1990s, and the early difficulties with the International Monetary Fund. However, earlier fears of an 'L-shaped' recovery have given way to optimistic assessments that, like Mexico, East Asia's post-crisis trajectory will be 'V-shaped'.

Nevertheless, the notion that the crisis was simply a passing 'blip' in the long sweep of East Asia's development, which will soon just be of interest to the region's economic historians, is quite mistaken, for at least three reasons.

First, there has been great diversity in regional outcomes. Four countries were seriously affected by the crisis — Indonesia, Malaysia,

---

* We are indebted to our fellow authors in this volume, on whose work we have drawn freely. Thanks also go to the colleagues in Australia and East Asia for many illuminating discussions.

1

South Korea (hereafter referred to as Korea), and Thailand. Of these, one (Korea) has recovered extremely quickly since 1998, another (Indonesia) has bottomed out but has yet to experience a significant recovery, while the other two are registering modest progress. Among the 'non-crisis' economies, the outcomes have also been equally diverse. Taiwan experienced only a very mild slowdown. Australia, whose economy is more deeply connected with the region than any other non-East Asian OECD economy, actually experienced a slight acceleration in its already strong growth rate. China and Vietnam slowed down, but still recorded quite strong growth. The Philippine and Singaporean economies were stationary in 1998, the latter bouncing back quickly in 1999. Nor, as will be obvious from these examples, are there any simple correlates of the severity of the crisis. If the region's economies are divided into those which (a) were crisis-affected, (b) continued to register positive growth, and (c) recorded zero (or near-zero) growth, then within each group there are both high- and low-income economies, and those which are more and less outward-looking.

There is clearly no such thing as 'the Asian crisis'. It therefore follows that sweeping generalizations concerning causes, effects, and prognostications are of little assistance. Rather, what is needed is a more nuanced country approach, but one which nevertheless appreciates the importance of global economic factors and regional economic interdependencies.

The second reason the crisis and its aftermath will be with us for some time to come is that, although the early signs of recovery are encouraging, the problems left in its wake are serious. In the most adversely affected economy, Indonesia, the modern commercial banking sector is still hardly functioning, and very little progress has been made with private sector debt workouts. Major financial reforms are required in several other economies. Just as markets overreacted in 1997 and early 1998, it is quite possible that they have rebounded too quickly since late 1998. The possibility of a 'W-shaped' recovery cannot be discounted. A significant element here is that some of the reforms demanded by the international financial institutions and investors are longer-term and institutional, and intrude deeply into domestic political structures. Much of the crisis management of the past focused upon essentially macroeconomic targets and levers—principally the control of money supply and fiscal deficits, and exchange rate depreciation.

Under the new rules of the game, these foreign influences and dictates are much more intrusive, micro, and complex. They involve major reforms, affecting the legal system and the civil service. Institutions which in the now developed countries took decades to evolve and mature are now expected to function according to international standards in the space of just a few years. Allegations of corruption may well interrupt the inflow of foreign capital to an extent unmanageable a decade ago. Even human rights and democratic practices are under scrutiny. Democracy and good governance are of course inherently desirable. But a major question hangs on whether all the East Asian economies will be up to the task of reforming as rapidly as the new and challenging international environment demands.

The third factor is that so much of the crisis remains unexplained. Just when economists thought they had developed reasonably coherent and credible explanations for East Asia's extraordinarily rapid growth, now the focus is on explaining the sharp change in fortunes. There is also uncertainty about the social impacts of the crisis. Quick-release social indicators are difficult to obtain in all the crisis economies. Moreover, differences in economic structure and institutions are such that, for a given economic shock, social outcomes may diverge significantly. Of particular importance here is the presence of government-supported social services, and the flexibility of markets — especially the labor market — in response to economic decline. Finally, there is now much less consensus on some key economic policy issues. While all but Malaysia among the crisis-affected economies are constrained by IMF-imposed conditionalities, there is by no means a consensus on some key economic policy issues: what sort of exchange rate regime should be adopted? Should the international capital account be opened? How quickly should financial deregulation proceed?

To examine these issues, this volume presents case studies of six major East Asian economies — Indonesia, Korea, Malaysia, the Philippines, Taiwan, and Thailand. The group is thus nicely representative of the region. For example, and to identify just a few differentiating variables, it includes economies which: are rich and poor; were seriously and lightly affected by the crisis; experienced slow and high growth in the decade leading up to the crisis; were in and out of IMF programs; and were very open and still somewhat inward-looking.

Each chapter contains an analysis of the events leading up to and during the crisis, the social impacts of the crisis, and an assessment of the path forward. Reflecting the authors' interests and expertise, special attention is paid to the social impacts. Within this common framework, however, there are differences of approach, as befits particular country circumstances and challenges. For example, the chapter on Korea focuses on how to reform the country's conglomerates (Jaebol), and the corruption of the financial system — and politics more generally — which has resulted from that country's highly interventionist policy regime. In the case of Taiwan, one of the main thrusts is to understand how and why it largely escaped from the crisis. The Indonesian chapter draws attention to the wider political economy ramifications, and their contribution to the most serious economic, financial, and social breakdowns among the six. The Philippine and Thai chapters provide illuminating and detailed analyses of the social impacts of the crisis. The Malaysian chapter traces the events leading up to that country's controversial decision to deviate from IMF orthodoxy through the imposition of controls on the movement of short-term capital.

2. THE CRISIS: CAUSES AND TRENDS

Tables 1.1 and 1.2 provide a summary picture of the six economies prior to and during the crisis. Several features are immediately evident. One is the diversity of outcomes during the peak of the crisis in 1998, when growth ranged from −13.2 percent (Indonesia) to +4.6 percent (Taiwan).

Table 1.1 Key economic indicators, 1991–99 (%)

	Ind	Kor	Mal	Phil	Tai	Thai
GDP growth:						
1992–96	7.3	7.1	8.7	3.5	6.3	7.9
1997	4.7	5.0	7.5	5.2	6.7	−1.8
1998	−13.2	−6.7	−7.5	−0.5	4.6	−10.4
1999	0.2	10.7	5.4	3.2	5.7	4.1
2000 (f)	4.0	7.5	6.0	3.8	6.3	4.5
Inflation:						
1992–96	9.0	5.3	3.9	8.4	3.6	4.8
1997	6.6	4.5	2.7	5.9	0.9	5.6
1998	58.5	7.5	5.3	9.8	1.7	8.1
1999	20.5	0.8	2.8	6.6	0.2	0.3
Current account/GDP:						
1992–96	−4.3	−2.0	−6.7	−4.2	3.2	−6.7
1997	−2.3	−1.7	−5.0	−5.3	2.4	−2.1
1998	4.1	12.8	12.9	1.7	1.3	12.7
1999	3.5	6.1	14.0	9.1	3.0	9.1
Govt balance/GDP:						
1992–96	0.3	−0.3	1.7	−1.6	−6.5	2.5
1997	0	−1.5	2.5	0.1	−3.8	−0.9
1998	−3.7	−4.2	−1.9	−1.8	−3.3	−3.4
1999	−2.3	−2.9	−4.9	−3.6	−4.2	−3.0

Sources: various issues of IMF *World Economic Outlook*, JP Morgan, *World Financial Markets*, ADB, *Asian Development Outlook*.

Table 1.2 Comparative financial data, 1997–2000

(a) Exchange rate	30/6/97	1/1/98	1/1/99	1/1/00	8/3/00
(indexed at 1/1/97=100)					
Indonesia	103	343	341	305	315
Korea	105	207	142	134	132
Malaysia	100	178	150	150	150
Philippines	100	172	149	153	156
Taiwan	101	125	117	112	112
Thailand	98	204	143	145	147
(b) REERs	1996	1997	1998	1999	
(1990 =100, end of year)					
Indonesia	105	62	70	79	
Korea	88	58	71	78	
Malaysia	112	85	83	85	
Philippines	117	90	86	87	
Taiwan	95	95	82	84	
Thailand	108	76	90	83	
(c) Stock market	30/6/97	1/1/98	1/1/99	1/1/00	8/3/00
(index in local currency; indexed at 1/1/97=100)					
Indonesia	112	62	62	106	89
Korea	108	63	86	151	141
Malaysia	86	42	45	66	75
Philippines	89	55	62	65	52
Taiwan	129	113	93	128	135
Thailand	60	44	43	56	46
(d) Stock market	30/6/97	1/1/98	1/1/99	1/1/00	8/3/00
(index in $; indexed at 1/1/97=100)					
Indonesia	109	18	18	35	28
Korea	103	30	61	113	107
Malaysia	86	24	30	44	50
Philippines	89	32	42	42	33
Taiwan	128	90	79	114	121
Thailand	61	18	30	39	31

Notes: Stock market and nominal exchange rate data refer to the nearest weekly closing figures for the date indicated. Increases in the nominal exchange rates indicate depreciation, whereas upward movements in the real exchange rate series refer to appreciation.

Sources: *The Economist*, various issues, for stock market and nominal exchange rate data; JP Morgan for real effective exchange rates.

The second is the magnitude of the turnaround in performance from pre-crisis trend growth rates to the crisis year — almost 25 percentage points in the case of Indonesia's per capita growth rates, over 20 percentage points in both Malaysia and Thailand, and about 15 percentage points in Korea. Sudden collapses of these orders of magnitude are very rare in any era of global economic history, and they draw attention to attendant social stresses. There are, moreover, few parallels in these countries' own histories. According to Suk Bum Yoon, some Koreans believe that the pain and economic loss associated with the crisis were worse than those experienced during that country's traumatic civil war of 1950–53. The convulsions in Indonesia during 1965–66, which led to the emergence of President Soeharto's so-called New Order regime, were associated with a decline of economic growth of no more than 2 percent of GDP, a figure which pales into insignificance compared to that of 1998. Thailand had not experienced a year of negative growth since 1960. Malaysia's last recession, of 1985–86, saw negative growth of no more than 2 percent. With the obvious exception of the Philippines, these were not events with which East Asian governments and peoples had much experience. In part because economic crises in the region were rare, there was a complacency (and perhaps even an arrogance) on the part of the region's policy-makers, businesses, and researchers. The emerging warning signs which Latin Americans — long familiar with such crises — would take seriously were not given much currency in the region (Edwards, 1999).

A third important observation is that there was no generalized loss of macroeconomic control. Except for Indonesia, inflation remained at single digits in all countries, in spite of very large nominal exchange rate depreciations. This was so even in the Philippines, a country which has had an inflation-prone history. This reflected a combination of adherence to prudent monetary policy, cautious (and significantly foreign-financed) fiscal expansions, and the collapse of demand and cost pressures. Indonesia was very much the outlier in this respect, and its experience was a significant departure from the orthodox macroeconomic policy regime which had characterized the 32-year Soeharto regime. At the root of its problem was the loss of monetary control, itself the result of indiscriminate bank bailouts over the period November 1997 to April 1998. Once monetary discipline was re-established, inflation quickly disappeared.

Fourth, there was a major adjustment in macroeconomic balances to accommodate this exogenous shock. Particularly pronounced were the movement in current account balances. Pre-crisis, all except Taiwan were running current account deficits, some substantial. All the crisis-affected economies quickly shifted to surpluses. This switch was driven primarily by the capital account—new flows dried up, and there was substantial capital repatriation. Official capital flows increased, but these took some time to commence, and were in any case much smaller than the private outflows. In effect, the rest of the world was no longer willing to allow these economies to run a deficit. Current account transactions supported these outcomes. Exports remained roughly constant in dollar terms (implying substantial increases in volume and local currency terms), while imports declined sharply in response to depreciating currencies and collapsing domestic demand.

The current account adjustments, from the pre-crisis trend deficits to 1998, were very large in all four crisis economies—equivalent to around 15 percent of GDP in Korea, Malaysia, and Thailand, and 10 percent in Indonesia. In the Philippines it was nearly 10 percent, even though economic growth did not collapse to the same extent. Taiwan experienced a slight decrease in its surplus. These figures illustrate starkly the adjustment costs which can result from international financial integration. By themselves, they do not constitute a case for closing fully or partially the international capital account. But they do carry a warning that capital account convertibility needs to proceed with caution. It is possible—though debatable—that pre-crisis current account deficits in some of these economies (notably Thailand) were 'too large'. But it can certainly be argued that the surpluses imposed by these shocks were too large. A current account surplus equivalent to more than 5 percent of GDP can hardly be recommended as a correction measure if it is achieved primarily through economic collapse and social hardship.

Government budgets generally shifted in the opposite direction, although by smaller orders of magnitude. Governments of the crisis economies were generally running balanced budgets or modest surpluses pre-crisis. (Ironically, the two which managed to avoid the worst effects, the Philippines and Taiwan, had the largest deficits.) They all shifted, slowly at first, to deficits. The shift was for essentially Keynesian-style countercyclical reasons, with increased expenditure mainly directed towards social programs. The slow response was explained by a number of factors—initial (and illogical) IMF opposition to deficits, the innate fiscal conservatism of finance ministries, and, in the absence of functioning social programs, the difficulty of quickly increasing social expenditures. Even in very open economies, there is a case for an 'old-fashioned' fiscal expansion, the more so if it is substantially foreign-financed. It is important, however, to ensure that this expansion is strictly time-bound, and does not become built into the macroeconomic policy framework (Corden, 1999). As recovery proceeds, the challenge has very quickly shifted towards containing fiscal deficits. This is particularly so in Indonesia, given the huge cost of bank restructuring and looming fiscal decentralization, and in the Philippines, where chronic deficits have been a continuous problem for over 30 years.

Changing risk premia and capital flight had profound effects on the region's foreign exchange and financial markets (table 1.2). Both fell in dramatic fashion in the second half of 1997. In the Thai case, the fall in the stock market pre-dated (and in fact precipitated) the currency decline, as the Bank of Thailand squandered its international reserves in a vain attempt to hang on to the pegged rate. In the other countries, the two series generally declined at about the same rate. The principal exception was Indonesia, where the exchange rate collapse was simply calamitous. As Hal Hill points out, at one point, the rupiah fell to as low as 17,000/$, from a pre-crisis rate of about 2,500/$. No economy, obviously, could withstand changes of this order of magnitude, and especially one in which there were large and unhedged foreign currency borrowings. Until about October 1998, the exchange rate was such as to offer little prospect of substantial debt workouts. However, the low inflation and stronger rupiah since then have transformed Indonesia's immediate economic prospects from quite hopeless to extremely difficult but potentially manageable.

None of the other countries has experienced such violent fluctuations in their exchange rates and stock market indices. Both series deteriorated in the second half of 1997, generally bottomed in early 1998, improved in the first four months of 1998, deteriorated somewhat around the middle of that year, and then picked up again from about October 1998, with rapid gains in the months April–June 1999. There was some softening of markets in early 2000. Table 1.2 provides summary point-to-point indicators for four important series over this period: stock markets in local currency and US dollar terms, together with nominal (*vis-à-vis* the US dollar) and real effective exchange rates. By early 2000, exchange rates in the region's affected economies were typically 30–50 percent below those prevailing pre-crisis, with Taiwan by then hardly affected but Indonesia still well below pre-crisis rates. Even allowing for inflation differentials, this had resulted in a significant boost to competitiveness in the depreciated currencies, as revealed by the real effective exchange rate series. At the early stages of the crisis, at the end of 1997, real rates in the crisis four had declined by at least 30 percent. Through 1998 there was a general tendency towards appreciation, mostly through some strengthening in nominal rates, though in the case of Indonesia principally via inflation. By the end of 1999, real rates of the four Southeast Asian countries were still about 70–80 percent of end-1996 levels, whereas those in Korea and Taiwan had recovered to about 90 percent of these levels. Stock markets in domestic currency terms had recovered most of their losses, with Korea and Taiwan well above end-1996 levels. Although not as severely affected by the crisis, the Philippine stock market has performed about the same as Indonesia and Thailand, and much worse than Malaysia.[1] Measured in US dollar terms, the markets of these four countries were still well below the levels of end-1996, with even the best-performing (Malaysia) at just half the previous total.

There is now a very large literature on the causes of and early response to the crisis, and the case studies presented in this volume are generally consistent with, and augment, this literature. In analyzing this subject, it is useful to divide it into pre-crisis vulnerabilities, a 'trigger' or precipitating event(s), and the subsequent management of the crisis.

Since it all started in Thailand, Medhi Krongkaew's comprehensive analysis is a useful point of departure. As he is careful to emphasize, there was a number of factors behind the crisis, and it is difficult to single out one, or even two or three, as key explanatory factors. Among the interrelated factors identified were: (a) premature financial deregulation, resulting in a sharp difference between foreign and domestic interest rates, and poor financial supervision; (b) rigid commitment to a fixed nominal exchange rate (*vis-à-vis* the US$) even when, in 1996, export performance deteriorated notably; (c) declining quality in the key macroeconomic policy-making institutions; (d) supply-side constraints (particularly urban infrastructure and post-primary education) in the face of rapidly rising real wage rates; and (e) a series of exceptionally large current account deficits, driven mainly by record capital inflows, which almost inevitably led to a deterioration in the quality of investment at the margin.

Problems started to emerge in late 1996, manifested in capital outflows and a falling stock exchange. At this point, it appears that the Bank of Thailand mismanaged things by attempting to hang on to the nominal currency peg at all costs. Its clumsy attempt to hide the real level of foreign exchange reserves further complicated the problem. The rest is history. On 2 July 1997 it finally let the baht float, thus triggering the formal beginning of the region's crisis. The baht began to depreciate quickly, and by early 1998 it was less than half its pre-crisis rate.

A fortunate development was a change of government in November 1997. This brought to power the cautious but highly regarded Chuan Leekpai to power, and with it a regime more willing to confront the political obstacles to reform. Indeed, from the early stages of the crisis, Thailand established a close and cooperative relationship with the IMF, and was hailed as that institution's 'model pupil'. A change in leadership in Korea at the end of 1997 had a similarly beneficial effect in facilitating the reform process.

The ripple effects began to spread quickly. Capital flight and exchange rate depreciation affected not just the other three crisis economies, but the Philippines and even the seemingly impregnable Singapore economy. For a short period, in late 1997 and early 1998, economies beyond the region were also affected, although this proved to be short-lived.

There were elements of the Thai story in the other economies, too, but it is important to emphasize that each one exhibited distinctive features. In Malaysia, as Ishak Shari emphasizes, there was an extraordinarily rapid growth in credit and the stock market. Relative to GDP, its ratios of credit outstanding and stock market capitalization were among the highest in the world. The former in particular rendered it somewhat vulnerable since, with the onset of a crisis, its room to maneuver with interest rate policy (to defend the currency) was thereby limited.

In the case of Korea, Suk Bum Yoon's primary emphasis is on the highly politicized nature of government–Jaebol relations, manifested most of all in an underdeveloped, inefficient, and distorted financial sector and widespread corruption. One consequence was that these Jaebol generally had very high debt–equity ratios, well above international norms. Another was a tendency to select projects on the basis of political, rather than financial, considerations. Thus, Korea was particularly vulnerable to a crisis-induced increase in real interest rates. As in Thailand, the crisis also coincided with the emergence of real sector/competitiveness issues. Following its 1980s political liberalization, trade unions had become quite powerful and real wages began to increase rapidly. Against this backdrop, throughout the 1990s Korea was caught between the challenge of low-end competition in international markets, particularly from China, and the imperative to match Japan and others at the top end.

The clearest case of crisis mismanagement occurred in Indonesia. As Hal Hill shows, the authorities lost control of monetary aggregates, and for a short period hyper-inflation threatened. Perhaps more important, the ailing Soeharto regime lost the trust of both the Indonesian people and international capital markets. It flirted with a currency board proposal, which for a period terminated its relationship with the IMF. Although re-elected in March 1998, Soeharto's new cabinet contained some blatant patronage appointments, including his eldest daughter and his closest business tycoon. Rising fuel prices in May were the final trigger for massive student protests, which quite suddenly tipped Soeharto out of power, being replaced by his recently appointed Vice-President, Dr B.J. Habibie. Although he was president for almost 18 months, and he managed to restore macroeconomic stability, Habibie's government lacked legitimacy and widespread support. Dreadful ethnic and regional tensions persisted over this period. It was not until late 1999 that a respected administration was in place. In retrospect, the Indonesian tragedy was that, at the most difficult time in the nation's history, it was in important respects leaderless for over two years. It was this factor, more than any technical financial–economic problems, which explains the country's 'outlier' status during the crisis.

Why and how did the Philippines and, especially, Taiwan manage to come through relatively unscathed? There are both common elements and differences in their country experiences, to which Arsenio Balisacan Rosemarie Edillon, and Yun-Peng Chu respectively draw attention. One common element, often forgotten, is that both economies had experienced a financial crisis within the past dozen years. In 1990–91, the Taiwan stock price index fell precipitously, from a peak of 11,983 to a low of just 2,912 (though, puzzlingly, real-estate prices hardly declined). The economic crisis in the Philippines, 1984–86, crippled many financial institutions and corporations. The crisis in the Philippines had two important consequences: it prompted the government to introduce improved standards of prudential regulation and management; and it rendered financial institutions and investors more cautious than their counterparts in the crisis economies.[2] In Taiwan, it meant that the government was more prepared to take swift and effective rescue actions when financial institutions were in trouble.

A second common element is that both economies relied less than their neighbors on foreign savings to finance their investments. Historically, of course, this was for very different reasons. Taiwan has one of the world's highest savings rates, and has run large current account surpluses since the early 1980s. As a result, it has huge international reserves, and is therefore able to defend its currency with comparative ease. The Philippines, by contrast, has one of the poorest savings rates in East Asia. But the absence of a long boom in the 1980s and 1990s meant that it had not attracted large capital flows in the years leading up to the crisis. The 'benefit' of missing out on East Asia's boom meant that its bust was correspondingly smaller.

Arsenio Balisacan and Rosemarie Edillon draw attention to another important feature of the Philippines, which was also relevant to Indonesia. Owing to the El Niño-induced drought, Philippine agricultural value added declined by 7 percent in 1997. This occurrence was quite unrelated to the crisis, but, in both cases, it exacerbated its management: the rural sector was unable to play a role as a 'cushion' for the displaced workers from the modern urban economy who returned to their villages in search of employment.

One of the most controversial aspects of the management of the crisis, to which Ishak Shari draws attention, was Malaysia's imposition of short-term capital controls and a fixed exchange rate (to the US$) in September 1998. As he notes, although the government eschewed an IMF program, under the stewardship of the now-imprisoned Finance Minister it adopted 'IMF-like' policies during the first year of the crisis. The Prime Minister's disenchantment with these policies and his Finance Minister saw the adoption of a more radical policy approach from mid-1998. The large trading of Malaysian shares across the border in Singapore, and over which Malaysia had no control, was an additional factor.

In retrospect, the decision to impose capital controls has had consequences neither as catastrophic nor as beneficial as its critics and supporters predicted. Here the most relevant comparator is probably Thailand. Notwithstanding differences in their economic development and structure, the two have been quite similar in terms of pre-crisis indicators, depth of recession, and speed of recovery. Nor is there much difference with regard to the pace of fundamental reform of institutions and the policy-making framework. At the margin the terms on which Malaysia can obtain access to international capital markets may have been jeopardized a little, and there is an international perception that its reflation process has been biased towards Mahathir/UMNO-related business entities, at the expense of those associated with the deposed Deputy Prime Minister and non-UMNO groups. Moreover, one would hesitate to draw general lessons from its experience. Malaysia is a special case because (a) it is one of the developing world's most open economies (and thus a black market exchange rate is unlikely to develop); (b) it maintained its very open policy towards FDI throughout, and foreign equity investors showed little concern with the controls; and (c) the reflation process was managed with caution, and fiscal and monetary aggregates were kept in close check.[3]

The country chapters all essentially share the view that the IMF mishandled the crisis in its early stages, but by early 1998 it had adjusted quickly to the new reality. That is, the Fund apparently was no better prepared for the crisis than anyone else; and its initial policy prescriptions emphasized fiscal austerity, as though it was dealing with profligate 'Latin American' governments (table 1.1 shows such a notion was quite mistaken). The Fund fairly quickly adopted a more accommodating approach to fiscal policy, and one year into the crisis its concern had shifted to one of urging governments to reflate faster. There is also a legitimate worry that the conditionalities have been too intrusive, and not centrally related to the Fund's principal mandate of averting and resolving balance of payments crises. For example, it is not obvious that an environmental law, a competition commission, or gender equality – to mention just a few elements of the conditionality packages — are key elements of a recovery plan, however desirable they may be. There is also a genuine suspicion in the region that the Fund is an instrument for OECD government interests in forcing open markets in East Asia.[4] Finally, as Malaysia has shown, it is possible to recover without an IMF package.

Nevertheless, for all these criticisms, the Fund is clearly an important part of East Asian reform and recovery. No other institution could have played the coordinating role that it has, in facilitating increased bilateral donor support and reassuring jittery financial markets. It is also arguably the case that the Fund has played an important policy anchor role in some countries, in ensuring that a coherent macroeconomic policy framework is maintained. Indonesia from mid-1998 is probably the best illustration of this proposition.

Finally, the interrelated issues of contagion and interdependence are also assessed in this volume. The initial transmission of contagion effects was clearly through the capital account. Indonesia and Thailand each take less than 2 percent of the other's merchandise exports, and so trade effects cannot account for the rapid spread of the crisis from Thailand to Indonesia and elsewhere. The mechanism was obviously risk perception: the notion that the two countries were sufficiently 'similar' that what happened in one could easily happen in the other. However, once these financial effects began to feed through into a slowing real economy, the current account story of strong trade interdependence does become relevant.[5] That is, these current account effects impinged on all economies, regardless of whether they were able to survive the initial capital account effects. There was thus a second round of negative shocks throughout the region, felt most of all in 1998, which contributed to the regional economic slowdown. Conversely, as economies began to recover from mid-1999, the resultant acceleration in trade growth hastened the process.

3. SOCIAL IMPACTS

A key contribution of this volume is its analysis of the social impacts of the crisis. As in the previous section, there are significant differences among our six-economy sample. Much obviously depends on the severity of the economic crisis. But in addition labor market structures and institutions, the capacity of governments to provide emergency social assistance, and pre-existing social conditions have all shaped the social outcomes. In addition, there have been various country-specific factors at work, to which we also draw attention.

It needs to be emphasized immediately that any assessment of social impacts is akin to shooting at a moving target. There is at least a three-month lag for quick-release social indicators, and more commonly 6–12 months. Often the quick-release data are of dubious quality, and of little more value than knowledgeable 'casual empiricism'. The various social indicators – poverty incidence, education enrollments, health status, nutrition, crime – do not necessarily move in the same direction. Nevertheless, it is possible to paint a reasonably rich and comprehensive picture, and also to suggest how the policy and data monitoring frameworks might be improved. We discuss these social impacts under four broad headings, of which the first two are arguably the most important and the best documented.[6]

3.1 Poverty and Inequality

The incidence of poverty rose in all cases where there was a significant economic slowdown. Using non-uniform poverty lines, and recognizing that the estimates during the crisis period are very approximate, we get a picture something like the following in the four most affected countries. The percentage of the population in poverty rose from about 11 percent to 18–20 percent in Indonesia, as would be expected the sharpest percentage increase among the four.[7] In urban Korea it rose from 9 percent to 19 percent. The impact in Malaysia appears to have been quite mild, with just a 1–2 percentage point increase from the pre-crisis estimate of 7 percent. Something similar is thought to have occurred in Thailand (from 11.4 percent to 12.9 percent, 1996–98), although as Medhi Krongkaew points out, the more relevant comparison might be the crisis estimate compared to what the figure would have been in the absence of the crisis. Instead of an increase in the poverty incidence of up to 13 percent, the rise then becomes almost 20 percent.

As important as the aggregate estimates are the impacts on particular groups and variables and the various social mechanisms for ameliorating these effects. All chapters discuss these issues where relevant, with the most detailed analysis provided by Arsenio Balisacan and Rosemarie Edillon, based on a rich data panel. They conclude that poorer households were disproportionately affected by price increases as compared to better off ones. They also draw attention to several other differential effects, to be noted shortly. In Thailand, it is thought that the very poor may have been the most adversely affected.

It is less clear what happened to inequality. Here the key determinant may be the extent of urbanization and industrialization. In Korea inequality apparently rose, whereas in Indonesia it seems to have fallen. In the latter case, the heaviest impacts were felt in urban Java, particularly in construction, manufacturing, and financial services, and many in these sectors were non-poor. By contrast, after the drought, and boosted by the large devaluation, the rural sectors — where the poor are disproportionately located — were able to survive more easily. But in Korea, the sharp rise in unemployment presumably widened the gap between rich and poor, given that relatively few opportunities exist outside the urban formal wage-employment sector.

Adjustment mechanisms have displayed some common patterns. In the Philippines, and especially in poorer households, longer hours were worked, and eating patterns changed (for example, less meat was consumed). Once again it is important to note that the conclusion is complicated by the effects of the serious 1997 drought. With its well-established labor export patterns, seeking employment abroad was more readily an option for its people than any other in our sample.

3.2 The Labor Market

Here the impact on employment was the largest in Korea. Suk Bum Yoon reports that unemployment rose sharply, from virtually full employment (2.1 percent) to 8 percent. In Indonesia, unemployment and underemployment hardly rose according to official estimates, as was also the case in Malaysia. The Philippines and Thailand adopted intermediate positions, but were closer to Indonesia.

One major factor affecting these outcomes was the flexibility of labor markets, and whether the primary adjustment mechanism to the onset of the crisis was in prices or quantities.[8] In all cases it was a bit of both — real wages did decline somewhat in Korea, while there was a marginal rise in Indonesia's unemployment. But the primary distinction was falling real wages in Indonesia, in the range 30–50 percent in 1998 (Manning, 2000), in contrast to rising unemployment in Korea. The general presumption, other things being equal, is that adjustment will be easier, and the social impacts less harmful, the more flexible are prices. Whether price flexibility is socially and politically acceptable in higher-income economies like Korea is of course another question.

As with rising poverty, the effects across different groups of workers and attributes varied considerably. In general, those with higher levels of education were more likely to experience increased unemployment in economies severely affected by the crisis. This reflects the impact of the crisis on the sectors in which they were employed, such as finance, property, and R&D-intensive industry. In the Philippines, the rise in unemployment was most pronounced in Metro Manila. In both that country and Malaysia, the gender effects impacted most severely on women.

Ishak Shari notes importantly that Malaysia's labor market has been cushioned somewhat by the very large migrant worker presence, estimated to be as much as 20 percent of its workforce. That is, in addition to the fact that it was a labor-scarce economy pre-crisis, adjustment was facilitated as much as anything else by simply repatriating some of these workers, and prohibiting new entrants. In reality, the process was not that simple: many of the migrants are illegal anyway, and therefore not easily removed, and in deference to Malay solidarity, Malaysia moderated its repatriation policy in recognition that conditions in the major source country, Indonesia, were far worse. On a per capita basis, the largest source of migrant labor in our sample is the Philippines, but because its migration patterns are so well established, and diversified across countries, the crisis did not exert a major negative impact on its labor market.

Since Taiwan largely escaped the crisis, it experienced little by way of negative labor market impacts. But as Yun-Peng Chu observes, the mini-financial turbulence in Taiwan triggered by the asian financial crisis exacerbated the unemployment problem, which mainly resulted from the recession in the construction industry, as the unemployment rate rose to about 3percent in 1998, the highest since 1985. Using both single-year unemployment data and a cross-year panel data of prime-age working people, he notes that unemployment was more severe among the lower-educated manual laborers in the construction industry. So its pattern is very different from the other crisis-struck economies where the higher-paid, high-end workers in the urban areas suffered the most.

3.3 Other Social Impacts

Education and health impacts have generally been negative, but by how much remains unclear. In the Philippines, Balisacan and Edillon report that the withdrawal of children from school was 'widespread' amongst the poorest 20 percent of the population. In Indonesia, there is hardly any evidence of departures from trend enrollment ratios, although quality (and levels of absenteeism) may have suffered. It is too early to discern any significant health impacts, although more expensive pharmaceutical products and frequent press reports of greater resort to traditional health providers and practices are suggestive of problems.

It is too early to be sure about the effects on *regional disparities*. But, generally, the higher the share of agriculture in a region's economy, the less serious the impact of the crisis has been. This is so because the rural economy was less connected to the modern financial sector, and because agriculture — especially its traded, export-oriented segments — has benefited from East Asia's exchange rate depreciations. Since these regions also usually had below average incomes, interregional disparities have thus narrowed as a result of the crisis. This process has most obviously occurred in Indonesia, but it has been evident to some extent in all countries. Whatever the merits of greater regional equality, however, this is hardly a desirable trend, since it has been a 'levelling down' rather than a 'lifting up' process. In both Korea and Thailand, there was also return migration to the rural areas in search of employment; in the latter it is thought that a measure of 'rural resilience' lessened the adverse social impacts of the crisis, particularly as much of the urban migration was quite recent. Conversely, the fact that all these economies have become rapidly more urbanized and industrialized over recent decades suggests that retreat to the traditional rural economy is now much less an option that it was in the past, even in Indonesia.

The only country in which severe ethnic and communal tensions have been evident is Indonesia. During 1997–98, a series of nasty anti-Chinese incidents occurred, most especially during the breakdown in civil order in May 1998 which triggered the hasty departure from office of President Soeharto. This ethnic tension has greatly complicated Indonesia's reform and recovery process, since the Sino Indonesian community, numbering 3–4 percent of the population, controls perhaps around 40 percent of the economy, in addition to being a major conduit for foreign investment. In Malaysia, where the memories of the May 1969 ethnic disturbances linger on, there is considerable pride that the crisis did not heighten intercommunal relations.[9] There have been other severe social tensions, including simmering Christian/Muslim differences throughout the country, manifested tragically in the distant eastern province of Maluku, and between the local Dayak community and immigrants from Madura in the province of West Kalimantan. As noted also, Indonesia is the only country to have experienced serious regional difficulties. East Timor voted to secede, an opportunity given to it in the wake of the political crisis, while in the provinces of Aceh and Irian Jaya (now renamed West Papua) the pressure for extensive autonomy, if not independence, remains ever-present.

The evidence also suggests that, *among firms of different size*, small–medium enterprises (SMEs) have generally been less affected. Here too the intuitive explanation is that these operations have 'benefited' by being less connected to the modern financial sector. In addition, they are much less likely to have borrowings denominated in foreign currencies; they are more likely to produce essentials (for example, food products), whose production has fallen less than in the luxury goods industries; and they are generally more nimble and less top-heavy than their larger counterparts. Where they have also established an export capacity, some SMEs have actually done very well out of the crisis.[10] Some writers, observing a boom in the SME and informal sectors (and some of agriculture), have drawn the inference that there has not been an economic crisis of any significance. However, such a normative judgement is quite inappropriate, since it is often overlooked that these are generally low-productivity (and wage) activities, and that what is really happening is a process of involution and rising poverty, of which this growth is a symptom.

Crime is reported to have risen in all the crisis-affected economies, particularly in urban areas. Again, Indonesia has probably been the worst affected, owing to the general breakdown in its social and political order for a period, and to its more severe economic contraction.

3.4 The Policy Framework

How quickly and effectively were governments able to respond to the social challenges thrown up by the crisis? Here too the evidence is mixed. In both Indonesia and the Philippines, there were major political distractions, a massive political transformation in the former, and a six-yearly presidential election in the latter.

In the Philippines, the survey results indicate that poor households received some government assistance. But so too did non-poor households, and in any case this assistance was not as great as that from friends and relatives. This suggests that the government had difficulty targeting its social assistance, and that informal networks — in particular through the extended family — were more important than official programs. Both conclusions almost certainly apply to the other lower-income economies.

With governments already under serious fiscal stress, real remuneration in the civil service declining, and bureaucracies possessing limited experience in devising and implementing social safety net (SSN) programs, it is not surprising that problems of poor targeting and corruption emerged. These criticisms do not necessarily constitute a convincing case against the various SSN initiatives, however. Targeting is everywhere a problem, even in rich countries with long experience and well-resourced bureaucracies. Moreover, some schemes seem to have worked quite well. One example is scholarships for the poor, where the responsibility is devolved to local educational institutions and the subsidies are modest. The results of various public works programs have been mixed, but on balance these are probably worthwhile initiatives.

It is important not to lose sight of the fact that the only sure way to overcome the social hardship is through a return to growth. On this criterion, Korea must be judged the most successful in our sample.

4. LOOKING TO THE FUTURE

Two sets of interrelated issues are relevant in considering future trends. First, how rapid and durable will the recovery be? Second, what are the major policy challenges and how substantial has reform been thus far in the crisis-affected economies? We alluded above to the region's unexpectedly fast recovery since mid-1999. We therefore focus here on the second of these questions, since it – along with the state of the (now buoyant) international economy – will largely shape the post-crisis growth trajectory.

By way of background, tables 1.3 and 1.4 provide some context to the magnitude of the challenges. Table 1.3 draws attention to the financial restructuring task in the four most affected countries. More than two years into the crisis, non-performing loans (as a percentage of total portfolios) remained unacceptably high, especially in Indonesia and Thailand. NPLs will decline as economic growth resumes, and as they are taken over by

Table 1.3 Financial sector restructuring

	Indonesia	Korea	Malaysia	Thailand
NPLs: I (%)	31.4 (9/99)	17.9 (5/99)	19.4 (5/99)	47.1 (7/99)
NPLs: II (%)	12.4	11.3	12.4	47.1
NPLs: III (%)	60–85	20–30	20–30	50–70
Closures:				
Banks	66 out of 237	none	none	1 out of 15
Other financial Institutions	n.a.	117	none	57 out of 91
Public funds for recapitalization	$27.6 bn	$36 bn	$1.6 bn	$20.6 bn
% of GDP	58	16	10	32
Existing weaknesses	many weak banks	many weak NBFIs	difficult to assess	some weak banks

Notes: Non-performing loans (NPLs) are as a percentage of total loans. 'NPLs I', 'NPLs II', 'NPLs III' refer respectively to estimated actual ratios on the dates indicated, to the ratios after transfers to asset management corporations, and to the peak estimates during the crisis.

Sources: World Bank (2000), p. 5; ADB, *Asian Development Outlook 2000*.

asset management corporations. But the latter requires complex negotiation procedures, and shifts an element of the problem on to the government's fiscal problems. Some bank restructuring has already occurred, as institutions have been closed or merged. But the public funds required for this process to be successfully completed are very large, especially in the context of budgets which are under pressure to meet other economic and social goals, and during a period of low growth when it is more difficult to meet fiscal targets. Here also Indonesia and Thailand stand out. Moreover, many of the existing banks remain very weak and undercapitalized, even after the initial rounds of reform.

If governance and institutional reform are the key challenges of the crisis economies, table 1.4 indicates that in some cases the starting-point is very low. According to the surveys on which these findings are based, the rule of law is considered to be weak and corruption rife in Indonesia and the Philippines. Only in Malaysia and to a lesser extent Taiwan is the judiciary regarded as competent. In no case are accounting standards particularly high. Among the lower-income countries, various commercial risks have to be factored in. These assessments, generally obtained during the boom times of the 1980s and 1990s, would no doubt be a good deal less favorable if judged by contemporary opinion.

Table 1.4 Legal and institutional ratings

	Ind	Kor	Mal	Phil	Tai	Thai
Rule of law	4.0	5.4	6.8	2.7	8.5	6.3
Judiciary	2.5	6.0	9.0	4.8	6.8	3.3
Corruption	2.2	5.3	7.4	2.9	6.9	5.2
Risk of expropriation	7.2	8.3	8.0	5.2	9.1	7.4
Risk of contract repudiation	6.1	8.6	7.4	4.8	9.1	7.6
Accounting standards	n.a.	6.2	7.6	6.5	6.5	6.4

Notes: Variables are scored in a range of 0 to 10. Higher scores indicate higher assessments in the case of the rule of law, judicial efficiency, and accounting standards variables. A lower score indicates more corruption and a higher risk of expropriation and contract repudiation. Data generally refer to the period 1982–95. For more explanation, see the source, and the original material on which it is based.
Source: Khan (1999), pp. 24–5.

It will be useful to assess future prospects according to a few key indicators of policy performance.

4.1 The Macroeconomic Policy Framework

This is probably the most encouraging facet of economic performance in the wake of the crisis. In no country is inflation now a serious problem. Except for Indonesia, monetary discipline was maintained throughout the crisis, and it does not appear to be threatened anywhere. As a corollary, exchange rate regimes are contributing to the maintenance of competitiveness. The latter is an important achievement, as these economies have managed the difficult transition to new arrangements, having abandoned the old fixed-but-adjustable regime. In most cases, reasonably free floats have been instituted, sometimes under IMF tutelage. Earlier fears that floating regimes would be plagued by instability have not thus far materialized, and the longer these regimes are maintained without difficulty, the more the market and the regulators will become accustomed to them. Malaysia's approach also worked quite satisfactorily albeit, as noted earlier, in part owing to its unique circumstances. These are transitional arrangements, and in the future Malaysia will most likely either adopt the fixed rate along with reasonably permanent restrictions on the movement of short-term capital, or switch over to a more flexible system.

4.2 Fiscal Sustainability

The other pillar of macroeconomic stability, fiscal policy, has also performed well, and some fiscal stress will be relieved as growth-induced 'automatic stabilizers' reduce deficits. However, the fiscal challenges remain daunting. The most serious arises from various banking restructuring and recapitalization programs, and in minimizing their impacts on government expenditure. There is clearly a case for government intervention to revitalize the banks, but the danger — especially in Indonesia and Thailand — is that private debts will be socialized and eventually funded by taxpayers. Since the amounts are potentially very large (see table 1.3), the region's exemplary history of fiscal caution could be jeopardized, and expenditure on necessary public goods could be squeezed. The continuing difficulties in the Philippines post-Marcos could be indicative of things to come elsewhere. In addition, emergency foreign aid, which had risen during the crisis, is beginning to taper off as recovery proceeds. It will therefore be important to ensure that the SSN initiatives do not develop their own, durable constituencies, which prolong their existence after their useful life. Internationally, it appears likely that interest rates will rise during 2000 and possibly beyond, thus putting further stress on public sector debt service. Finally,

Indonesia faces a very challenging period as it negotiates various decentralization reforms, which will entail handing back a significant portion of central government resources to the provinces.

4.3 Legal and Civil Service Reform

This is perhaps the most difficult challenge, the more so in the poorer Southeast Asian countries, to which the following comments are mainly directed. Whereas macroeconomic policy entails adjustment of a few key policy levers, and is somewhat more insulated from sectional interests, the more micro the policy reforms, the more difficult the process. Civil services in the crisis economies cannot be reformed quickly, yet they are the key to implementation of much of the reform agenda laid out by international donors, and demanded by more strident legislatures. Even more so in the wake of the crisis, public sector salaries are uncompetitive, especially at upper echelons. Promotion is based mainly on seniority, rather than competence. Deep-seated bureaucratic cultures are resistant to change, particularly if their access to resources and power are threatened.

The legal system is central to resolving much of the debt crisis. If debtors believe that there is little likelihood of successful prosecution – because of political protection, legal corruption, or simply tedious procedures – then they have little incentive to negotiate. The operation of bankruptcy courts in Indonesia and Thailand thus far suggests that debt workouts will be painfully slow, thus holding back the injection of new funds and therefore the pace of economic recovery. The problem here does not appear to be the quality of the law, but its implementation. This may be overcome in part by specialized training of judges and court officials. But, as with civil service reform, the problems go deeper than this. There is a vast gap between the salaries of judges and top lawyers. The court system itself is massively underresourced. There are few legal precedents and case histories on which to base judgements. Land titles and other forms of collateral are poorly defined, while auditing quality is still generally weak. And in the case of disputes there is an inclination to side with domestic debtors, particularly if the creditors are large multinational corporations or wealthy non-indigenous citizens.

There also appears to be a naïve expectation that the democratization process which has gathered strength in the wake of the crisis will automatically ensure that old problems of corruption will quickly abate. While it is unlikely that the highly personalized authority and corruption of figures such as former Indonesian president Soeharto will be repeated, corruption is likely to remain an ever-present problem. Civil society remains weak. Civil services as noted remained underresourced and unresponsive. Attempts to decentralize power and finances away from central governments, while in principle desirable, may in the short term actually exacerbate the problem, as new and inexperienced administrations subject to even fewer checks and balances than those at the center suddenly have substantial resources at their command. As the experience of the Estrada Administration in the Philippines seems to suggest, even a very democratic process, a vigorous and free press, and a talented cabinet cannot easily solve deep-seated problems of cronyism.

4.4 Whence Industry Policy?

Korea pre-crisis was frequently hailed as a case of a successful 'interventionist' industry policy. While there were no doubt many successes in the past regimes, anybody reading Suk Bum Yoon's chapter in this volume will be convinced that there is no going back to the old system of highly politicized interventions through the credit market and other incentives schemes. In other countries, it is unlikely that governments will want to revisit their spectacular industry policy disasters. There is very little support for the proposition that selective industry assistance — via tariffs, fiscal incentives, credit subsidies, and so on — has paid off. Indeed, very often the most assisted industries have performed the worst. Moreover, constrained budgets, privatizations and IMF-mandated trade liberalizations are removing many policy options in this area.

Not all forms of selective intervention in East Asia have been unsuccessful. In Singapore, with its very open economy, well-paid bureaucracy and fierce anti-corruption campaigns, it may well be that certain selective interventions have paid off — such as the goal of establishing the country as a major electronics center, and pushing the industry to upgrade quickly. Taiwan is noted for its innovative R&D programs, many of which have been commercialized through its flexible SME-dominated industrial structure. Agricultural extension programs in several Southeast Asian countries have successfully induced farmers to innovate, especially in the adoption of higher-yielding varieties. The real challenge for the policy-makers in the region is to identify genuine cases of market failure, and to develop programs which do not exceed domestic bureaucratic capacities. The weaker these capacities — and most in the region's poorer countries at the micro level are weak — the more likely the problem of government failure overshadowing that of market failure.

NOTES

1. One explanation is not crisis-related. The Philippines experienced a serious and prolonged market scandal from late 1999, which pushed prices down more than occurred in neighboring markets.

2. Conversely, the prolonged stock exchange scandal in the Philippines, which emerged in late 1999 and, at the time of writing (March 2000) has yet to be resolved, casts doubt on that country's financial regulatory capacity.

3. See Athukorala (2000) for an extended discussion of these issues.

4. In the words of Suk Bum Yoon, a widespread Korean perception was that the IMF 'more or less represented the interests of the superpower economies rather than trying to revive the Korean economy'.

5. For example, in 1998 East Asia accounted for the following export shares among our six economies: Indonesia – 53 percent, Korea – 38 percent, Malaysia – 48 percent, Philippines – 41 percent, Taiwan – 42 percent, Thailand – 42 percent.

    In passing, it might also be noted that it is sometimes conjectured that a contributing factor to the Philippines escaping the worst effects of the crisis is that the booming US economy absorbs the largest share of its exports (34 percent) among any East Asian economy.

6. For general surveys and analyses of the social impacts of the crisis, see Booth (1999) and Knowles, Pernia and Racelis (1999).

7. The range of initial poverty estimates was also the greatest in Indonesia. As Hal Hill shows, during 1998 the estimates of poverty incidence rose to as high as 48 percent. Part of the explanation for this range was the difficulty of computing estimates during a period of accelerating inflation. Flawed methodologies, and even a policy agenda for which it was advantageous to overstate the severity of the impacts, also contributed to the confusion. By 1999, better data and cooler heads contributed to more accurate figures (see Suryahadi et al., 1999).

    Medhi Krongkaew also notes an initial tendency to overstate the negative social impacts of the crisis in Thailand.

8. See Manning (2000) for a more formal treatment of this issue, followed by detailed empirical application to Indonesia. It needs to be noted that, while the most important dimension of labor market flexibility, mobility (sectoral, spatial, occupational) is also a significant variable.

9. Some argue that the country's affirmative action program (the New Economic/Development Policies) contributed significantly to its greater social harmony. While this is probably true, it needs to be recognized that Indonesia's political and economic stresses over this period were much greater.

10. For one such successful Indonesian SME case study, of the Jepara (Central Java) furniture-makers, see Sandee, Andadari and Sulandjari (2000).

REFERENCES

Athukorala, P.-C. (2000), 'The Malaysian Experiment', in P. Drysdale (ed.), *Reform and Recovery in East Asia: The Role of the State and Economic Enterprise*, Routledge, London, forthcoming.

Booth, A. (1999), 'The Social Impact of the Asian Crisis: What Do We Know Two Years On?', *Asian-Pacific Economic Literature*, 13 (2), pp. 16–29.

Corden, M. (1999), *The Asian Crisis: Is There a Way Out?*, Institute of Southeast Asian Studies, Singapore.

Edwards, S. (1999), 'On Crisis Prevention: Lessons from Mexico and East Asia', in A. Harwood, R.E. Litan, and M. Pomerleano (eds), *Financial Markets and Development: The Crisis in Emerging Markets*, Brookings Institution Press, Washington DC, pp. 269–334.

Khan, H.A. (1999), 'Corporate Governance of Family Businesses in Asia: What's Right and What's Wrong?', *ADB Institute Working Paper 3*, Tokyo.

Knowles, J.C., E.M. Pernia, and M. Racelis (1999), 'Social Consequences of the Financial Crisis in Asia', *Economic Staff Paper* No. 60, Asian Development Bank, Manila.

Manning, C. (2000), 'Labor Market Adjustment to Indonesia's Economic Crisis: Context, Trends, and Implications', *Bulletin of Indonesian Economic Studies*, 36 (1), pp. 105–36.

Sandee, H., R.K. Andadari, and S. Sulandjari (2000), 'Small Firm Development during Good Times and Bad: The Jepara Furniture Industry', in C. Manning and P. van Diermen (eds), *Indonesia in Transition: Social Aspects of Reformasi and Crisis*, Institute of Southeast Asian Studies, Singapore, pp. 184–98.

Suryahadi, A., Sudarno S., Y. Suharso, and L. Pritchett (1999), 'The Evolution of Poverty during the Crisis in Indonesia, 1996 to 1999', *Working Paper*, Social Monitoring and Early Response Unit, Jakarta.

World Bank (2000), *East Asia Quarterly Brief*, 31 January, East Asia and Pacific Region, Washington DC.

2. A tale of an economic crisis: how the economic crisis started, developed and is ending in Thailand*

Medhi Krongkaew

1. THE CRISIS

It was the best of times, then it was the worst of times. It was the age of wisdom, then it was the age of stupidity. It was the season of light, then it was the season of darkness. It was the era of new hope, then it was the era of despair. It was the beginning of bold ideas, then it was the end of bold ideas. It was the rise to richness, then it was the fall into poverty. We had everything before us, then we had nothing before us. We were experiencing the advent of economic prosperity, a dizzying boom, which had disintegrated into economic crisis, a pitiful bust. In the short period of two years, Thailand had gone from a promising and lively economy to a wretched economy, simply struggling to survive.

We need this Dickensian opening to dramatize and capture the seriousness of the crisis. To be sure, no one had really expected or predicted that this kind of crisis would happen in Thailand. Some might have had an inkling that the Thai economy would experience some problems associated with its huge current account deficit in early 1997, but the crisis of the existing magnitude was something no one in his or her right mind would think possible. When the Thai government announced its unpegging of its currency from the US dollar-denominated basket to a managed float system, some would call this the outcome of a currency crisis. When the financial system of Thailand was also debilitated as a result of the run of the banks and finance companies and huge losses from

*An earlier version was presented at the Workshop on Economic Crisis and Impacts on Social Welfare organized by the Program for Southeast Asian Area Studies (PROSEA), Academia Sinica, Taipei, 14–15 June 1999.

27

banking operations and massive outflows of foreign capital, the currency crisis had become a financial crisis. But when the economy had sharply contracted with widespread business collapses and job losses, the financial crisis had become an economic crisis. We need a clearer definition of economic crisis, of course, but no one would doubt that what Thailand had experienced from July 1997 onward was anything but an economic crisis, no matter how strict the term crisis is defined.

In the past two years, several Thai and non-Thai scholars and researchers have written about this economic crisis in Thailand.[1] These authors have had different ways of analysing the Thai crisis and presenting their findings. It is difficult to say whose view and analysis capture the truth or essence of the Thai crisis. It is the duty of the reader to distinguish between which factors are more important than the others in causing the crisis, or how effective one policy measure is over the others, or how long the crisis will run until some semblance of economic recovery is experienced. Therefore, there can never be an over-explanation of the Thai crisis. Different assignment of weight to different causes or factors will elicit different policy responses which will result in different outcomes, or the same outcomes but with different speeds of adjustment or correction. This chapter is like that. It will give the reader a view on the origin of the current Thai economic crisis, the course of development of the crisis, the effectiveness of the government's policies to counter these problems, and the consequences of this crisis on the Thai people as a whole.

2.   THE CAUSES

Before the collapse of the baht defense in July 1997, many economic experts still believed that the economic slowdown in 1996 and the first half of 1997 was still nothing near the severity of the economic crisis of the first half of the 1980s. As is well known, the Mexican peso collapsed towards the end of 1994, leading many international analysts to speculate that Thailand could be the next Mexico because it was suffering from a severe and chronic current account deficit of the same magnitude as Mexico. That had generated a series of rejections and rebuttals from the Thai authorities saying that there were many differences between Thailand and Mexico (see box 1), such that the likelihood of Thailand being another Mexico was remote. The situation at the end of 1995 could warrant this confidence, but the situation in 1996 and 1997 could not. The succession of events in 1996 and the early part of 1997 had worked to bring about the economic collapse in July 1997.

Box 1: Why the Bank of Thailand Did Not Worry Too Much About the Current Account Deficit Earlier On

It is now well known that one of the factors that brought about the collapse of the Thai economy in 1997 was its inability to shake off its large and chronic current account deficit (CAD). Although no one would argue in defense of this large and chronic CAD, the Bank of Thailand, the Thai monetary authority, did try to allay the fears about it, as the following account shows.

A major financial crisis broke out in Thailand in January 1995. An article appeared in the *Asian Wall Street Journal* which analyzed the reasons behind the Mexican financial crisis and the subsequent collapse of the peso, and attempted to link the Mexican economic conditions with those of Thailand, particularly the similar chronic balance of current account deficits that might lead to the same currency devaluation. This had an immediate devastating effect on the confidence of several foreign investors in the Thai stock market as they began to dump their large stocks in the domestic market, effectively triggering panic selling in all markets. The fear of baht devaluation generated a massive rush to convert the baht to US dollars, putting serious pressure on domestic liquidity and dollar reserves. The Thai authorities had to announce that devaluation would not happen, and various emergency measures were put in place such as the injection of money through repurchase market and loan windows, and a 24-hour swap facility between baht and US dollars. These measures brought back the investors' confidence, and the crisis was over within a few weeks.

It is true that such a deficit is large and chronic, but can it be said that this level of deficit in a growing and dynamic economy like Thailand is unacceptable? The crisis in January 1995 and the subsequent calming down of the stock and exchange markets after strong reaction by the Thai authorities had proved that the root cause of this event was a crisis of confidence rather than a real crisis. This was indeed the position of officials of the Bank of Thailand, who wanted to give the impression that although Thailand's current account deficit was large it was not unsustainable. What was the basis for this thinking? And how valid was it?

In its first issue of a new publication called *Bank of Thailand Economic Focus* published just before Christmas 1995, the Economic Research Department tackled the problems of Thailand's current account deficit head-on. It first gave its analysis of the causes of the high deficit in 1995 by noting the following three important features:

1. With exports rising strongly by 25.3 percent – almost double the growth of world trade in volume terms, the rise in the trade deficit in 1995 did not reflect a change in Thailand's international competitiveness. Instead, it reflected the strength of domestic demand, as well as the effects of other temporary factors.
2. Among the various demand components, private investment was perhaps the most important factor behind the growth in imports and the deficit. Private consumption and other temporary factors such as government imports were also important, but secondary, factors.
3. A terms of trade shock caused by a surge in the price of raw materials as well as the appreciation of the yen and the Deutsche Mark during the first half of the year also contributed importantly to the deficit through higher import prices. Import price in local currency was estimated to have increased by 10 percent during the first nine months.

Based on the above interpretation, the Bank raised an important question whether the deficit was sustainable; that is, could it be managed without seriously risking the overall health of the economy? Sustainability, of course, is often assessed in terms of the cause of the deficit, the financing of the deficit, the strength of the real economy, and the soundness of the economy's overall financial position. Under these criteria, the Bank was of the opinion that the present current account deficit was sustainable, and the following evidence was given:

- The deficit reflected the strengthening of investment and not increased consumption;
- The deficit occurred against the backdrop of strong GDP and export growth;
- In the absence of fiscal problems, Thailand's fiscal position was strong;
- High-quality capital inflows more than financed the deficit;
- Thailand had high international reserves and low external debt.

The Bank of Thailand said in conclusion, therefore, that the current account deficit in 1995 should not be allowed to mask the strong economic fundamentals of the Thai economy. It pointed out that during the past three decades, Thailand had recorded perhaps one of the most impressive macroeconomic performances in terms of growth and stability. Real GDP growth averaged 7.7 percent annually, with inflation averaging 3.3 percent. This strong performance was facilitated by a number of important attributes that continue to remain: tradition of cautious and conservative financial policies; liberal and outward-looking trade and investment policies; high saving ratios; large and expanding domestic market; able pool of human capital; and a governance that encouraged private sector development with minimum government intervention.

With the benefit of hindsight, it was obvious that the Bank of Thailand had made a grave error in predicting a strong export growth and economic expansion in 1997. This mistake had led to its defence of the baht in 1997. By early 1997, the future of Thailand lay in the hands of currency speculators. There was nothing anyone could do to prevent the impending doom. This was the crisis that Thailand had to have.

2.1 Contributing Factors

There are at least six factors that contributed to the 1997 economic collapse. Each of these factors will be discussed in turn as follows.

(a) Financial sector mismanagement
Partly as a result of the economic boom in the latter half of the 1980s and partly as a result of the financial liberalization of the Thai monetary authorities in the early 1990s, financial institutions in Thailand, especially commercial banks and finance companies, and private individuals and companies, were given vast opportunities to engage in high-risk, high-return property and stock markets. Lending was made to the real-estate sector and to property developers in large number without much scrutiny as to the economic worthiness of the projects in the long run. This was possible because the money from foreign sources was abundant and cheap, and the desire of many financial institutions, especially finance companies, to maintain their market share of commercial lending caused the loans to be approved quickly and much caution was thrown to the wind. Real-estate projects such as office buildings, condominiums, housing villages, golf courses, and other recreational property development projects mushroomed in the late 1980s and the early 1990s. Because of the rising economic prosperity with the rising income of the people, the demand for these immovable properties (and also movable

properties such as cars) also increased, pushing the prices of these properties higher. These high prices and high profits further generated more investments from old and new developers, and the credit supports from the banks and finance companies. This is a classic example of how a bubble economy is created. Realizing the over-investment in these areas, in 1994 the Bank of Thailand attempted to slow it down by making it more difficult for the banks and finance companies to lend for property development purposes, but this was the case of policy that is too little and too late. When the economy slowed down in 1996, property development was more or less at its peak. The reduced demand saw the oversupply of property units, and the growing inability of property developers to service their debts to the banks or finance companies, or, in some cases where loans were raised offshore, to foreign creditors. The Thai financial sector was swamped with non-performing loans (NPLs). It was reported that at the end of June 1997, about 12 percent of bank loans and 20 percent of finance companies were non-performing, worth in total about 1 trillion baht or about 20 percent of GDP.[2]

The above only applies to one property sector. There are other business and investment activities that showed Thai industrialists, entrepreneurs and investors in very aggressive investment movements.[3] These aggressive activities gave an aura of success, at least in the short run. They showed how bright and innovative such people are.[4] Of all the new employment opportunities in Thailand in the early 1990s, none could be more profitable than to work in finance companies. The salary scale was at least twice that for other private employments requiring similar skills, and in some finance companies, the annual bonuses were 12 to 18 months of salary. When these finance companies collapsed, the highly paid workers were caught in a dire state because they were already used to the life of high spending.

Failure in commercial banks and other financial institutions is nothing new; it has happened before. But bank failure had never come before an attempt by the monetary authorities to rescue the threatened institution. Until the 1997 collapse, it was a standing philosophy of the Thai monetary authorities, in this case, the Bank of Thailand, not to allow a public financial institution to go under for fear that the public would suffer and the erosion of confidence could hurt the financial system and the overall economy.[5] With the state acting as an implicit partner in an investment or business operation, the relative risk of these banks or finance companies became much less. This has created what Paul Krugman called the problem of moral hazard in the investment decisions of these financial intermediaries.[6] They became bolder and underestimated the repercussions of a business failure (or overestimated the likelihood of success) because the perceived certainty of government or public bailout figured prominently in their investment decisions. The crisis was brought on when the government had exhausted its bailout money, or suddenly realized that it had used too much money and was not willing to keep on doing it. Panic set in and the run on the existing banks or finance companies started, hastening crisis in other sectors as well.[7]

It may appear as if the supervisory system is not working well in Thailand. On a closer examination of the supervisory system practised at the Bank of Thailand, it is quite obvious that the framework and mechanism of financial institution supervision are in place and working. The Bank has more than 300 examiners looking after the commercial banks and some other 200 examiners looking after non-bank institutions both on-site and off-site. The real problem may lie not with the lack of professional expertise of monitoring or supervising good banking practices, but with what to do and how fast the correction is once irregularities are discovered. It is often believed that the first serious banking crisis started with the Bangkok Bank of Commerce in late 1994, when questionable loans were granted to questionable people, and the top bank management itself used the bank funds for improper activities. The governor of the Bank of Thailand himself was implicated in this impropriety through his personal friendship with the management personnel of BBC, and through this connection and the inability of the Central Bank in dealing with growing problems in the financial and property sectors, the governor was forced to resign. That may have some part to do with the tardiness of the central bank action in redressing the problems occurring in this bank: not only that the bank management and other related parties were not legally persecuted right away, but that the bank had received several billion baht worth of financial assistance from the Financial Institution Development Fund (FIDF). It was believed that if this BBC crisis was dealt with resolutely and quickly in early 1995, further problems in the banking and finance sector may have been lessened and the crisis could have been avoided.

(b) Current account deficit (CAD)

It may be true that the CAD of Thailand at the end of 1995 was as sustainable as the Bank of Thailand had claimed (see box 1), but the economic conditions of the country had deteriorated a great deal after that, putting pressure on the confidence of foreign investors and encouraging international speculators to attack the baht. We know that there are two components of current account, the trade balance and the service balance. The trade balance is almost always in deficit for Thailand, whereas the service balance is almost always in surplus, but the trade deficit is so much larger than the service surplus that the overall current account is almost always in deficit, as mentioned earlier. And this deposit is growing bigger. At the end of 1996, the CAD for Thailand stood at about 372 billion baht or about 7.9 of GDP for that year. This was in fact an improvement over the level of 1995 where the CAD reached 8.0 percent of GDP, but as can be seen later, the outlook was not good, as the export growth of Thailand was in decline at the end of 1996.

Although it could be argued that the majority of imports into Thailand were mainly for investment, not consumption, the line between the two is not clear. The bank ATM machine is probably classified as an investment good, but so many of these imported machines widely available to the Thai users at almost every street corner may put the worthiness of this investment in a doubtful light. The conspicuous consumption of such expensive items as passenger cars, mobile telephones and foreign travel all work against a sound current account balance. The Thais are simply spending beyond their means, or at least the means of the country to finance it out of its own savings. They live on money borrowed from other people's savings, and the chronic CAD is a constant reminder of a long-term saving–investment gap. If and when the creditors no longer believe in the credibility of the Thai borrowers and want their money back, the economy will be in trouble. This is partly what happened in Thailand with regard to the CAD.

Theoretically, there are many ways of reducing the CAD. The trade balance can be improved by increasing exports and cutting imports, and the service balance can be enhanced by reducing service payments while increasing service receipts. The relaxation of exchange control as part of broader financial liberalization in Thailand made the above difficult to achieve. The economic boom of the latter half of the 1980s and earlier 1990s had created a spreading group of the 'new rich', especially in Bangkok, where conspicuous overconsumption had become the norm. It is this group of people who have suffered most from this current crisis because their sources of income suddenly disappeared through job losses and weakened currency.

(c) High domestic interest rate and uncontrolled capital inflows

Since the First Plan, economic growth has been one of the most, if not the most, important objective of government leaders and policy-makers. When the economy is in crisis, and the desired growth cannot be obtained, the Thai authorities will try to stabilize the economy quickly so that growth can resume. Income distribution or concern about poverty and social welfare has never taken priority over these two economic objectives in modern Thai economic history. In the case of Thailand, like many other developing economies, there are saving and foreign exchange shortages. Therefore, to generate domestic growth quickly, the authorities may induce or attract foreign capital inflow by setting the domestic interest rate higher than the overseas interest rate. Assuming that the capital movement is unrestricted or unrestrained, the interest differential between the domestic and foreign markets will induce the inflow of foreign capital.

But the role of the high domestic interest rate in inducing the inflow of foreign capital is not without cost. By raising the cost of money domestically (through a high interest rate), local investors will find it less attractive or more difficult to invest or take risks. The beneficial effects of foreign capital could be offset as a result. Moreover, the uncontrolled inflow of foreign capital could create the feeling and atmosphere of easy money, prompting wasteful or uneconomic overspending. Excess inflow of foreign capital also puts pressure on the local currency to appreciate, which could hurt its export performance. Although the monetary authorities could sterilize or neutralize the adverse effects of capital inflows, this sterilization or neutralization policy may not always work. The hidden danger of easy inflow is that it can also lead to easy outflow, with devastating effects if the inflow is used unwisely.

All things considered, it seems that the benefits of a high domestic interest rate in enticing capital inflow to spur growth have outweighed the costs in the eyes of policy-makers. The adoption of a high interest rate also works to calm the internal inflationary pressure which is another very important objective of the monetary authorities of Thailand. As long as there is a threat of inflation, the monetary authority of Thailand is likely to maintain a tight monetary policy, of which a high interest rate regime is one of the policy measures.

(d) The rigidity of the exchange rate

The exchange rate regime of Thailand has gone through several changes in its modern history. It was fixed to the British pound and gold in the 1920s but was forced to cut the link when the global economic crisis in the aftermath of the Great Depression made it impossible for the government to maintain its convertibility to gold. It went back to the gold standard again after the devaluation in the early 1930s, which goes to show that the British influence and sentiment of a fixed exchange rate was very strong in Thailand. Discounting the untypical period during and after the Second World War, the baht remained fixed with gold and, later, the US dollar until the oil price crisis in the early 1980s. When again forced to devalue against the US dollar in 1984, the Bank of Thailand 'abandoned' the fixed exchange rate system with the US dollar and adopted a system of exchange rates based on a basket of currencies. But since the US dollar is a major currency in the basket, and the BOT has the full authority confidentially to adjust the weight of each currency in the basket, the fixed exchange rate with the US dollar still remained in practice. Therefore, the baht went up and down with the US dollar. At times, Thailand benefited from an undervalued currency when the US dollar depreciated, as in 1995, but it also suffered an overvaluation when the US dollar appreciated, as in 1997.

Politically, the devaluation of the baht has very limited appeal, and no Thai government wants to do it unless there is no other choice. Devaluation was often looked upon as the government's failure to manage the economy, and the political fallout could be severe. The monetary authorities themselves also may not like devaluation because devaluation means instability in the exchange rate system. Experiences or even hints of devaluation or a movement away from the certainty of the fixed exchange rate system may affect external trade and investment. This is the same as saying that the fixed exchange rate system had served the country well in the past, in bringing about confidence and certainty in individual or firms' economic decisions, in reducing the cost of business operations when the fear and uncertainty of exchange rate fluctuations are removed, and in promoting the continuous growth path of the economy.

But in the globalized world of today, where fund managers and international speculators can move in and out of any country and any currency quickly, a fixed exchange rate system can be subject to short-term speculative attacks. Unless the country is well supplied with foreign exchange reserves and its economy is in healthy shape, no country can escape a concentrated attack that could bring that currency down. In the case of Thailand, although the size of its foreign reserves at the end of June 1997 was quite large (about 37.8 billion US dollars), which could deter speculators, its economy was ailing, and the deterrence did not work. When the US dollar appreciated in early 1997, the baht had gone up with it, and it was obvious to everyone that the baht was overvalued and must eventually depreciate. With no remedy to the present economic conditions in sight, the pertinent belief was not whether the baht would depreciate or devalue, but when.

Several waves of attacks on the baht were encountered in foreign exchange markets in London, New York, and Singapore in December 1996, February 1997, and May 1997. Each time the Bank of Thailand was reportedly able to repulse the attack without yielding to the pressure to devalue the baht. The Thai monetary authorities actually even helped facilitate contracts to sell US dollars forward to domestic as well as international buyers. This is like bluffing in the game of poker when an air of confidence (of having a good hand) may deter the attackers. The speculative attack in May 1997 was quite interesting in the sense that after the contracts were made, the Bank of Thailand reverted to a measure of currency control by closing the offshore transaction of the baht. This, in effect, created a two-tier exchange rate system where the baht was no longer available outside Thailand. A contract made offshore must secure the baht for forward purchase within Thailand, which had become exorbitantly expensive. In short, the speculators got badly burned with this financial ploy. But the position of the Bank of Thailand was not tenable; the economy was too weak to sustain continuous attacks like these. So, in late June, when practically all of the foreign reserves of Thailand were committed to forward contracts, the baht could no longer be defended. The prime minister was consulted and eventually agreed to delink the baht from the US dollar. They called this a flotation of the baht, not a devaluation of the baht. But instead of floating, the baht started to sink from that day onward.

(e) Lack of economic leadership from political leaders

Note that the prime minister was consulted at the last minute to float the baht when the country could no longer hold on to the baht defense. In the eyes of many outsiders, it may be desirable that politicians be kept out of important economic decision-making, and the technocrats and bureaucrats given free rein to decide on economic policies. In theory, this is as it should be, so that the independence of such policy-making organizations as the Bank of Thailand be upheld and not tampered with. This principle and practice had worked well in the past. However, the current economic crisis has shown that the Bank of Thailand had made mistakes by not dealing with banking irregularities resolutely and in a timely manner, by defending the baht for too long, by injecting too much money into rescuing failed banks and finance companies, and by not being able to control or regulate the borrowing and spending of private companies and financial institutions, especially from overseas.

There is no question about the professionalism and integrity of the high-ranking personnel of the Bank of Thailand, but these able technocrats had few opportunities to come into contact with other technocrats or intellectuals outside the Bank. Many important decisions by the Bank were made by a few high-ranking officials without the benefit of outside inputs, opinions, and ideas. Decisions such as whether or not or to what extent the Bank should spend to rescue the currency or financial institutions were some of those decisions. A system that basically maintains the independence of these monetary authorities but at the same time provides more transparency in the way these decisions are made, and opportunities for necessary participation from other government bodies, especially from knowledgeable (and honest) political leaders who have to live by their performance records, may be an improvement over the present system.

There is a danger that the above suggestion be misinterpreted as a proposal for an unrestrained intervention by political forces. On the contrary, it is a suggestion for reforms on both sides. While the technocrats and bureaucrats are to be given required independence, they need to be told that they must be accountable for what they have done and allow others to share their views or participate in the process of decision-making when possible or feasible. The politicians also will have to be reformed. The political system should be reformed until there is a reasonable chance that honest and able politicians are given the opportunities to run the country. In the present internationalized world, the concept that any politician can run any ministry in Thailand is not only outdated but dangerous. The new political leaders must be able to understand the more complex economic situations and participate more actively in economic decision-making in conjunction with the more accountable technocrats. The practice of inviting outsiders who are not professional politicians to come in to run the country should also be phased out because these outsiders cannot provide long-term solutions to the system. The long-term solution must be found in a system where good people are able to enter politics and become good leaders.

(f) The decline in export performance
In an open economy like Thailand, where foreign trade is very important for the health of the economy, export growth or the lack of it can spell boom or gloom to the overall economy. The growth of exports of Thailand had been consistently quite high throughout the latter half of the 1980s and the first half of the 1990s. In the 10-year period from 1986 to 1995, the average growth rate of Thai exports was 22.4 percent, with the lowest growth rate of 13.0 percent recorded in 1993. In 1996, however, Thailand suffered a drastic drop in its exports, a drop which was much larger than many had expected. The export growth rate of Thailand in 1996 was only 0.4 percent over the export level of 1995. The detrimental effects of this export slowdown include not only the ensuing slowdown in the overall economic growth rate, but perhaps more importantly, the serious erosion of confidence in the Thai economy from within the country as well as from outside it. Some may even go so far as to say that it does not matter how large the current account deficit is; as long as the exports keep growing at a reasonable rate which is greater than the import growth rate, there should not be any genuine cause for concern. Certainly what

happened to the Thai export growth rate in 1996 was not like that, and indeed this slowdown in the export growth rate was the last straw that broke the back of the Thai economy.

There were many reasons for this slowing down of Thai exports. Kakwani and Medhi Krongkaew have shown in tables 2.1 and 2.2 that there were great changes in both the composition of Thai exports to the world market and the contributions of various groups of exports to the total growth rate. In table 2.1, for example, there was a drop in the share of labor-intensive exports of Thailand which, in the early 1990s, was the largest group of exports from Thailand, from 25.4 percent to 22.0 percent between 1995 and 1996. In table 2.2, it was shown that this drop in the export of labor-intensive products gave the highest negative contribution (−3.26 percentage points) to the overall growth rate of exports for 1996. On further investigation, Kakwani and Medhi Krongkaew found that Thailand had lost the market share of these labor-intensive products (especially textile products and footwear) to China. Perhaps this loss of cost competitiveness to China was something to be expected because of the generally lower wage structure in China and the large devaluation of the Chinese currency in 1994.

Apart from the rise in real wages in Thailand, other reasons for the slowdown in Thai exports in 1996 could include the slowdown in the demand for Thai exports from importing countries, the high costs of Thai exports that came as a result of congestion and a shortage of infrastructure, and real appreciation of the Thai baht against the Japanese yen in 1996. Interestingly, it had been argued also that the fast slowdown of the Thai exports was a result of falsified export data for the purpose of value-added tax rebate.[8] If this is true, then the true export value of Thailand in 1995 would be about 150 billion baht less than the reported level, which means that the true export growth rates of Thai exports for 1995 and 1996 would have been about 10.4 and 11.4 percent, respectively, not 23.6 and 0.34 percent as officially reported.

At any rate, the apparent impact of export slowdown was drastic. When these data were reported towards the end of 1996, many people started to panic. With the current account showing no improvement, the economic position of Thailand weakened. The baht came under repeated attacks, and capital started to flow out. In December 1996, Thailand recorded a deficit in its balance of payments for the first time in many years. The property market remained in the doldrums with no solution in sight, and many large finance companies showed serious signs of breaking down through their inability to service their debts. The instability of the government under General Chavalit Yongchaiyudh offered no help as his economic management team began to unravel. The speculative attacks on the baht in February and May 1997 had crippled the Thai defense of its currency. On the early morning of 2 July 1997, the government announced the unpegging of the baht to the US dollar. The crisis began.

Table 2.1 Composition of Thailand's exports to the world

	1992	1993	1994	1995	1996
Primary agricultural products	20.3	17.1	16.8	16.0	15.8
Agro-industry products	10.5	8.8	8.7	8.8	9.3
Labor-intensive products	31.2	29.2	28.0	25.4	22.0
Medium–high-tech products	30.3	34.2	35.7	37.6	39.4
Mineral products and fuels	0.7	0.5	0.5	0.4	0.6
Others	7.0	10.2	10.2	11.9	12.8
Total	100.0	100.0	100.0	100.0	100.0

Source: N. Kakwani and Medhi Krongkaew, National Economic and Social Development Board (NESDB), 1996.

Table 2.2 Contribution to Thailand's total export growth rates

	1993	1994	1995	1996
Primary agricultural products	−0.81	3.24	2.94	−0.09
Agro-industry products	−0.42	1.72	2.10	0.55
Labor-intensive products	2.17	4.71	3.31	−3.26
Medium–high-tech products	8.71	9.05	10.73	1.98
Mineral products and fuels	−0.14	0.08	0.04	0.17
Others	4.59	2.12	4.50	0.99
Total	14.09	20.91	23.62	0.34

Source: N. Kakwani and Medhi Krongkaew, National Economic and Social Development Board (NESDB), 1996.

3.   THE COURSE

Much had happened during the crisis — much more than many had thought or even imagined. When the Bank of Thailand was fighting with currency speculators such as George Soros and other hedge fund managers throughout 1996 and early 1997, most Thais never realized that their lives were at stake as almost all of the country's foreign reserves were gambled away in the international currency markets in so short a time and by so few people. Later on, the Thai people were told also that close to 800 billion baht were used by the monetary authority to keep afloat the operations of more than half of all finance companies in the country at the time, plus some commercial banks. When these finance companies and commercial banks eventually failed, the losses were beyond anyone's comprehension. Roughly 30 percent of GDP was wiped out in a period of a few weeks. These events were used to make the point that this enormous financial mismanagement had shocked the country into incredulous panic and massive retractive actions.

First, when the government was told, for the first time, that the country has less than 3 billion US dollars left after the failed attempt to defend the baht, it had no other choice but to replenish the country's foreign reserve quickly or the trading and overall economic systems would collapse. Then it had promptly to attend to the problems in the mismanagement of banking and finance sectors to restore the confidence of the depositors who were already running on the banks. Bad finance companies, and later bad commercial banks, were closed down permanently and their assets liquidated to help pay back their debts to the monetary authority. As more than half of the finance companies were closed down, this put an immediate and tremendous squeeze on many commercial and industrial establishments who depended on these finance companies for their credits. They could not turn to the commercial banks either, as the government became very strict about the ways these banks lent and managed their lending. Commercial loans became scarce and interest rates became very high, as a necessary measure to prop up the value of the domestic currency and keep foreign capital at home. With foreign capital starting to flow out of the country with blinding speed and viability of business enterprises in doubt (as seen through continuous downgrading of their credit ratings), it was difficult to get money anywhere. The era of easy and cheap money from overseas was over.

With no money to run the existing businesses, or to pay back the debts that became due, many of these enterprises folded. Those who could survive did so through cuts in operations and employment. Staff, sales, and factory workers were retrenched, or wages and salaries reduced. Even the public servants who were not major players in the above events and were, on the whole, not directly affected by the crisis, were troubled by the cut in government fringe benefits and stringent control on their official operations brought about early on by the government's attempt to trim its public expenditures. Hardest hit were, of course, the employees of the finance companies which were closed down. Several thousands of these workers had enjoyed large salaries and bonuses in the olden days of the bubble economy. The chance of returning to the old glorious past was slim even if and when the economy emerged from the gloom of recession.

Why? What had led to this sorry state was excess in the private sector: excess in careless borrowing; excess in careless investment and spending; excess in not planning for the future, and so on. The new economy is certain to have a public sector that is alert and unlikely to allow the private sector to fall into similar excess again. The private sector will also be in a situation where competition will be keener but more transparent, so that only those who are economically efficient will survive. In this respect, the present crisis will serve as a very good lesson for everyone concerned.

Before we jump ahead of ourselves in the final analysis of the current economic crisis, let us slow down a little and look back at what had happened to various economic aspects in different economic sectors. The following aspects will be discussed in turn: exchange rate and balance of payments, external trade, interest rate and credit expansion, production, price, employment, and investment.

(a) On the exchange rate and balance of payments

The floating of the baht on July 2, 1997 signalled the defeat of Thailand against international speculators and fund managers. It would be several weeks after this that the Thai people were informed of the full extent of the disaster. During the first attack on the baht in December 1996, the Bank of Thailand lost about US$0.9 billion. In February 1997, it lost another US$1.1 billion, and in May 1997 another US$4 billion. The defence of the baht also took the form of forward swap contracts which amounted to US$4.75 billion by the end of 1996. This increased to US$ 12.2 billion by February 1997 and US$25.5 billion by May 15, 1997. With total foreign exchange reserves of US$32.4 billion remaining at the end of June 1997 and US$400–500 million reportedly flowing out daily, free foreign exchange reserves (total foreign exchange reserves net of forward obligations) dropped to an alarming level. The Bank of Thailand had no choice but to float the baht.

Thus began the free fall of the baht. As can be seen from table 2.3a, the average exchange rate of the Thai baht against the US dollar was 30.27 baht for July 1997 compared to 25.78 baht for June 1997. The baht continued to weaken throughout 1997, reaching the lowest point on January 8, 1998, when 55.5 baht was exchanged for one US dollar. In six months, the baht had lost more than half of its original value. After

January 1998, the baht started to strengthen. This came partly as a result of the original overshoot of the exchange rate and the high interest policy to keep existing capital in Thailand and to induce inflows of new capital. By April 1998, the baht had appreciated to a level below 40 baht for one US dollar. It had, however, fallen to a level between 42.36 and 40.41 baht during June–September 1998, mainly as a result of the weakening of the Japanese yen. From October 1998 onward, the baht had stabilized around 36–38 baht for one US dollar. The stabilization of the baht seemed to have materialized during the last quarter of 1998.

The weakened baht had had an almost immediate effect on the current account balance. From the deficit in the vicinity of 8 percent of GDP, the current account of Thailand had turned into surplus in September 1997, mainly as a result of the increase in exports, especially in volume terms, and the drastic fall in imports. This surplus in the current account balance continued to grow every month from September 1997 onward, reaching its highest level at US$1.502 million in February 1998. The surplus had maintained at a level over 1 billion US dollars every month until a year later in March 1999, when a beginning of the economic recovery caused imports to increase faster than exports.

The surplus in the current account balance did help compensate the enormous outflow of foreign capital in the aftermath of the baht flotation. As mentioned earlier, capital had already started to flow out in late 1996 when the economy experienced its first sign of difficulty through the slowdown in exports. According to Dr Pichit Likhitkitsomboon, an economist at Thammasat University who has been following the capital movements in and out of Thailand, there were private capital outflows of approximately US$2 billion monthly throughout the second half of 1997 and the whole of 1998. In 1997, THB274.6 billion (US$7.3 billion) of private capital flowed out of the country, most of it towards repaying debts and withdrawals from non-resident baht deposit accounts. Consequently, private external debt declined to US$67.3 billion at the end of 1997 from US$73.7 billion at the end of 1996. Private capital registered a net outflow throughout the first ten months of 1998, amounting to US$12.0 billion as against US$2.9 billion for the same period of 1997. Apart from the largest monthly net outflow of US$2.6 billion in January 1998, July and October also exhibited large net outflows of US$2.2 billion and US$2.4 billion, respectively. These were a result of Thai corporations paying back their foreign debts. On the other hand, the current account deficit fell to 0.8 percent of gross domestic product in 1997 while consecutive monthly current account surpluses have been registered since September 1997 as imports collapsed by 30 percent per annum. Thus the current account deficit, which had been the norm for Thailand during the last three decades, turned into a surplus large enough to compensate for the private capital outflow and resulting in a small balance of payment surplus of US$0.7 billion for the first ten months of 1998.

(b) On trade

From table 2.3a–2.3d it may be seen that the crisis had caused drastic changes in the ways Thailand traded with the outside world. As a result of the floating and subsequent depreciation of the baht, imports had become much more expensive to the Thai people, so that the demand for these imports fell as early as August 1997. Coupled with the government and others' calls for patriotic gestures of 'buy Thai' and the natural slowing down of import demand in time of crisis, the value of imports dropped dramatically. In June 1997, the import value stood at 5,892 million baht, falling to 3,590 million baht in July 1998. With exports continuing to grow in volume terms (though not in US dollar value terms because the rate of currency depreciation was very high), the trade balance began to show surpluses starting in September 1997. Surpluses in trade in goods and also in services helped eliminate current account deficits from September 1997 onward, as mentioned earlier. During that month, the current account deficit had turned into a current account surplus of US$81 million, and this surplus continued unabated, reaching the highest level with US$1,502 million in February 1998. However, the crisis that had directly affected the confidence of foreign investors had caused these capital owners to pull out from Thailand, resulting in continuous capital outflows almost every month since December 1996, as mentioned above. The balance of payments of Thailand, therefore, showed deficits in most months after July 1997, except in the months when Thailand received new tranches of financial assistance from the IMF or other international sources. The official reserves had recovered somewhat from the currency-defense débâcle in early 1997, reaching US$26.8 billion or about seven months of imports in July 1998 and US$30.2 billion in April 1999.

(c) On interest rate and credit expansion

In order to help slow the depreciation of the baht after its flotation in July 1997, the Bank of Thailand maintained a very high interest rate regime. This was also what the IMF had prescribed for Thailand in the early months of the crisis. The average interbank rate shot up from the already high level of 15.1 percent in June 1997 to 23.87 percent in September 1997 and fluctuated around 20 percent until July 1998, when it began to fall markedly. This high interest rate regime of the Thai government had come under much criticism for contributing to the rapid contraction of the

Table 2.3a Current economic statistics[1]

	1997 Jun.	Jul.	Aug.	Sept.	Oct.	Nov.
Activity and Prices	(% change from the same period of last year)					
Manufacturing Production Index, seasonally adjusted[2]	108.0	108.0	101.9	99.2	98.4	94.6
Manufacturing Production Index without seasonal adjustment	5.0	3.8	−5.1	−6.7	−11.6	−14.4
(12-month moving average)	6.8	6.7	5.6	4.3	2.7	0.8
Private Investment[3]	4.1	4.1	2.5	1.3	−0.4	−0.9
Government cash balance (bn)	29.5	−18.7	−21.9	21.4	−17.4	−11.9
Consumer Price Index[4]	4.4	4.9	6.6	7.0	7.2	7.6
Food	5.7	6.9	9.5	9.2	8.0	7.9
Non-food	3.4	3.5	4.4	5.3	6.7	7.3
External Accounts	(In millions of US$)					
Exports	4753	4745	4790	4986	5141	4786
(%△US$)	−4	7.9	2.2	11.5	11.7	0.8
Imports	5892	5273	5336	4767	4520	3942
(%△US$)	5.8	−8.7	−13.3	−12.2	−24.5	−30.4
Trade Balance	−749	−528	−546	219	621	844
Current Account Balance	−20.1	−387	−413	81	701	997
Balance of Payments[4]	−24.6	−1706	−4508	3674	1556	4716
Official Reserves (bnUS$)[4]	32.4	30.4	25.9	29.6	31.3	26.3
Monetary Statistics	(In billions of baht)					
M1[5]	396.4	393.5	428.4	400.5	407.3	407.9
(%△)	0.8	−3.6	7.3	−1.9	−3.0	0.3
M2[5]	3958.1	4047.5	4139.4	4166.3	4239.7	4250.2
(%△)	11.9	14.5	16.7	16.6	18.1	16.6
M2A[5]						
(%△)						
Monetary Base[5]	514.3	468.5	435.6	433.8	443.5	441.9
(%△)	29.8	14.6	9.9	7.4	5.5	5.7
Bank deposits	3986.9	4059.4	4035	4065.5	4144.1	4155.5
(%△)	15.9	18.2	16.9	16.5	18.9	16.7
Commercial bank credits	5076.1	5308.6	5420.3	5539.2	5708.1	5678.6
(%△)	10.4	15.3	16.4	17.0	19.6	17.6
excluding BIBF's	4246.2	4281.3	4326	4391.8	4425.8	4440.5
(%△)	11.1	11.5	11.3	10.9	11.0	10.0
Interest Rates[4]	(End of period)					
Prime Rate (MLR)[6]	12.75	13.75	13.75	14.25	14.25	14.75
Minimum Retail Rate (MRR)[6]	13–13.5	14–14.5	14–14.5	14.5	15	15–15.5
Fixed Deposit Rate (1 year)[6]	8–8.75	10–11.5	10–11.5	10–11.5	10–11.5	10–11.5
Interbank Rate (average)	15.1	18.66	15.43	23.87	18.72	19.99
Exchange Rate (average baht : US$)[4]	25.78	30.27	32.48	36.28	37.55	39.3

Notes:
1. Except for actual figures, data shown in this table are subject to revision.
2. Revised series of the Level of the Manufacturing Production Index with seasonal adjustment.
3. % △ of private investment as indicated by the Private Investment Index.
4. Actual figures.
5. Revised series.
6. As quoted by the 4 largest banks.

Source: Bank of Thailand's Monthly Statistical Release.

The social impact of the Asian financial crisis

Table 2.3b Current economic statistics[1] (continued)

	1997 Dec.	1998 Jan.	Feb.	Mar.	Apr.	May
Activity and Prices	(% change from the same period of last year)					
Manufacturing Production Index, seasonally adjusted[2]	99.9	98.0	100.2	89.6	95.6	94.4
Manufacturing Production Index without seasonal adjustment	−8.4	−15.8	−13.7	−21.3	−16.1	−17.3
(12-month moving average)	−0.4	−2.4	−3.9	(−6.7)	(−8.6)	(−10.6)
Private Investment[3]	−2.1	−5.0	−6.7	−8.9	−12.0	−14.4
Government cash balance (bn.)	2.6	−3.5	0.4	3.2	5.0	3.0
Consumer Price Index[4]	7.7	8.6	8.9	9.5	10.1	10.2
Food	7.8	9.7	10.4	11.6	12.1	13.1
Non-food	7.5	7.8	8.0	8.2	8.7	8.6
External Accounts	(In millions of US$)					
Exports	4970	4190	4351	4708	4255	4203
(% Δ US$)	7.8	−7.9	3.2	(−3.5)	(−0.1)	(−11.9)
Imports	3937	3321	3211	3589	3543	3244
(% Δ US$)	−27.9	−45.1	−36.1	(−37.6)	(−39.1)	(−39.7)
Trade Balance	1033	869	1140	1119	712	959
Current Account Balance	1179	1229	1502	1479	937	1020
Balance of Payments[4]	1038	−364	−577	1714	1806	−1869
Official Reserves (bn US$)[4]	27.0	26.7	26.2	27.7	29.5	27.5
Monetary Statistics	(In billions of baht)					
M1[5]	428.8	443.8	430.6	405.9	409.6	389.1
(% Δ)	1.2	6.1	0.6	(−4.9)	(−2.1)	(−9.5)
M2[5]	4339.3	4416.3	4414.2	4408.7	4416.2	4433.0
(% Δ)	16.4	19.0	18.0	(15.7)	(14.5)	(13.4)
M2A[5]				4898.2	4902.2	4896.0
(% Δ)				(3.8)	(2.9)	(2.2)
Monetary Base[5]	474.1	471.3	465.4	447.7	448.9	448.2
(% Δ)	4.7	2.6	1.7	(−3.1)	(1.7)	(−1.4)
Bank deposits	4224.7	4287.8	4299.5	4283.3	4275.0	4310.3
(% Δ)	16.0	18.4	17.5	(14.2)	(12.8)	(13.0)
Commercial bank credits	5953.8	6187.6	5794.0	5669.6	5654.2	5683.1
(% Δ)	21.2	25.9	17.0	(13.1)	(11.7)	(11.2)
excluding BIBF's	4542.2	4606.0	4579.1	4603.4	4602.6	4628.0
(% Δ)	10.7	12.6	11.1	(10.3)	(9.3)	(8.5)
Interest Rates[4]	(End of period)					
Prime Rate (MLR)[6]	15.25	15.25	15.25–15.5	15.25–15.5	15.25–15.5	15.25–15.5
Minimum Retail Rate (MRR)[6]	15.0–15.5	15.5–16	15.5–16.25	15.5–16.25	15.5–16.25	15.5–16.25
Fixed Deposit Rate (1 year)[6]	10.0–13.0	10.0–11.5	10.0–12.25	10.0–12.25	10.0–12.25	10.0–12.25
Interbank Rate (average)	21.73	21.51	19.83	20.57	19.11	16.40
Exchange Rate (average baht : US$)[4]	45.29	53.71	46.30	41.33	39.48	39.14

Notes:
1. Except for actual figures, data shown in this table are subject to revision.
2. Revised series of the Level of the Manufacturing Production Index with seasonal adjustment.
3. % Δ of private investment as indicated by the Private Investment Index.
4. Actual figures.
5. Revised series.
6. As quoted by the 4 largest banks.

Source: Bank of Thailand's Monthly Statistical Release.

Table 2.3c Current economic statistics[1] (continued)

	1998 Jun.	Jul.	Aug.	Sep.	Oct.	Nov.
Activity and Prices	(% change from the same period of last year)					
Manufacturing Production Index, seasonally adjusted[2]	98.3	94.9	93.9	95.5	98.5	95.5
Manufacturing Production Index without seasonal adjustment	−12.3	−13.9	−10.4	−8.3	−3.1	−5.3
(12-month moving average)	−12.0	−13.4	−13.7	(−10.9)	(−10.5)	(−10.1)
Private Investment[3]	−16.9	−19.6	−20.8	−22.3	−23.0	−23.4
Government cash balance (bn)	−1.3	−10.7	−32.8	−51.6	−18.8	−2.0
Consumer Price Index[4]	10.7	10.0	7.6	7.0	5.9	4.7
Food	13.6	11.8	7.4	7.3	6.7	5.8
Non-food	8.8	9.0	8.2	7.0	5.8	4.1
External Accounts	(In millions of US$)					
Exports	4493	4560	4229	4470	4493	4379
(% Δ US$)	−3.1	−3.8	−11.7	(−10.3)	(−12.6)	(−8.5)
Imports	3565	3590	3294	3228	3402	3341
(% Δ US$)	−35.9	−31.9	−38.3	(−32.3)	(−24.8)	(−15.2)
Trade Balance	928	970	935	1242	1091	1038
Current Account Balance	853	1184	1123	1103	1275	1136
Balance of Payments[4]	−808	266	−176	376	342	831
Official Reserves (bn US$)[4]	26.6	26.8	26.7	27.3	28.5	28.9
Monetary Statistics	(In billions of baht)					
M1[5]	381.7	398.9	389.9	389.3	399.2	406.1
(% Δ)	−3.7	1.4	−9.0	(−2.8)	(−2.0)	(−0.4)
M2[5]	4502.5	4587.5	4602.9	4689.3	4718.2	4729.3
(% Δ)	13.8	13.3	11.2	(12.6)	(11.3)	(11.3)
M2A[5]	4929.4	4968.2	5003.9	5059.6	5092.9	5074.3
(% Δ)	4.4	5.8	6.7	(8.1)	(7.7)	(7.2)
Monetary Base[5]	427.5	448.1	442.1	440.0	450.2	467.3
(% Δ)	−16.9	−4.4	1.5	(1.4)	(1.5)	(5.7)
Bank deposits	4377.6	4457.4	4496.8	4580.3	4585.6	4603.7
(% Δ)	9.8	9.8	11.4	(12.7)	(10.7)	(10.8)
Commercial bank credits	5723.1	5639.2	5642.5	5653.0	5537.1	5476.8
(% Δ)	12.7	6.2	4.1	(0.8)	(−4.3)	(−4.9)
excluding BIBF's	4653.8	4640.3	4643.5	4734.3	4690.3	4682.1
(% Δ)	9.6	8.4	7.3	(6.1)	(4.2)	(3.5)
Interest Rates[4]	(End of period)					
Prime Rate (MLR)[6]	15.25–15.5	15.25–15.5	14.75–15.0	14.5–14.75	13.75–14.0	11.75–12.75
Minimum Retail Rate (MRR)[6]	15.5–16.25	15.5–16.25	15.25–16.25	15.0–15.75	14.25–15.25	12.25–14.00
Fixed Deposit Rate (1 year)[6]	10.0–11.5	10.0–12.5	9.5–11.5	7.0–8.5	6.75–7.75	6.00–6.75
Interbank Rate (average)	18.58	11.72	9.81	7.17	5.35	3.55
Exchange Rate (average baht : US$)[4]	42.36	41.19	41.58	40.41	38.14	36.46

Notes:

1. Except for actual figures, data shown in this table are subject to revision.
2. Revised series of the Level of the Manufacturing Production Index with seasonal adjustment.
3. % Δ of private investment as indicated by the Private Investment Index.
4. Actual figures.
5. Revised series.
6. As quoted by the 4 largest banks.

Source: Bank of Thailand's Monthly Statistical Release.

Table 2.3d Current economic statistics[1] (continued)

	1998 Dec.	1999 Jan.	Feb.	Mar.	Apr.
Activity and Prices	(% change from the same period of last year)				
Manufacturing Production Index, seasonally adjusted[2]	100.6	98.6	100.5	99.8	102.9
Manufacturing Production Index without seasonal adjustment	−2.7	−0.1	2.7	9.2	7.7
(12-month moving average)	(−10.0)	(−9.2)	(−8.1)	(−5.6)	(−3.9)
Private Investment[3]	−23.5	−22.9	−22.4	−21.0	n.a.
Government cash balance (bn)	−19.9	−1.9	−2.1	3.9	−26.0
Consumer Price Index[4]	4.3	3.5	2.9	1.6	0.4
Food	6.1	4.7	3.5	0.9	−0.3
Non-food	3.2	2.9	2.5	2.1	0.8
External Accounts	(In millions of US$)				
Exports	4543	3976	4103	4635	4359
(%△US$)	(−8.5)	(−5.1)	(−5.7)	(−1.6)	(2.5)
Imports	3313	3190	3144	3687	3875
(%△US$)	(−15.8)	(−3.9)	(−2.1)	(2.7)	(9.4)
Trade Balance	1230	786	959	948	484
Current Account Balance	1450	1202	1354	905	n.a.
Balance of Payments[4]	193	−447	−48	1304	229
Official Reserves (bn US$)[4]	29.5	29.0	28.7	29.9	30.2
Monetary Statistics	(In billions of baht)				
M1[5]	441.8	437.0	426.9	458.1	432.5
(%△)	(3.0)	(−1.5)	(−0.9)	(12.9)	(5.6)
M2[5]	4753.4	4741.9	4784.9	4789.1	4809.5
(%△)	(9.5)	(7.4)	(8.4)	(8.6)	(8.9)
M2A[5]	5118.1	5092.2	5128.3	5126.3	5136.3
(%△)	(6.1)	(4.8)	(5.3)	(4.9)	(5.0)
Monetary Base[5]	475.3	475.7	464.3	489.1	432.4
(%△)	(0.3)	(0.9)	(−0.2)	(9.2)	(−3.7)
Bank deposits	4595.9	4580.8	4641.9	4646.8	4652.8
(%△)	(8.8)	(6.8)	(8.0)	(8.5)	(9.1)
Commercial bank credits	5472.7	5457.2	5489.8	5474.6	5456.6
(%△)	(−9.7)	(−13.2)	(6.5)	(−4.2)	(−4.3)
excluding BIBF's	4705.7	4706.4	4755.1	4765.6	4791.5
(%△)	(1.2)	(0.1)	(2.1)	(2.5)	(3.0)
Interest Rates[4]	(End of period)				
Prime Rate (MLR)[6]	11.50–12.00	11.00–11.50	10.00–10.50	9.50–10.00	9.00–9.75
Minimum Retail Rate (MRR)[6]	12.00–13.25	11.50–12.75	10.50–11.75	10.00–11.25	9.50–10.75
Fixed Deposit Rate (1 year)[6]	6.00	5.50–6.00	5.00–5.25	5.00	5.00
Interbank Rate (average)	2.63	2.73	3.09	2.25	1.65
Exchange Rate (average baht : US$)[4]	36.25	36.59	37.06	37.51	37.60

Notes:

1. Except for actual figures, data shown in this table are subject to revision.
2. Revised series of the Level of the Manufacturing Production Index with seasonal adjustment.
3. % △ of private investment as indicated by the Private Investment Index.
4. Actual figures.
5. Revised series.
6. As quoted by the 4 largest banks.

Source: Bank of Thailand's Monthly Statistical Release.

economy, and for not helping the slowing down of the baht slide. However, the Thai government insisted that it did. As a result of this high interest rate, liquidity in the financial system was extremely tight during early 1997–June 1998. We have alluded to the steady increase in the overnight interbank rate above. This was followed by a rapid decline in deposit rates, as shown by the benchmark 3-month deposit rate calculated by the BOT falling from a peak at 13.25–13.50 percent during February– June 1998 to 12.75 percent on July 27, 1998, 11.25 percent at the end of August, 8.75 percent at the end of September, and 8.00 percent at the end of 1998. The tight liquidity was due to stringent new loan-loss provisioning requirements as well as a new non-performing loan definition for Thai banks introduced by the BOT on 1 November 1997, which were intended to force them to recapitalize. Furthermore, capital continues to flow out of the country from loan repayments and non-resident baht deposit account withdrawals.

(d) On production

The credit crunch brought on by the crisis had slowed down or stopped numerous manufacturing productions. Of all the eight groups of industrial production, namely food, beverages, tobacco, construction materials, automotive, textile, petroleum products, and others, only the beverage and textile sectors had shown consistent positive trends of industrial growth and expansion during the crisis. But this was not enough to help buckle the downward trends of overall manufacturing activities. From table 2.3a it may be seen that the seasonally unadjusted manufacturing index (calculated from 38 major manufacturing products) had started to turn negative from August 1997, one month after the onset of the crisis, and continued to slide downward ever since.

The slowdown in manufacturing activities was most severe in March 1998, when the seasonally adjusted manufacturing index reached 89.6 based on the 1985 value of 100. In terms of a manufacturing index without seasonal adjustment, the figure for March 1998 was –21.3, confirming the lowest manufacturing activities compared to the situation one year before. While the said activities are still contracting, the rate of decline has become slower. The latest seasonally adjusted manufacturing index for July 1998 was 94.9, slightly lower than the index for June 1998 of 98.3. The index without seasonal adjustment may show a higher figure of –13.9 in July 1998, and indeed the 12-month moving average was the second worst for this month (at –13.4); this is expected and it should be understood that the manufacturing activities are at or near the bottom of manufacturing contraction. In August 1998, the manufacturing production index without seasonal adjustment began to decline, reaching the lowest point in January 1999 at –0.1. From February 1999 onward, this index turned positive for three months in a row. In April 1999, the 12-month moving average of this manufacturing production index was still negative (at –3.9). With the improving trend in manufacturing production in general, the 12-month moving average figure should become positive by June 1999.

(e) On price

When the baht depreciated rapidly after July 2, 1997, there were fears that the highly depreciated domestic currency would bring about high inflation. This was certainly true in the first few months after the crisis, as the consumer price index went up from 4.9 percent in July 1997 to 6.6 percent in August 1997, then to 7.0 percent in September 1997, and so on (see tables 2.3a and 2.3b). But while the rise in CPI was obvious, it was quite gradual and never jerky. The highest CPI reached was in June 1998 at 10.7 percent. In August 1998, the CPI fell below a 2-digit level and continued falling in later months (see tables 2.3c and 2.3d). The CPI for April 1999 was only 0.4 percent, perhaps the lowest CPI ever experienced by Thailand so far.[9] There are several reasons for this. One is Thailand's abundant food supply. Second, the severe economic contraction had caused the real income of the Thai people to decline across the board, making price increases difficult. Third, the government had appealed for price restraints and many producers had responded positively, slowing down the price hike. Fourth, the industrial workers were relatively quiet on their wage demand, knowing that any wage push could result in companies closing down and job losses. Fifth, the tight monetary policy acted as an effective brake on the threats of price increases. And so on. This relatively low rate of inflation despite more than 30 percent depreciation of local currency is something that has taken many by surprise. Various hardships have been avoided with relatively low inflation during the economic crisis.

(f) On investment

Along with the slowdown in manufacturing activities, overall private investment had shown the same trend. As shown in table 2.3, the rate of change in the private investment index started to go into the negative in October 1997, three months after the contraction in the manufacturing activities. This index started to slide continuously downward as the recession deepened, reaching the highest negative growth rate of –23.5 percent in December 1998. In January 1999, the negative growth rate became smaller at –22.9 and continued to fall thereafter. In March 1999, where the latest information was available, the growth rate of private investment index was −21.0 percent. Assuming that this negative rate continues to improve (becomes smaller and eventually turns positive), this is one indication which showed that the worst of the crisis has been reached in December 1998.

(g) On employment
That the crisis has caused increased unemployment in the economy is beyond any doubt, but the incidence and the rate of unemployment differ from one sector to another. Unemployment figures are never accurate in the Thai situation because the definitions of employment and unemployment change from time to time. More importantly, the patterns of employment of many Thai workers often exhibit high degrees of underemployment, shifting, or seasonal employment from circular migration (between rural and urban areas at different seasons of the year), and so on. The lack of unemployment insurance facilities also contributes to poor workers having to find new odd jobs as soon as old jobs are lost. This type of employment is difficult to gauge.

Nevertheless, the increase in formal registration of unemployed persons at government employment centers throughout the country, especially in Bangkok during the past 12 months, testifies to the severity of unemployment as a result of economic crisis. The figure of between 1.5 to 2 million unemployed workers is often used to show the size of unemployment in Thailand in time of crisis. These figures normally came from the Labour Force Surveys conducted twice yearly by the National Statistical Office. But they could be misleading because the effects of seasonality have not been taken out of the unemployment situation. In other words, unemployment usually increases during the dry season and falls during the wet season. To account for the impact of economic crisis, this seasonal effect must be taken into consideration.

Recently, Professor Nanak Kakwani of the University of New South Wales has attempted to measure the impact of the economic crisis on employment and unemployment in Thailand by taking the seasonality effect into consideration. We can see from the preliminary results of his study, shown in tables 3.2 and 3.3, that the number of unemployed persons during the first quarter of 1998, which could be rightly called the crisis period, was estimated at 1.48 million. But this was a dry season figure which is expected to go down naturally during the next survey period, which will be wet season. Professor Kakwani had used the employment trends of the periods before the crisis to project the employment and unemployment situations in the crisis period (the first quarter of 1998). The difference between this projected figure and the actual figure can be understood as reflecting the effects of the economic crisis. In this way, it was shown that the unemployed persons as a result of economic crisis numbered about 810,000, divided into 510,000 males and 300,000 females (see table 2.4). This is much lower than the often quoted number of between 1.5 and 2 million persons. While this result has shown the unemployment to be quite serious, and that the crisis had also led to a decline in total employment, the effect of the crisis on total employment was statistically insignificant. This could mean that the nature of the crisis was cyclical and not structural. The normal trend would show a general increase in employment.

Table 2.4 Effects of economic crisis on employment and unemployment (unit: million persons)

	Employment			Unemployment			Total labor force		
	Male	Female	Total	Male	Female	Total	Male	Female	Total
1. Seasonal Index	0.83	2.19	3.02	−0.25	−0.26	−0.52	0.24	1.07	1.3
t-value	2.43	3.04	2.93	−1.97	−2.26	−2.15	1.3	3.02	2.85
2. Crisis Index	−0.47	−0.19	−0.67	0.51	0.3	0.81	0.09	0.08	0.17
t-value	−1.67	−0.62	−1.16	7.13	2.87	4.71	0.47	0.45	0.48
3. Trend Index	0.09	0.02	0.11	−0.02	−0.02	−0.04	0.06	0	0.06
t-value	3.96	0.98	2.48	−2.93	−2.83	−2.94	4.3	−0.31	2.1
Memo items: Employment situation in:									
Wet season 1997	18.12	15.04	33.06	0.15	0.14	0.29	18.31	15.25	33.56
Dry season 1998	16.88	12.53	29.41	0.85	0.63	1.48	18.1	14.04	32.14

Notes: The Seasonal Index is computed from the additions of centered-two-period moving averages from 12 labor force surveys divided into 6 dry seasons and 6 wet seasons. As this index is supposed to show the differential effect on employment generation between the more active wet season and the less active dry season, the Seasonal Index shows the additional employment in millions that is generated in the wet season compared to that in the dry season.

The Crisis Index is computed from using the trend line which covers the seasonally adjusted employment series from the third quarter of 1992 to the third quarter of 1997 to predict the forecasted or expected employment value for the first quarter of 1998 (the crisis period). The difference between the actual value from the Labor Force Survey of the first quarter 1998 and the expected or forecasted value is the Crisis Index.

The Trend Index is computed from the 12 employment series. It shows the average rate at which employment has changed over the entire period from the first quarter of 1992 to the third quarter of 1997.

Source: Adapted from Nanak Kakwani, 'Impact of Economic Crisis on Employment, Unemployment and Real Income', Development Evaluation Division, National Economic and Social Development Board and Asian Development Bank, September 1998.

In table 2.5, it can be seen that the contribution of the economic crisis to the unemployment rate by different sector varies from sector to sector. The crisis hit the hardest in the construction sector, with the crisis contribution to unemployment of 11.4 percent, followed by the banking and insurance sector with 4.48 percent. The mining and manufacturing were next at 3.77 and 3.44 percent, respectively. It is interesting to note that the services sector and the agricultural sectors were the two sectors least affected by the crisis. This is intuitively convincing as the agricultural sector is very large and agricultural production and exports have in fact benefited from depreciated local currency. So, it can absorb unemployed workers from other sectors in the cities. The situation is similar with regard to the services sector.

Table 2.5 Effects of seasonality, crisis, and trends on unemployment rate by sector

	Seasonal Index	Crisis Index	Trend Index
1. Agriculture	−2.70	1.49	−0.18
2. Mining	2.18	3.77	−0.45
3. Manufacturing	−0.78	3.44	−0.07
4. Construction	−1.87	11.40	−0.26
5. Utilities	−0.21	0.63	−0.03
6. Trade	−0.32	1.70	−0.04
7. Banking and insurance	−0.43	4.48	−0.02
8. Property	−0.32	2.01	−0.06
9. Transport and communications	−0.31	1.64	−0.06
10. Services	−0.68	1.00	−0.05

Source: Adapted from Nanak Kakwani, 'Impact of Economic Crisis on Employment, Unemployment and Real Income', Development Evaluation Division, National Economic and Social Development Board and Asian Development Bank, September 1998.

4.   THE CORRECTIONS

As mentioned earlier, when the Thai monetary authorities floated the baht in early July 1997, it was an act of a forced surrender precipitated by the exhaustion of foreign reserves. As such, the government did not have any plan or strategy concerning the next course of action once the baht was floated. It did not even know whether the country needed an infusion of foreign funds to keep the economy solvent and functioning. After about two weeks, as the baht started to slide badly downward, the government realized that the country needed immediate financial assistance from outside. It quickly asked the Japanese government to work with the International Monetary Fund to organise a rescue package consisting of traditional emergency loans from the Japanese government and the IMF and other standby credits from other friendly countries totalling 17.2 billion US dollars. The negotiations as to the terms and conditions of this lending took place in Bangkok between officials of the IMF and the Thai government. The usual 'IMF Conditionalities' were of course discussed and applied, but were supplemented by terms that reflect the specific nature and characteristics of the Thai problems.[10] The First Letter of Intent to borrow from the IMF was submitted on August 5, 1998 requesting the first tranche of emergency loan of about 4 billion US dollars. Thus started the bailout operations for the Thai economy under the supervision of the IMF.

This does not mean that the Thai authorities did not realize that the country's economic problems were already near critical stage. They did, and indeed several measures had already been meted out to cope with these problems. Take, for example, the suspension of several troubled finance companies (pending their restructuring and recapitalization plans) undertaken before the baht flotation, or the reduction in the government budget in response (as well as anticipation) of the decline in public revenues, or the government support of the merger of financial institutions for more efficient management. But perhaps these measures were too little and too late. Therefore, when the first batch of finance companies was suspended, local depositors started to panic and set off the run on all other finance companies. It was learned later that in order to sustain the operations of most finance companies, the Financial Institution Development Fund (FIDF), which operates under the jurisdiction of the Bank of Thailand, provided almost 500 billion baht emergency loans to resuscitate these finance companies. When this point was reached with no solution in sight, it was quite obvious that the collapse of this segment of the financial sector was imminent and nothing could stop this from occurring.

What happened after the flotation of the baht was a series of policy measures that aimed at preserving the confidence and subsequent stability in the financial sector and the exchange market. Confidence is important in this case because it was indeed the lack of confidence of foreign investors and creditors that caused the massive outflows of capital. If confidence is restored, this breeding might stop, foreign capital return, and the local currency stop its downward slide. The first set of macroeconomic conditions under the IMF was a good indication of how confidence in the improved health of the economy could lead to overall economic stability. The IMF had specifically ordered that its money must not be used to bail out failed finance companies or other financial institutions. The government must cut its budget on most expenditure categories except on health and education, and raise certain taxes so that the fiscal surplus of about 1 percent of GDP is achieved at the end of the current fiscal year (1997). Subsidies on public services would not be allowed except those services that clearly benefit the poor (such as the basic Bangkok bus and third-class national train services). The contraction of the economy was expected, with the growth rate of GDP for 1997 estimated at about 2–3 percent, and the inflation rate about 10 percent. The current account deficit must also be reduced from 8 percent of GDP to about 5 percent at the end of 1997 and about 3 percent of GDP at the end of 1998. The privatization movement which has already started will continue at a greater speed. Finally, the foreign exchange reserves of Thailand will be maintained at about 26 billion US dollars, equivalent to about four months of imports.

When the agreements with the IMF were reached in early August 1997, many had expected that the infusion of these emergency funds from the IMF, the World Bank, and the ADB would stop the sliding of the baht. It did not. By September 1997, the first psychological benchmark exchange rate of 35 baht to the US dollar was passed.[11] In November 1997, another psychological benchmark of 40 baht to a dollar was also passed. At that time the contagion effect of the baht flotation and ensuing crisis had spread throughout the East Asian region, with Korea and Indonesia as two new victims. The crisis in Indonesia had further pulled the baht exchange rate beyond 55 baht per US dollar at the end of January 1998.

By this time both the IMF and the Thai government had realized that the perceived currency crisis had turned into a full-fledged economic crisis. All the earlier macroeconomic projections and estimates were wrong and several policy measures adopted during the last quarter of 1997 were also wrong. Many of these macroeconomic projections and estimates had to be changed quickly and frequently, and with them, new policy measures and adjustments. As can be seen from tables 2.6a–2.6c, macroeconomic frameworks for 1997 and 1998 were changed many times, each change reflecting the greater-than-expected severity of the economic crisis. For example, the projected rate of growth of GDP for 1997 which was first estimated at 2.5 percent was revised downward to 0.6 percent in the period of the third Letter of Intent, and finally to –0.4 percent during

The social impact of the Asian financial crisis

Table 2.6a Thailand's macroeconomic framework, 1996–98

	1996 First estimate Loi2	1996 Revised Loi3	1997 First Estimate Loi2	1997 First review Loi3	1997 Revised Loi4
Real GDP growth (%)	6.4	5.5	2.5	0.6	−0.4
Consumption	6.2	6.7	3.3	0.5	0.1
Gross fixed investment	6.7	6.0	−10.2	−13.3	−16.0
CPI inflation (end of period, %)	4.8	4.8	9.5	10.0	7.7
CPI inflation (period average, %)	5.9	5.9	7.0	6.0	5.6
Saving and investment (% of GDP)					
Gross domestic investment	41.0	41.7	36.3	35.8	35.0
Private	31.3	31.5	26.4	25.3	23.5
Public	9.7	10.2	9.9	10.5	11.5
Gross national saving	33.1	33.7	31.3	31.8	32.9
Private	21.5	20.6	21.0	21.3	22.2
Public	11.6	13.1	10.2	10.6	10.7
Foreign saving	7.9	7.9	5.0	3.9	2.0
Fiscal accounts (% of GDP) [1]					
Central government balance	2.3	2.4	−1.1	−0.9	−0.9
Revenue and grants	19.1	19.5	17.3	17.6	18.3
Expenditure and net lending	16.8	17.1	18.4	18.5	19.2
Overall public sector balance	2.7	2.7	−1.6	−1.5	−2.1
Monetary accounts (end of period, %)					
M2A growth	12.7	12.7	7.0	1.5	2.1
Reserve money growth	12.0	12.0	8.0	4.4	4.7
Balance of payments (billion of US$)					
Exports	54.7	54.7	56.2	56.4	56.7
Growth rate (in dollar terms)	−1.3	−1.9	2.8	3.2	3.8
Growth rate (in volume terms)		−5.1			9.2
Imports	70.8	70.8	66.5	64.2	61.3
Growth rate (in dollar terms)	1.8	0.6	−6.1	−9.3	−13.4
Growth rate (in volume terms)		−4.0			−11.8
Current account balance	−14.4	−14.4	−9.0	−6.4	−3.0
(% of GDP)	−7.9	−7.9	−5.0	−3.9	−2.0
Capital account balance	18.0	16.5	−16.4	−17.9	−15.6
Medium- and long-term	12.2	11.3	5.5	6.5	6.3
Short-term [2]	5.8	5.2	−21.9	−24.4	−21.9

Table 2.6a Thailand's macroeconomic framework, 1996–98 (continued)

	1996 First estimate	1996 Revised	1997 First Estimate	1997 First review	1997 Revised
Overall balance	2.2	2.2	−24.7	−24.6	−18.6
Gross official reserves (end-year)	38.7	38.7	23.0	23.0	27.0
(Months of imports)	6.6	6.6	4.2	4.3	5.3
(% of short-term external debt)	103	103	69	75	90.1
Forward position of BOT (end-year)		−4.9		−18.0	−18.0
External debt (% of GDP)	48.9	49.9	55.5	58.6	59.6
Total debt (billions of US$) [4]	90.6	90.5	99.1	94.9	91.8
Public sector	16.9	16.8	27.3	27.8	24.5
Private sector	73.7	73.7	71.7	67.1	67.3
Medium- and long-term	36.1	36.2	38.5	38.0	37.4
Short-term	37.6	37.6	33.2	29.1	29.9
Debt-service ratio [5]	12.3	12.1	15.5	15.0	15.8

Notes:

1. On a fiscal-year basis.
2. Including outflows associated with the closing of swap and forward contracts by the Bank of Thailand.
3. The difference in the overall balance relative to the First Review (-US$7.7 billion) is being financed by gross reserves at end-1997 (US$4.0 billion), a lower reserve target for end-1998 (US$1.8 billion), greater-than-expected disbursement under the existing financing package (US$0.4 billion), and additional official external financing (US$1.0 billion from the ADB and US$0.6 billion from JEXIM).
4. Excluding loans (estimated at around US$4 billion at end-1997), proceeds of which were not brought by Thai corporations into Thailand.
5. Percent of exports of goods and services.

Source: IMF, from information provided by the Thai authorities.

the fourth Letter of Intent. Similarly, the forecasted GDP for 1998 was revised five times between the second Letter of Intent and the seventh Letter of Intent, from 3.5 percent to −8.0 percent. Other macroeconomic estimates contained in tables 2.6a–2.6c tell the same story of miscalculation and underestimation of the crisis. Probably everyone is so bewildered by this strange new economic crisis.[12]

It was undeniable that the IMF came to Thailand's aid with a traditional box of tools. Currency devaluation, cuts in government spending, increases in taxes, financial restructuring, and privatization of

Table 2.6b Thailand's macroeconomic framework, 1998

	1998 First estimate	First review	Second review	Third review	Revised
Real GDP growth (%)	3.5	0–1	–3 to–3.5	–7 to –8	– 8
Consumption	0.8	–1.1	– 5.0		
Gross fixed investment	–0.8	–6.5	–21.0		
CPI inflation (end of period, %)	5.0	6.0	10.6		
CPI inflation (period average, %)	8.0	10.0	11.6	8.0	8.0
Saving and investment (% of GDP)					
Gross domestic investment	35.9	34.3	29.1		
Private	26.1	24.7	17.6		
Public	9.8	9.6	11.5		
Gross national saving	32.9	32.5	33.0		
Private	21.5	21.7	23.0		
Public	11.5	10.8	10.0		
Foreign saving	3.0	1.8	–3.9		
Fiscal accounts (% of GDP) [1]					
Central government balance	1.0	1.0	–1.6		
Revenue and grants	17.8	16.6	15.8		
Expenditure and net lending	16.8	15.6	17.4		
Overall public sector balance	1.0	1.0	–2.0		
Monetary accounts (end of period, %)					
M2A growth	11.0	6.8	5.1		
Reserve money growth	11.0	6.8	6.6		
Balance of payments (billion of US$)					
Exports	61.0	60.9	60.1		
Growth rate (in dollar terms)	8.6	7.9	6.2		
Growth rate (in volume terms)			10.6		
Imports	67.6	64.3	56.8		
Growth rate (in dollar terms)	1.6	0.2	–7.7		
Growth rate (in volume terms)			–5.2		
Current account balance	–5.3	–2.5	4.4	13.5	14.0
(% of GDP)	–3.0	–1.8	3.9	11.5	12.0
Capital account balance	1.8	0.3	–12 to–14		
Medium- and long-term	5.3	8.5	2-3		
Short-term [2]	–3.5	–8.2	–15 to–16		

Table 2.6b Thailand's macroeconomic framework, 1998 (continued)

	1998 First estimate	First review	Second review	Third review	Revised
Overall balance	−3.5	−2.2	−8 to −10		
Gross official reserves (end-year)	24.5	24.8	23–25	28.5	29.0
(Months of imports)	4.3	4.6	4.9–5.3	8.5	8
(% of short-term external debt)	74	87	109–118	113	123
Forward position of BOT (end-year)		−9.0	−9.0	−10	−11
External debt (% of GDP)	59.6	76.4	76.3		
Total debt (billions of US$) [4]	105.5	102.5	85.9		
Public sector	33.4	35.4	31.7		
Private sector	72.1	67.1	54.2		
Medium- and long-term	39.2	39.0	33.6		
Short-term	32.8	28.1	20.6		
Debt–service ratio [5]	16.5	16.8	18.8		

Notes:
1. On a fiscal-year basis.
2. Including outflows associated with the closing of swap and forward contracts by the Bank of Thailand.
3. The difference in the overall balance relative to the First Review (-US$7.7 billion) is being financed by gross reserves at end-1997 (US$4.0 billion), a lower reserve target for end-1998 (US$1.8 billion), greater-than-expected disbursement under the existing financing package (US$0.4 billion), and additional official external financing (US$1.0 billion from the ADB and US$0.6 billion from JEXIM).
4. Excluding loans (estimated at around US$4 billion at end-1997), proceeds of which were not brought by Thai corporations into Thailand.
5. Percent of exports of goods and services.

Source: IMF, from information provided by the Thai authorities.

Table 2.6c Thailand's macroeconomic framework, 1999

	1998 First estimate Loi2	First review Loi3	Second review Loi4	Third review Loi6	Revised Loi7
Real GDP growth (%)	1.0	1.0			
CPI inflation (period average, %)	2.5–3.0	2.0			
Current account balance	11.0	12.0			
(% of GDP)	8.5	9.0			
Gross official reserves (end-year)	32–34	32–34			
(Months of imports)	8.5	9			
(% of short-term external debt)	178	191–203			
Forward position of BOT (end-year)	−3 to −4	−4			

Source: IMF, from information provided by the Thai authorities.

state enterprises are some of the standard measures that the IMF has used all over the world, and all of these were used in Thailand. A cut in government spending was certainly a mistake, as the government was not one of the problems. It did in fact enjoy some fiscal surplus before the crisis, and its spending behavior was under control. Earlier on, it was argued that by cutting government spending it did not have to compete for scarce funds in the private market, thus enabling the private sector to utilize the available funds in the market. But the economic contraction was too severe, and the government was deprived of an early opportunity to slow down such contractions through its deficit spending. The raising of the Value Added Tax from 7 to 10 percent was also a mistake. While the government could enjoy an increase in tax revenue, this measure had the effect of further suppressing the domestic economy and fuelling inflationary pressure due to domestic price increase. However, both the government and the IMF worked closely to monitor macroeconomic movements during the crisis, and were willing to make necessary adjustments such as the reversal to increased government spending through deficit financing, and to introduce measures that would provide social assistance to the rural sector and the unemployed.

Meanwhile, the most concentrated efforts of the government and the IMF were still in the financial restructuring of the banking and finance sector in the economy. By the third Letter of Intent to the IMF in February 1998, most planned corrections were in place, and subsequent letters of intent simply dwelt on how these planned corrections had progressed. It is now an appropriate time to discuss these planned corrections and how they changed the economic conditions in Thailand.

4.1 Macroeconomic Policies

(a) Financial restructuring
After closing down troubled finance companies and setting up the Financial Restructuring Authority (FRA) to auction off good assets to pay back their existing debts, the government went ahead to recapitalize the remaining commercial banks with a new set of rules concerning capital adequacy and treatment of non-performing loans. When several small and medium-sized banks failed to raise the required capital, the government took over their operations by forcing the write-down of the existing capital before injecting necessary funds into them with a clear plan that when these newly taken-over banks became healthy they would be sold back into private hands. The Financial Institution Development Fund (FIDF), which had already lost a lot of money in its past attempt to rescue finance companies and commercial banks, still needed a lot of money to

help out weak commercial banks. Since liquidity had become very tight in the aftermath of massive loss of foreign reserves and capital outflows, the FIDF needed all the money it could get its hands on. The remaining healthy commercial banks would find it convenient to lend to the FIDF rather than lending to private borrowers, especially borrowers in the real sector, as it was safer and had higher returns. This had created a short-term distortion in the financial market, where the FIDF had all the money but not the rest of the economy. To correct this distortion and to help reduce the interest obligations of the FIDF, the government needed to generate domestic credits quickly to relieve domestic credit crunch. It had done this through the power of several emergency decrees enabling the government to issue 500 billion baht worth of bonds for the FIDF.

In a way the government had decided that it had no choice but to use public money to help prop up commercial banks so that they were able to start lending to the public again. The government had realized that without a healthy commercial bank system, there was little hope for the country to recover quickly. Critics of this policy would argue that this was no different from the technique used by the FIDF before the crisis. But according to the government, it was. The new banking rescue operations called for stringent control of new lending, stricter treatment of non-performing loans and a forced corporate debt restructuring. As stated in its 5th Letter of Intent to the IMF, the Thai government, through its comprehensive financial measures announced on August 14, 1998, aimed to do four things. First, it wanted to consolidate commercial banks and finance companies through additional Bank of Thailand interventions and proposed mergers. Second, it continued to encourage private investment and entry (domestic and foreign) into the banking system. Third, it had decided to use public funds to recapitalize all remaining financial institutions but with appropriate safeguards and conditions and with links to progress in corporate debt restructuring. And fourth, it had set a framework for the creation of private asset management companies.

(b) Corporate debt restructuring

The point made in the 14 August comprehensive financial plan on corporate debt restructuring needs further discussion. The government was of opinion that, as the debt burden of the corporate sector had risen rapidly, corporate debt restructuring had become crucial if normal market conditions were to be re-established and normal credit flows resumed. The government was committed to facilitating this process through legal, tax, and other institutional reforms. The recently established Corporate Debt Restructuring Advisory Committee (CDRAC) was said to aim at promoting market-based corporate debt restructuring with a view to supporting the economy and employment. At the moment more than 800 debtors have begun the process of debt restructuring with their creditors, with the help of the Bank of Thailand and the CDRAC. The change in bankruptcy law should also help the debt restructuring process as the debtor's position may be strengthened through a chance to put forward his business reorganization plan, whereas for the creditors the judicial procedure regarding foreclosure and enforcement of security rights may be accelerated.

(c) Exchange rate and monetary policy

One of the hallmarks of the earlier Thai government–IMF policy to cope with the economic crisis was the maintenance of a high interest rate to stabilize the exchange rate. This policy was subject to acerbic attacks from many quarters, but the government persisted. According to the government's thinking, without stability in the exchange rate, no confidence in the foreign investors could be forthcoming. And if recovery must depend on external sources of funds, this exchange rate policy must be pursued rigorously and resolutely. Obviously, the government's persistence had achieved its objective as the baht had become quite stable during the last six months or so, despite unstable political and economic situations around Thailand. Because of this stability the government could now afford to reduce the domestic interest rate to help increase private sector borrowing. As can be seen from table 2.3, the average interbank rate in August 1998 had fallen to 9.81 percent from 18.58 percent in June and 11.72 percent in July.[13]

The Bank of Thailand's careful monetary policy in maintaining an appropriate level of money supply had also paid off in terms of reduced pressure on the price level. It has been shown that inflation hurts the poor and the low-income relatively more than the rich and the high-income. So, the fastidious inclination by the Bank of Thailand to keep inflation in check is something not difficult to understand. Now that inflation is slowing, the Bank can afford to focus more on restoring liquidity and be more effective in setting the target for reserve money.

(d) External sector policy

The sharp reduction in imports with the continuing satisfactory performance in exports (at least in volume terms) had helped explain a rapid change in the country's balance of current account from deficit to surplus. This current account surplus will continue and is expected to reach 9 billion US dollars or about 7 percent of GDP in 1999. The level of foreign reserves at the level of 26–28 billion US dollars was considered sufficient for the current level of economic activities. As the recovery gathers pace, the Bank of Thailand reserves could rise further in 1999.

Policy regarding foreign direct investment could be classified under this heading. The overall foreign direct investment under the Board of Investment (BOI) scheme was substantially reduced during the economic crisis. In an effort to boost direct investment from overseas, as well as other strategies to stimulate economic recovery, the BOI had announced a series of measures since late 1997 to achieve the said purposes. Some of these measures included:

- Agro-business projects exporting at least 80 percent of their output would now receive import-duty exemption on machinery, regardless of zone;
- Existing BOI-promoted companies in Zone 1 and 2 may now apply for promotion of expansion projects;
- BOI-promoted projects in three sectors – textiles, footwear, and food processing – are now eligible for exemption from import duty on replacement machinery utilizing higher technology;
- Promoted export projects may now be located in any zone, with incentives following the existing criteria for each zone (until 31 December 1999);
- Alien Business Law will be revised or a decree issued allowing promoted foreign companies to engage in businesses that promote Thai exports;
- Foreign companies will be enabled to buy a specified number of existing buildings within a given time frame;
- Projects on the BOI List of Activities Eligible for Promotion, that were previously required to be located in Zone 2 or 3, may now be located in Zone 1 or Zone 2, providing that at least 80 percent of all sales each year are from exports.

The above measures, coupled with the general improvement in the economic conditions of the country, had helped attract a rapid increase in foreign direct investment.

(e) Fiscal policy
One of the major changes in the ways the Thai government used to cope with economic crisis is the switch on fiscal policy from fiscal surplus to balanced budget to fiscal deficit. As mentioned earlier, it had become obvious three months into the crisis that the austerity program on the public sector side was not suitable for the type of remedy the Thai economy needed. The severe contraction in the domestic economy required the government to stimulate aggregate domestic demand if the

economy were to recover quickly. Public sector fiscal deficit is now expected to reach 3 percent of GDP by the end of 1998. There were lingering doubts, of course, that increased public debts would affect the fiscal discipline of the government. However, past experience had shown that fiscal discipline of the Thai public sector should remain intact despite large public debts.

In order to facilitate corporate debt restructuring, the government had eliminated or temporarily suspended taxes that could hinder debt restructuring efforts and mergers and acquisitions. To improve fiscal strength and efficiency in the tax system in the future, the government had planned several tax reforms including the phasing out of tax exemptions, the introduction of capitalization rules limiting interest deductibility, and the streamlining of the VAT collection and refund procedures. Also included was the appointment of a customs adviser to implement a program for institutional and procedural improvements in customs administration.

On 30 March 1999, the Thai government announced another major fiscal policy package. The package contained three categories of fiscal measures to stimulate domestic demand and to help the economy to recover quickly. The first category was the use of loans from Japan under the Miyazawa Initiative (or Miyazawa Plan) and the World Bank to the tune of some 53 billion baht. This loan money was allocated to every ministry, to be expended quickly to create employment mainly in the rural areas and to augment the income of the people. The second category was the reduction of VAT from 10 percent to 7 percent, and the exemption of the first 50,000 baht of personal income from income taxation. This should have had the immediate effect of lowering the prices of most goods and services and increasing the purchasing power of the people. And the third category was the reduction in the price of oil and gas for industrial as well as household consumption. The reduced costs of production will not only help stimulate domestic demand but could also lower the production costs of exportables from Thailand, improving the export performance, which does not look promising lately. All things considered, this economic stimulus package should add to the recovery attempt of the government to bring the economy back from a −7.8 percent growth rate in 1998 to somewhere between +0.2 to +1.2 at the end of 1999.

4.2 Social Policies

The above section is concerned mainly with macroeconomic management with an aim to stabilize the economy so that it can start growing again.

While this stabilization policy is very important and indeed should be undertaken before any other policies, the government must also take care of the immediate welfare of the people: how they live and work during the crisis. This is when the social safety net policy comes into play. The government has managed to borrow a substantial amount of money from such international organizations as the World Bank and the Asian Development Bank, and these foreign loans will be used to relieve the pain of economic recession suffered by the majority of the population. There are many components of this public welfare policy.

(a) Social investment and social safety net programs
This current crisis has hurt many people in different sectors differently. In the public sector, public servants who are normally paid less than their counterparts in the private sector may lose some of the fringe benefits that come with the jobs such as medical allowances, supplementary salaries based on special qualifications or entertainment expenses due to government budget cuts, but they will maintain their jobs. The long-standing policy of the government to freeze the number of public officials by allowing no more than a 2 percent increase in the existing workforce annually actually helps those who remained in the jobs because the government does not need to incur heavy additional costs to look after new officials. In order to absorb the overflow of unemployed workers from the private sector, the government may be pressured to increase employment in the public sector. The political officials or politicians will be forced to be more careful in their spending, as they will be subject to increasing scrutiny. They are believed to be more socially conscious as well. The adoption of the new Constitution in October 1997 would not have gone smoothly if the economy had not been in crisis and the politicians had had more time to engage in political debates.

As for the private sector, three groups of people can be distinguished: the professional and business people and entrepreneurs in the modern production, service or financial sectors; the wage and salary workers; and the farmers. The first group are those who are most adversely affected by the current economic crisis because the economic slowdown is translated into fewer economic activities and less income. Those who had borrowed overseas without exchange rate cover would find that their foreign debts increased along with the depreciation of the baht. If the understanding creditors allow for debt rollovers, then the hardship can be postponed. If not, the debt burden could bankrupt their businesses. The tight monetary policy and credit crunch could also work against these business entrepreneurs as they face the genuine danger of debt default if necessary credit is not ready to come by. That is why ready credit in time of recession is so important to maintaining the activities of the economy. The increase in business bankruptcies as a result of the current economic crisis had prompted the Thai government to seriously consider amending its current bankruptcy law. The current law is said to be slow and inefficient, and favors the creditors more than debtors. The new Bankruptcy Law will permit corporate reorganizations as opposed to liquidations, increase the scope for out-of-court settlements, and also ensure fair treatment of creditors.

The wage and salary workers are also affected by job losses. These people may benefit from availability of credits but only through the regeneration of jobs and employment by the first group of people. Lack of unemployment benefits in the Thai social security system makes these workers very vulnerable to hardship. Some may have to find a completely new job in order to survive, and a majority of these unemployed wage and salary workers may have to depend on their families at least in the short run until business activities improve, or a new job is found. Wage workers who came from the countryside may choose to return to the rural areas where family supports are still available.

Finally, the farmers may be the only group of people who could benefit from this crisis. Assuming that their production inputs are mainly land and labor, which have little import content, their products would be in greater demand through a depreciated exchange rate (as is actually the case with regard to the production and export of high-quality rice). However, they could not escape the impact of inflation brought about by the increase in the costs of production of other necessary household goods and services. Moreover, the burden of the farm sector in the rural areas in looking after members of the families who had gone to work in cities but returned home after job losses could put a great deal of pressure on these farmers, who are generally the least well off in the society.

It was the concern for the welfare of these farmers and retrenched industrial workers that mainly prompted the government to set up separate social investment and social safety net programs. These programs can be considered as consisting of four important elements as follows.

(b) Social Investment Project (SIP)

The government is expected to receive about 21.7 billion baht worth of loans and grants from the World Bank, ADB, the OECD, UNDP, and the Australian Agency for International Development (Ausaid) in a project called the Social Investment Project (SIP) for the purpose of helping those who are affected by the crisis. The immediate aims of the SIP are to reduce the rate of unemployment in the country by creating jobs; to improve the delivery of social services by strengthening local governments and local authorities; to invite participation from the local people; and to encourage transparency in policy-making.

The first part of the funds will be managed by the Ministry of Finance with money to go to the Ministries of Interior, Public Health, and Labor and Social Welfare; the Tourist Authority of Thailand; and the Bangkok Metropolitan Administration (BMA). The second portion (about 6 billion baht) will go the Social Investment Fund (SIF) and the Regional Urban Development Fund (RUDF) and will be managed by the Social Fund Office (SOFO) under the responsibility of the Government Savings Bank (GSB). The SIF, with a budget allocation of about 5 billion baht, will be administered as grants to community development projects to be carried out by the community organizations, whereas the RUDF's about 1 billion baht budget will be used in the form of loans to municipal administrations throughout the country to spend on urban development projects. The SIF projects will be proposed and prepared by local community organizations under the guidelines provided by the SOFO. These projects may be classified into four types or categories. Project Type 1 will aim at encouraging career education and community economic development. Project Type 2 is about social welfare and community security. Project Type 3 concerns natural resources and environmental management and cultural support. And finally, Project Type 4 will promote community capability and networking development.

The SIF has generated a great deal of interest among academics and other development practitioners. As mentioned above, this fund will be managed by a special office set up under the overall administration of the GSB. Many had doubted the ability of the officers of the GSB to screen and monitor public works or community-oriented projects. Even when the ability to do so was never in doubt, many had doubted whether this was a proper job for the GSB officers. Reference was made to the Rural Job Creation Programs (RJCP) which preceded this SIF projects and a question was raised whether the Department of Local Administration with its extensive staff and prior experience in conducting this kind of rural public works project would be more suited to do this kind of social spending. Some scholars had criticized this SIF as a pilot project to be used for business expansion of foreign investors, and thought that, eventually, it would do more harm than good to local communities.[14] These types of questions and criticisms have been raised before with regard to past rural public works programs such as the RJCP and the Green Esan Programs (GEP). The conclusions from these rural public works programs seem to show that, while this type of public expenditure was based on capital-intensive techniques, the local people and communities did not totally object to it because they could make use of the complete infrastructure projects later. On the whole, the rural population were in favor of rural public works projects such as those in the RJCP or GEP. However, the SIF projects will be different from the earlier public works projects in that, in a crisis situation as at present, the supply of local labor may be available to work on the projects. Moreover, the size of the budget for these SIF projects is much larger than the RJCP or GEP, so that it can make a difference in terms of the impact on local economies or societies.

(c) Social sector program loan

The government had decided to borrow 500 US dollars from the ADB to be used in the reform of the three areas, namely in labor market and social welfare, in education, and in public health. The first tranche of 300 US dollars has already been disbursed, with the remaining 200 US dollars to be withdrawn soon. Regarding the labor market and social welfare, the government had agreed with the ADB to do the following: (a) set up centers for retrenched workers in various provinces to provide information on new employment and job training; (b) extend the social security coverage to retrenched workers to include sickness outside work, maternity leave, invalidity and death benefits; (c) increase competition in the labor market by reconsidering the overall labor and minimum wage policies; (d) encourage investment in on-the-job training along the lines supported in the Job Training Act B.E. 2537, and the participation of the private sector in the skill development of labor.

On education, the government will increase the budget for education loans to help students who may have to leave school due to financial problems. The quality of education may be improved also by the improvement in instruction techniques and qualifications of instructors, the greater autonomy in administrative and financial matters, and the greater role of the private sector in educational services and administration. On public health, the government had decided to help the poor and low-income people by increasing the budget on the Public Assistance Scheme from 4.9 to 7.0 billion US dollars, and increasing the number of Health Cards from 1.5 to 2 million, which are expected to cover 9 million people by March 1998. The ADB had also agreed to give 700,000 US dollars worth of technical assistance to each of the three areas.[15]

(d) Raising the efficiency of public financial institutions to help farmers and low-income people

The Bank for Agriculture and Agricultural Cooperatives (BAAC) is well known for its role in providing rural credits for farmers throughout the country. During this current crisis, the government has plans to help the sugarcane farmers during the 1998/99 growing season by agreeing to provide 4 billion baht to the BAAC to purchase on a discounted basis the so-called sugar support checks from sugar farmers. Other agriculture-related projects include, for example,

- The 3.3 billion baht structural adjustment loan (SAL) project from the World Bank to create rural employment;
- The 12.3 billion baht credit program from the ADB to promote occupations related to agriculture;
- The 6.23 billion baht loan project from the OECD to promote reforestation and the protection of the environment;
- The change in the BAAC Act to increase its role in the promotion of the agricultural occupation and the augmentation of farm income, and the raising of the quality of farm life in general.

In conclusion, it may be seen that the government has tried its utmost to help the farmers, the retrenched workers, the poor and the needy during this economic crisis. Although the amount of money involved in this social investment and social safety net objective is much less than that involved in the rescue of the financial sector, it is still much larger than at any other time in its modern history. The Thai government is expected to take many years to pay off the debts to the World Bank, ADB, and OECD. But this indebtedness is justified in the sense that it will go to help the majority of the Thai people who had no part in bringing about the collapse of the Thai economy. However, the government still has to be careful about efficiency in the spending of this borrowed money because it has to be paid back by the future generation of the Thai people. We have no right to burden the future generation with the mistakes that we have committed in our generation.

From the above account, it is quite obvious that the Thai government has been trying very hard to cope with the worsening crisis and to get the economy out of it as quickly as possible. Two conditions apart from the good functioning of the above prescribed policies have worked to help the present government. One is the relative stability of the government, and the other is the patience of the Thai people. Despite the coalition nature of the government, Mr Chuan Leekpai as the Prime Minister and head of the coalition had commanded respect from both within the country and outside it for his leadership, honesty, and hard work. Until recently, the opposition parties were rendered ineffectual in mounting any challenge to the government's rule. The patience of the Thai people has helped the government to concentrate on the work at hand without having to worry about popular protests or strikes. Thailand is lucky still to have a large rural sector where a large portion of industrial workers can always return. The Thai government's faithful adherence to external obligations and liberal regimes of trade and investment has helped to win back foreign confidence quickly.

5.   THE CONSEQUENCES

The above crisis has affected different groups of people in different ways. It is probably impossible to recount in detail who these people are and in what ways they have been affected. However, we may be able to look at the broad picture of how the current economic crisis has brought about some changes in the Thai society and economy. This section will discuss some changes in the political and business sectors in Thailand, and changes in the welfare of certain groups of people.

5.1 Political Changes

In the past four sections, we have on various occasions mentioned the difficulties faced by the government headed by General Chavalit Yongchaiyudh in tackling both economic and political problems. It was difficult enough to have to face currency, financial, and economic problems that went beyond the confines of national boundaries and national authority. The government needed all the technical expertise and the total political support of the people. The technical expertise might have been available but it was disarrayed and uncoordinated due to the lack of political and economic leadership. Political support was weak, as many ministers were alleged to be involved in various corrupt practices, and the prime minister himself was unable to bring unity and order into his government and his country. The crisis which started in July 1997 was in fact not the first crisis that hit the government; it had suffered the resignation of two ministers of finance and two governors of the Bank of Thailand. The inability to forestall the crisis (the failed defense of the baht) eroded the credibility and legitimacy of the government. With the impending abandonment of support from the coalition parties of the government in Parliament, the Prime Minister had no choice but to resign in November 1997.

As a matter of fact, General Chavalit's government might have had to go earlier had it not been for the fact that the draft new constitution was already completed and being debated in Parliament. For this new constitution to pass, it would need the support of the government with a majority vote to push it through. If Parliament were to be dissolved before the promulgation of the new constitution bill, the whole process of constitution drafting would have to start again. It would create too much trauma for the country to go through the whole attempt again, and chaos was likely to break out. In short, the government was kept in power long enough for the passing of the new constitution in October 1997, and when it was properly enacted, the old government was ready to go, and the new government was installed.

Although long-standing political tradition dictates that the political party which has the second largest vote in Parliament (in this case the Democrat Party) has the chance to form a new government, this was not as easy as it appeared to be because the Democrat Party could not muster enough majority votes to form a coalition government. This political deadlock, however, was broken when the Democrat Party was able to woo a sufficient number of members of parliament from an opposition party to form a majority. The new government was therefore formed with Mr Chuan Leekpai appointed as Prime Minister for the second time.

The general public was mostly in support of the new government led by Mr Chuan, who was known to be an honest and incorruptible man. However, as a lawyer, he was also known to be a very cautious man who could not make decisions quickly. With his second chance as Prime Minister, however, he had become more experienced and would probably be quicker in his decision-making. There were several politicians in the Democrat Party who were also top-flight economists or monetary experts, and two of them were appointed Minister of Finance and Minister of Commerce, two of the most important ministries in the Thai political structure. Eventually it was the Minister of Finance (Mr Tarrin Nimmarnhaemindra) who was given the primary responsibility to bring the Thai economy out of crisis. The story about the clashes between this Minister of Finance (Mr Tarrin) and the Minister of Commerce (Dr Supachai Panitchpakdi) on the proper way to solve the Thai economic crisis is well known. But since Tarrin basically had the primary support of the Prime Minister, he was able to carry out most of his ideas uninterrupted. Any success or failure in the economic management of the Thai economy during the crisis would be principally attributable to the work of Mr Tarrin acting with Mr Chuan's support.

The year 1998 was probably the toughest year for the Democrat-led government. While it had no difficulty agreeing with the basic policy recommendations of the IMF, the government faced numerous obstacles in tackling the Thai economic problems. For example, many laws had to be enacted or changed to enable the government legally to implement the policies (mainly in the banking and financial sectors). Often the government could not wait for the laws to be initiated, debated, and passed in the usual way; it had to use the power of royal decree in case of emergency while in the less urgent cases the law could be passed in the normal way. One of the major legal changes that could bring success or spell doom to the overall efforts of the government to solve the corporate and financial debt problems in the Thai economy was the change in the existing bankruptcy law that would allow more effective debt restructuring and resettlement, business rehabilitation, and foreclosure of the failing businesses. The proposed change by the government was resisted by several influential senators in the Senate. A new, compromise bankruptcy law was eventually passed, thus ending a deadlock that saw lack of activity by debtors and creditors in debt restructuring for several months. More problems still remain, such as the government reforms and privatization of state enterprises, but with the honest and able personalities of the prime minister and his minister of finance, the prospects of future solutions to the Thai economic problems are quite good.

5.2 Business and Economic Changes

The crisis had caused dramatic changes in the financial sector in Thailand. The closure of almost all finance companies in Thailand attests the weaknesses in the operations of these financial institutions, weaknesses which were brought about mainly by careless borrowing and careless lending. Several commercial banks were also in trouble. Bigger and more established banks were able to raise sufficient capital to satisfy the capital adequacy requirements to remain in operation. Several smaller banks which were burdened with huge non-performing loans (NPLs) and inability to recapitalize were either closed down, taken over by the government, or merged with larger banks. The banking and finance sector which, until the crisis, was the fastest growing and the leading sector in the Thai economy, had suddenly become the most problematic and a drag on the Thai economy. The aura of trustworthy and invincible Thai bankers of the past was gone. Along with these bankers and financiers or financial wizards who had fallen into disgrace were flamboyant business people, industrialists, and entrepreneurs who had suffered from careless borrowing and spending. The crisis had taught these people a good lesson of business conservatism and a good practice of corporate governance.

It can be argued that the above business trouble would have been avoided if the government had not followed the impossible economic policy of maintaining a fixed exchange rate, with free capital movement and a flexible interest rate. There is some truth in this. But in the free enterprise system where rewards are proportional to the risks involved, it is the duty and responsibility of these business entrepreneurs to take care of their own decisions. It was sad that the people who worked in various financial institutions, especially the finance companies, also had to share the burden of this failure. These were the people at the forefront of the business and economic boom of the late 1980s and early 1990s. If they had saved well during their good times, the burden of this crisis might not have been too severe. At least everyone in the business circle would have to learn to behave differently in the future and be more professional in their approach.[16]

5.3 Welfare Effects on the People

Professor Nanak Kakwani of the University of New South Wales in Sydney started to take an interest in the study of poverty and income distribution in Thailand in 1994, and together with the present author continued to work on poverty and income inequality in Thailand using the data from the latest Socio-Economic Survey (SES). In 1996 their work on the new technique for poverty line estimation in Thailand was presented in a conference and later published locally.[17] From 1997 onward, Professor Kakwani was contracted by the Asian Development Bank to work as a consultant to the Development Evaluation Division (DED) of the National Economic and Social Development Board (NESDB). Not only has he continued to conduct further research on poverty and income distribution in Thailand, but he has also been able to train the staff of the DED in the necessary techniques of poverty and income distribution studies so that this division will be able to carry out his work when his contract ends in 1999. After the crisis broke in 1997, Professor Kakwani expanded his research areas to cover employment and wages as well by using Labour Force Surveys (LFS) and many of the analyses on the impact of the economic crisis on employment, welfare and standard of living of the Thai people, including the effects on child labor.

Based on the latest LFS for 1998, Kakwani was able to compare the situation in 1997 before the crisis with the situation in 1998 when the crisis had generated some impact.[18] Using the wage income in these surveys, he showed that the real wage income of Thai workers began to fall in the first quarter of 1998 (Q1/98) and continued to fall further in the third quarter of 1998 (Q3/98). As can be seen from table 2.7, the seasonally adjusted real wage income of Thai workers fell from 2,876 baht per month in Q3/97 to 2,546 baht in Q1/98 and 2,485 baht in Q3/98. The drop in real wage income between Q3/98 and Q1/98 was –11.5 percent but the rate of decline became slower at –2.4 percent between

Table 2.7 Per capita real wage income, whole kingdom

Period	Actual values	Seasonally adjusted values	Growth rate
Q3/92	2045	2115	
Q1/93	2339	2216	6.9
Q3/93	2289	2368	4.7
Q1/94	2442	2361	−0.3
Q3/94	2351	2431	3.0
Q1/95	2644	2556	5.1
Q3/95	2709	2802	9.6
Q1/96	2909	2812	0.4
Q3/96	2735	2829	0.6
Q1/97	2930	2833	0.1
Q3/97	2780	2876	1.5
Q1/98	2633	2546	−11.5
Q3/98	2402	2485	−2.4

Source: Labour Force Surveys, various years. Estimated by Nanak Kakwani and DED.

Q1/98 and Q3/98. Further study showed that per capita real wage income for the whole kingdom had been increasing at an annual rate of 6.3 percent in the pre-crisis period. The long-term growth rate was 7.6 percent in villages compared with only 3.2 percent in municipal areas and 5.2 percent in health districts. Kakwani concluded that

> the high economic growth in the past has contributed to a substantial improvement in the standard of living especially in the rural areas. The economic crisis has now halted this impressive performance. It will tend to increase the already high disparity in the standard of living between rural and urban areas.[19]

In order to isolate the effects of the crisis, Kakwani used the growth trend of actual real wage income from Q3/92 to Q3/97 to compute the expected real wage income for Q1/98. This is a counterfactual estimate on the assumption that the crisis did not happen. The difference between the actual real wage income in Q1/98 and the expected real wage income for the same period would measure the effects of the crisis, other things being equal. In this way the so-called Crisis Index for Q1/98 was estimated as −19.2 percent, which means that the crisis had caused the real wage income to fall by 19.2 percent from the usual trend if the crisis had not happened. For Q3/98, this Crisis Index was −24.8 percent, which means that the standard of living worsened as the crisis progressed.

The LFS is basically an employment survey, and the income here is basically wage income, which does not include other non-cash or in-kind income. Obviously, this income from LFS understates the true income of households and population in Thailand. Household and individual income from the Socio-Economic Surveys (SES) also by the National Statistical Office (NSO) is more complete as non-cash or in-kind income and other transfers are included. Using data from various SES including the latest one for 1998, Kakwani was able to compute the average standard of living as represented by per capita individual real income. From table 2.8 it may be seen that the per capita real income for the whole kingdom had fallen from 3803 baht per person per month in 1996 to 3,753 baht per person per month or a fall of about −2.0 percent per annum. In terms of per capita welfare defined as the ratio of per capita income of a household to the per capita poverty line of that household, this decline is also apparent. In 1996, the per capita welfare index was 386 percent, meaning that the average real income of the population in 1996 was about 386 percent over the national poverty line. In 1998, this index had fallen to 370 percent. In terms of the impact of the crisis, the Crisis Index for per capita real

Table 2.8 Average standard of living: whole kingdom

Period	Per capita real income	Per capita welfare
1988	1997	212
1990	2449	254
1992	2911	295
1994	3407	344
1996	3803	386
1998	3753	370
Percentage change		
1988–90	22.6	19.9
1990–92	18.9	16.2
1992–94	17.0	16.5
1994–96	12.4	12.2
1996–98	−2.0	−4.2
Crisis Index	−6.2	−7.9

Source: Socio-Economic Surveys, various years. Estimated by Nanak Kakwani and DED.

income was −6.2 percent, whereas the Crisis Index for per capita welfare was −7.9 percent.

This general fall in average per capita real income had caused both the poverty incidence and the income inequality to increase.[20] The incidence of poverty measured by the proportion of the population whose income fell below the poverty line increased from 11.4 percent in 1996 to 12.9 percent in 1998. This increase of 1.5 percentage points reflects the increase of poverty incidence by about 13.2 percent in the actual comparison. But if the pre-crisis falling trend of poverty incidence is taken into account, the effect of the crisis on poverty is larger. The Crisis Index in this was estimated at 19.7 percent. In other words, it could be said that the crisis had caused poverty incidence in Thailand to increase by close to 20 percent. The income distribution on the post-crisis situation was also slightly worsened compared to the pre-crisis situation as the Gini coefficient of individuals of Thailand in 1998 had increased to 0.481 from 0.477 in 1996.

In all, the economic crisis which started in July 1997 caused an across-the-board reduction in welfare of the Thai people, although some suffered more than others. Kakwani pointed out that the impact of the crisis was more severe for the ultrapoor, defined as those whose income is below 80 percent of the official poverty line. It was estimated that in the absence of the economic crisis, Thailand would have had only 3.4 million ultrapoor instead of 4.3 ultrapoor in 1998. Thus, the crisis had contributed to an increase in the ultrapoor by 0.9 million.

In May 1998, Professor Pitaksit Chayaputi of Khon Kaen University and his associates conducted field surveys of the poorest households in more than 70 villages in the four provinces in the Northeast.[21] Pitaksit's study offers a few interesting findings. First of all, we can draw some conclusions about the overall size of retrenched workers in the Northeast by counting the number of those retrenched workers in sampled villages and make some kind of interpolation for the whole country. Pitaksit and associates selected about 70 villages in four provinces at random. In each village they received the information on the number of returned workers from village headmen (Puyai Baan) either from the records that these village headmen had put down, or from direct counting at the time of the interview. These numbers were of course not totally accurate, but they could be used to approximate the size of retrenched workers in that village. On this basis, it was found that there were about 532 retrenched workers in these 70 villages, averaging about seven or eight retrenched workers in each village, which was not large. Yet if one multiplies this number by the total number of villages in the country, the total number of retrenched workers who had returned to their homes could reach 420,000 to 480,000 persons.

Other interesting findings by Pitaksit et al. included the fact that these retrenched workers mostly had only primary education, and used to work in factories (mainly textile, construction materials, and parts and components) and in services sectors (mainly construction and transportation, e.g. taxi driving) before losing their jobs. The average salary of these people was slightly over 6,000 baht per month, which was relatively low (less than 200 baht per day). Very few of these retrenched workers were child workers. In fact in percentage terms, less than 5 percentwere in the 15–19-year-old age group. The majority of these retrenched workers were in the 20–29-year-old age group (more than 55 percent). On the assumption that this group of people is still young and mobile, the chances that they could get other jobs would be better than for those who were older workers. This could be one of the reasons why almost half of the retrenched workers in the samples did not show excessive anxiety and stress as a result of their job losses.[22] This relatively low level of anxiety was also believed to be the result of emotional as well as financial support from families. It was also discovered that at least in the early period of the crisis these retrenched workers did not seek assistance from the government, believing that the government probably could not be of any help.

In all, the above studies and analyses have shown that the crisis has hit various groups of people with differing degrees of severity. On the whole, however, the Thai people have weathered this crisis well, accepting the consequences of the crisis with less anguish and discontent than many people had thought. If the economy recovers quickly, then the suffering will be short-lived, and the people can withstand this short-cycle crisis without too much permanent damage.

NOTES

1. See, for example, Manuel F. Montes, *The Currency Crisis in Southeast Asia*, updated edition, Singapore: Institute of Southeast Asian Studies, 1998; Jomo, K.S. (ed.), *Tigers in Trouble: Financial Governance, Liberalisation and Crisis in East Asia*, Kuala Lumpur: Zed Books, 1999; Medhi Krongkaew, 'Three Pieces on Thai Economic Crisis', in *East*, journal of the Japanese Studies Centre, Institute of East Asian Studies, Thammasat University, September 1998; Peter G. Warr, 'Thailand', a chapter in Ross McLeod and Ross Garnaut (eds), *East Asia in Crisis: from being a miracle to needing one?* London and New York: Routledge, 1998; and Bhanupong Nidhiprabha, 'Economic Crisis and the Debt-Deflation Episode in Thailand', in H.W. Arndt and Hal Hill (eds), *Southeast*

Asia's Economic Crisis: Origin, Lessons, and the Way Forward, Singapore: Institute of Southeast Asian Studies, 1999, pp. 67–80.

2. As reported in the Economist Intelligence Unit, Thailand Country Report, 3rd Quarter, 1997, p. 22.

3. Cases in point are the acquisition of one of the largest tuna canning companies in the US by a Thai company, and the setting up of a multimedia empire by a Thai company that launched a regional business newspaper challenging such well-known newspapers as the *Asian Wall Street Journal* or the *International Herald Tribune*.

4. Again, a case in point is a young financier who made news by taking over various ailing companies and expanding his financial activities with blinding speed.   He became a billionaire overnight and was known as a financial wizard. A few years later his financial empire was ruined due to over-expansion and his finance company, once the largest in Thailand, is now bankrupt.

5. A statement by Karel Jansen, who had worked on Thai financial development, reads: 'Supervision of financial institutions by the Bank of Thailand aimed at building confidence in them. This implies that when these institutions were in trouble, the BOT organized rescue operations rather than allowing weak institutions to default'. See Karel Jansen, *Finance, Growth and Stability: Financing Economic Development in Thailand, 1960–86*, Aldershot: Gower Publishing, 1990, p. 76.

6. See Paul Krugman, 'What Happened to Asia?', paper from his personal webpage, January 1998.

7. This may have happened in the case of the rescue operation on the Bangkok Bank of Commerce (BBC), which experienced severe liquidity problems due to non-performing loans and heavy losses in several bank-supported activities (see next paragraph). An estimated 178 billion baht from the Financial Institution Development Fund (FIDF), a separate rescue operation entity but managed by the Bank of Thailand, were used on the BBC. Together with other bailout money to all other ailing finance companies, the amount used by the FIDF totalled more than 500 billion baht by mid-1997, a huge amount that shocked everybody when it was disclosed. With resources running dry, it was not surprising that many finance companies could not be helped. The suspension of these finance companies, 16 in June 1997 and 58 in August 1997, set off the panic and crisis as explained by Krugman.

8. See Peter G. Warr, 'The End of the Thai Miracle?', Thailand Information Paper no. 5, National Thai Studies Centre, Australian National University, July 1997.

9. This falling CPI since mid-1998 had raised some fear of deflation in the Thai economy. This is somewhat far-fetched. Instead this low inflation had given the government a greater latitude to stimulate the economy and bring it out of recession without the fear of inflation.

10. Standard conditionalities include, for example, devaluation of the overvalued

currency to improve external balance through increased exports and reduced imports; reduction in fiscal deficit and switching public spending to more efficient uses; increase taxes to reduce domestic consumption and increase public revenue; reduction in the rate of monetary expansion to control inflation; reduction in subsidies of public services to make them more efficient; and continuation of privatization of state enterprises. In short, the IMF conditionalities rely on orthodox stabilization policy that aims at fiscal and monetary discipline and conservatism.

11. The Governor of the Bank of Thailand was reported to have said that if the baht had dropped below 35 baht to one US dollar he might resign. It did drop below, but he did not resign. This is just to show that the extent of the actual depreciation of the baht was beyond most people's expectation.

12. It is interesting to link changes in macroeconomic frameworks with changes in political situations in the country. The political development in Thailand during the crisis has various repercussions on the course of its economic actions which resulted in the nature and speed of economic policies. However, this discussion is outside the main focus of this chapter.

13. It was still argued, however, that while the government had helped flood the market with liquidity and bring down the interest rate, the lending rate by commercial banks was still at a very high level of 15 to 16 percent. With the concerted cut in deposit rate to about 7 to 8 percent, the spread was between 7 to 8 percent, too large to be called a competitive level.

14. View from Dr Worapol Promigabutr of the Faculty of Sociology and Anthropology, Thammasat University as reported in *the Bangkok Post*, 26 July 1998.

15. With the NESDB responsible for the social reform project, the National Educational Council for the educational management and finance project, and the Ministry of Public Health for the health management and finance project.

16. The subject of good corporate governance is currently much talked about in Thailand. The business of the future must be conditioned by transparency in decision-making, clear accountability, full disclosure, acceptable accounting standards, and so on.

17. Nanak Kakwani and Medhi Krongkaew, 'Poverty in Thailand: Defining, Measuring and Analysing', paper prepared for the Development Evaluation Division, National Economic and Social Development Board, October 1996.

18. Development Evaluation Division, NESDB, 'Impact of Economic Crisis on the Standard of Living in Thailand', newsletter of the Development Evaluation Division (DED), vol. 2, no. 4, October 1998.

19. Ibid, pp. 2–3.

20. Development Evaluation Division, NESDB, 'Poverty and Inequality During the Economic Crisis in Thailand', vol. 3, no. 1, January 1999.

21. Pitaksit Chayaputi et al., 'The Study of Socio-Economic Characteristics of

Crisis-Caused Retrenched Workers in the Northeast', research report submitted to the Thailand Research Fund, January 1999.

22.   To the question of how these retrenched workers felt when they knew that they would lose their jobs, more than 45 percent replied that they felt calm, as they had already realized the possibility and prepared themselves for this eventuality. About 21 percent would feel sad or sorry to lose their jobs, and about 10 to 15 percent would feel angry, frustrated or desperate.

3. Financial crisis and its social impact in Malaysia

Ishak Shari

1. INTRODUCTION

The financial crisis, which began in Thailand in July 1997, and then spread to other countries in Southeast Asia, South Korea, and later to other parts of the world, seems to be the most severe in terms of magnitude and harshness since the Great Depression of the 1930s. The financial crisis in Southeast and East Asia quickly deteriorated into an economic and social crisis and had repercussions on the financial markets around the world as well as undermining the growth of the world economy. In fact, at one stage, there was some discussion of the risk that the crisis in Asia could turn into global depression. Although there are now an increasing number of reports suggesting that the worst is over and that there are signs that some of the affected countries are beginning to recover from the crisis, it is generally believed that the crisis will have significant economic and social impacts on the affected countries.

This chapter attempts to review the nature and extent of the financial and economic crisis in Malaysia and to provide an initial assessment of its social impact in the country. In particular, the discussion on the social impact will focus on such issues as unemployment, poverty, public expenditure affecting human development, and social capital. In doing so, the chapter will also identify various channels through which the crisis has affected the various population groups in Malaysian society. The first part of the chapter will discuss briefly the origin and development of the crisis in Malaysia as well as the policy responses of the Malaysian government. It is important to emphasize that the discussion on the origin of the financial and economic crisis in Malaysia cannot be seen from within a national context alone. Notwithstanding the differences between the various affected countries, the crisis is increasingly being recognized as global in scope and character. Thus the issues associated with rapid financial liberalization and deregulation, as well as the weaknesses in the architecture of the global financial system, cannot be ignored. The second and third parts of the chapter will detail some of the immediate and short- to medium-term economic and social impacts of the crisis, followed by some description of the impact on certain poor and vulnerable groups. The fourth section will highlight some emerging issues related to the crisis as well as identifying the potentially new poor groups and the shifting patterns of vulnerability. The concluding section will focus on some major issues which need further systematic research in order to provide useful input in the formulation of appropriate policies and programs to address the social impact arising from the financial and economic crisis affecting the country.

It is important to stress here that the social impact of the current crisis, unlike the macroeconomic impact, is not easy to identify due to insufficient data and information on social indicators. Furthermore, the distributional consequences of macroeconomic and structural policies and the interrelationships between financial and economic shocks and the social impact have yet to be identified clearly. In this chapter, the empirical data on the social impact of the crisis at the macro level are derived from available published official statistics. The micro-level data used in this chapter will be drawn substantially from a rapid assessment study conducted in October–November 1998. This study involves conducting focus group discussions with selected target groups, in-depth interviews with key informants well placed to identify cutting-edge issues, making systematic observations of what is happening in the various regions throughout the country, and doing content analysis of newspapers and periodicals. While this particular research approach makes it possible to reveal greater insights or new dimensions not usually captured in a traditional survey method, particularly on groups most adversely affected by the crisis, it must be stressed that the data from the rapid assessment do have limitations. As the samples for the study are not selected using the probabilistic random sampling based on a definitive population, they may not be totally representative. Hence, recognizing the limitations of the research method employed in this assessment, it is important to stress that the findings, which can serve as useful pointers in highlighting several key issues impacting the society as the result of the crisis, should be considered tentative.

2. ORIGIN AND EXTENT OF THE FINANCIAL CRISIS IN MALAYSIA

The economic situation in Malaysia has changed considerably since the devaluation of the Thai baht on July 2, 1997. During the first half of 1997, important macroeconomic indicators did not indicate Malaysia's vulnerability to crisis. For example, there was some moderation in real GDP growth from 9.4 percent in 1995 to 8.6 percent in 1996 and the current account deficit in the balance of payments fell from 10.4 percent of GNP in 1995 to 5.1 percent in 1996. Furthermore, the country's fiscal position has been strong over the years and recorded surpluses in five consecutive years. The unemployment and inflationary rates in the country in 1996 were low at 2.6 percent and 2.7 percent respectively (see table 3.1). The country's foreign reserves were generally adequate, being sufficient to cover about four months of imports and 154 percent coverage of short-term liabilities of residents. Malaysia also recorded a low debt level at 32.7 percent of GDP in 1997, of which external debt was US$3.3 billion, accounting for less than 14.4 percent of the total.

Despite these strong macroeconomic fundamentals, the Malaysian ringgit and the stock market have both seen significant decline since the start of the Thai crisis. In August 1997, the ringgit depreciated against the US dollar to breach the previous low of US$1=RM2.7945 recorded on July 4, 1991. Adverse market reaction to a series of events in the remaining four months of 1997 and early 1998 pushed the ringgit to successive lows of US$1=RM3.93 on December 15, 1997 and subsequently to its lowest level of US$1=4.8800 on January 7, 1998. There was also evidence of serious capital flight. It is estimated that more than RM25 billion ringgit flowed to Singapore where foreign banks were offering interest rates of 20–40 percent per annum (Ong, 1999, p. 158). Between July 2 1997 and September 1 1998, the ringgit depreciated by 45.2 percent against the US dollar, while the Composite Index of the Kuala Lumpur Stock Exchange (KLSE) plunged by 54.7 percent and its market capitalization dropped by 57.9 percent (see table 3.2). It is thus obvious that the contagion effects of developments in the region were transmitted quickly to Malaysia.

However, when the 1998 Malaysian budget was presented in October 1997, it was projected that the economy would grow by 7.0 percent in 1998. Such optimism was most probably based on the assumption that the financial crisis in Thailand would have limited impact on the Malaysian economy. The political leaders and planners in Malaysia appeared to have underestimated the 'contagion effect' of the devaluation of the Thai baht. They were constantly pointing to the relatively strong economic fundamentals of the Malaysian economy as compared to other neighboring countries. The development during the 18 months since the crisis began, however, shows that Malaysia and her neighbors in the region were faced with an economic shock of unprecedented severity. The

Table 3.1 Malaysia: main macroeconomic indicators, 1989–98

	1989	1990	1991	1992	1993	1994	1995	1996	1997	1998[1]
Growth rates:										
Real GDP (%)	9.2	9.7	8.7	7.8	8.3	9.2	9.5	8.6	7.7	–4.8
Agriculture (%)	6.0	0.4	0	4.7	4.3	–1.0	1.1	2.2	1.3	–5.9
Mining (%)	8.5	5.1	2.4	1.6	–0.4	2.5	9.0	4.5	1.0	–0.8
Manufacturing (%)	14.2	15.7	13.9	10.5	12.9	14.9	14.2	12.2	12.5	–5.8
Construction (%)	11.6	19.0	14.4	11.7	11.2	14.1	17.3	14.2	9.5	–19.2
Service (%)	8.1	11.5	10.3	8.8	9.8	9.7	9.4	9.7	8.0	2.1
Export growth rate (%)	22.7	17.4	18.6	9.7	17.0	27.0	20.2	6.5	12.4	40.9[2]
Trade balance (RM million)	11871	7093	1449	8609	8231	4460	97	10154	11337	42724
Current account balance (RM million)	698	–2483	–11644	–5622	–7926	–14770	–21647	–12196	–14153	20065
Current account balance as % of GDP	1.0	–3.1	–9.2	–3.8	–4.8	–6.3	–8.5	–4.9	–5.1	15.0
Gross international reserves (US$ billion)	7.8	9.8	10.9	17.2	27.2	25.4	23.8	27.8	21.7	22.6
Total external debt (US$ billion)	15.6	15.4	16.0	16.4	20.2	22.5	27.4	29.1	44.7	31.5
Unemployment	6.7	5.1	4.3	3.7	3.0	2.9	2.8	2.6	2.6	4.9
Savings–Investment Gap	–431	–4522	–12459	–5622	–7926	–14770	–21646	–12197	–14151	36068
(% of GNP)	–0.4	–4.1	–10.1	–4.0	–5.0	–8.2	–10.5	–5.1	–5.1	13.7
Consumer Price Index (CPI) (%)	2.8	3.1	4.4	4.7	3.6	3.7	3.4	3.5	2.7	5.2[3]
CPI–Food items (%)	3.7	4.3	4.8	6.5	2.3	5.6	4.9	5.7	4.1	8.9
Fiscal balances (% of GNP)	–3.5	–3.1	–2.2	–0.8	0.2	2.3	0.9	0.7	2.4	3.7

Note: 1. Estimation
2. For the period Jan. –July 1998
3. For the period Jan. –Sept. 1998

Sources: *Economic Report, 1998/99*; Bank Negara Malaysia (BNM), *Monthly Statistical Bulletin*, April 1999; BNM, *Annual Report 1999*; Malaysia (1999).

Table 3.2 Financial meltdown in Malaysia, 1997

	12/31/96–7/2/97	7/2/97–12/3/97	7/2/97–1/9/98
	Percent change		
Ringgit/US$	−0.2	−35.4	−45.2
Ringgit/yen	+1.2	−26.4	−36.8
Ringgit/UK£	−2.1	−34.9	−43.7
Ringgit/S$	+1.8	−23.9	−31.9
KLSE composite index	−12.4	−45.2	−54.7
Market capitalization	−9.9	−49.4	−57.9
Market capitalization	−79.6	−359.6	−421.0
RM billion	−32.3	−193.0	−220.7
US$ billion	23.74	10.31	10.22$_p$

Note: The PE ratio was 28.56 at end December 1996. *p*. preliminary
Source: Ong (1999: 159).

depreciation of the ringgit and other regional currencies, for example, was massive by any standard.

The sequence of events leading to and worsening the crisis in Malaysia seemed to involve several important developments at both the global and the national level. Some recent works (Montes, 1998; Jomo, 1998) show that the crises in Malaysia have been due to the undermining of previous systems of international and national economic governance due to deregulation and other developments associated with financial liberalization and globalization. As in the other affected economies, Malaysia has been carrying out a process of financial liberalization since the mid-1980s. This includes, among others, moves for greater capital account convertibility and encouraging more foreign institutional investors to have greater access to the Malaysian stock market. These moves facilitated the large inflow of funds, particularly in the form of portfolio investment in the local stock markets. For example, out of the massive inflow of capital during the 1990–95 period, portfolio equity finance accounted for 88 percent of the identified gross capital inflows. The inflow of portfolio investment rose from RM19 billion in 1991 to RM238 billion in 1994 before declining to RM145 billion in 1996 (see table 3.3).

Table 3.3 Malaysia: external portfolio investment 1991–98 (RM million)

		Receipts	Payments
1991		19,346	21,274
1992		60,935	53,043
1993		187,779	162,128
1994		238,454	224,425
1995		106,414	101,054
1996		144,933	136,167
1997	1st Quarter	47,431	45,786
	2nd Quarter	41,792	30,377
	3rd Quarter	35,820	55,615
	4th Quarter	27,316	32,809
1997	Total	156,154	184,587
1998	1st Quarter	27,005	21,140
	2nd Quarter	12,284	15,560
	3rd Quarter	8,919	12,587
	4th Quarter	5,363	6,370
1998	Total	53,861	55,927

Notes: i. Pre-July 1996: (1) corporate shares and securities, (2) government securities. ii. Post-July 1996: (1) corporate securities, (2) Malaysian government instruments, (3) foreign government securities, (4) private debt securities, (5) money market instruments, and (6) financial derivatives.

Sources: BNM, *Monthly Statistical Bulletin*, September 1998, Table VIII.15, pp. 121–4, and April 1999, Table VII.16, p. 128.

It is important to note that despite stricter prudential banking regulations in Malaysia compared to other countries affected by the crisis, some companies and local banks borrowed heavily from abroad, thus further increasing foreign capital inflows. According to the central bank, Bank Negara Malaysia (BNM), commercial banks' foreign liabilities increased from RM10.3 billion at the end of 1995 to RM25.5 billion in June 1997, while their net external reserves position deteriorated from –RM5.3 billion to –RM17.7 billion over the same period. However, fortunately for Malaysia, the BNM retained control in one crucial area; that is, private companies wanting to borrow foreign-currency loans exceeding RM5 million must obtain its approval. Generally, approval was given only to those borrowings intended for investment projects that would generate sufficient foreign exchange receipts to service the debts.

Thus there was a policy of limiting private sector external loans to corporations and individuals with foreign exchange earnings which has enabled Malaysia to meet its external obligations. It was argued that this ruling saved Malaysia from the kind of excessive short-term private sector borrowing that led the other neighboring countries into a debt crisis. As a result of these controls, Malaysia's external debt has been kept to manageable levels (Khor, 1998).

At the same time, months before the crisis, there had been concerns that the Malaysian economy was growing at unsustainable levels and was overheating, resulting in growing imbalances in both the domestic and external sectors. For example, Malaysia's economic growth rate since 1991 has consistently exceeded its potential output. According to the BNM, Malaysia's actual GDP growth rate in 1996 was estimated as being about 10 percent above its potential output (BNM, 1998). This growth was derived from massive inflows of foreign capital and foreign labor. In 1996, net private flow into the country constituted 9.6 percent of GDP, while foreign workers constituted more than 20 percent of the country's labor force.

There were other emerging concerns in the Malaysian economy which subsequently affected investor confidence. These concerns include:

(a) Problems associated with a slowdown in exports and decline in export competitiveness (resulting from the quasi-pegging of the ringgit to the US dollar and the significant appreciation of the latter prior to the crisis), resulting in a large current account deficit in the balance of payments (see table 3.1);

(b) Loss of efficiency in the economy as indicated by declining total factor productivity (TFP) growth from 4.7 percent in 1988 to 1 percent in 1997 as well as rising incremental capital–output ratio from 3.0 in 1988 to 6.5 in 1997 (National Economic Action Council, 1998, pp. 10–11). Consequently, TFP contribution to real GDP growth declined from 28.7 percent during 1991–95 to 19.5 percent during 1996–97 (Malaysia, 1999, p. 36);

(c) Excessive credit expansion, especially to non-productive sectors, such as the property sector, consumption credit, and loans for the purchase of shares (see tables 3.4 and 3.5). The financial sector witnessed credit growth averaging 30 percent per annum during the 1995–97 period. During the 1993–97 period, loans for the purchase of shares grew at an average rate of 38 percent per annum and amounted to 8.4 percent of the total commercial bank loans at the end of 1997. For most of 1997, loans to the property sector grew by 30 percent and amounted to 32.2 percent of total commercial

Table 3.4 Credit extended by the banking sector and development institutions and growth indicators, 1987–97(RM billion and percent, end of period)

	1987	1988	1989	1990	1991	1992	1993	1994	1995	1996	1997
Credit extended by:											
Banking institutions	70.2	77.5	92.5	114.0	138.8	152.4	170.8	195.9	251.9	332.9	421.0
Commercial banks	52.2	56.8	67.1	80.7	97.2	105.7	117.2	134.2	175.0	228.3	289.5
Finance companies	13.6	15.8	19.9	27.0	34.1	38.2	43.8	50.1	62.8	85.8	108.4
Merchant banks	4.4	4.9	5.5	6.3	7.5	8.5	9.8	11.6	14.1	18.8	23.1
Islamic banking	0.5	0.6	0.7	0.8	0.8	1.0	1.1	1.7	3.5	6.1	10.8
Industrial finance institutions	0.7	0.7	0.8	1.0	1.2	2.5	2.7	3.1	3.9	5.0	6.1
Rural credit institutions	0.9	0.7	0.9	0.5	0.5	0.7	0.9	1.0	1.2	1.6	2.1
Growth indicators											
GDP at current market prices	79.6	90.8	102.5	115.7	132.3	148.5	165.2	190.2	218.7	249.8	277.0
GDP growth rate (%)	5.4	8.9	9.2	9.7	8.7	7.8	8.1	9.2	9.5	8.6	7.8
Banking loans/GDP (%)	88.2	85.3	90.2	98.5	104.9	102.6	103.4	103.0	115.2	133.3	152.0
Commercial bank loan growth (%)	−0.3	8.9	18.1	20.3	20.4	8.8	10.9	14.4	30.5	24.5	32.9
M3 growth (%)	4.5	8.1	20.6	18.2	15.3	19.6	23.5	13.1	22.3	21.2	18.4
Government development finance	4.1	4.0	5.7	7.9	8.4	8.4	9.1	10.0	12.5	12.6	14.4
Fiscal surplus/GDP (%)	−2.6	0.8	2.2	3.9	4.4	4.8	5.7	7.6	6.6	5.8	7.6

Source: Ong (1999, 148).

Table 3.5 Distribution of commercial bank loans by sector, 1990–June 1998 (percent)

	1990	1991	1992	1993	1994	1995	1996	1997	June 1998
Manufacturing	23.2	24.2	24.0	26.5	24.0	24.2	22.0	20.1	19.2
Finance, insurance, business services	11.3	11.9	12.9	14.5	12.6	13.6	15.6	9.8	9.8
General commerce	14.4	13.2	12.2	11.7	11.2	10.9	10.2	10.3	10.3
Property sector	30.0	29.1	30.0	29.9	26.3	26.5	27.1	32.2	28.1
Construction	6.8	6.9	8.1	7.9	7.7	8.0	8.9	10.1	10.3
Real estate	11.3	10.3	10.4	9.7	8.1	9.1	9.7	4.3	3.9
Housing	11.9	11.9	11.5	12.3	10.5	9.4	8.5	13.1	9.1
Housing loans sold to Cagamas	n.a.	n.a.	n.a.	n.a.	n.a.	n.a.	n.a.	4.7	4.8
Purchase of stocks & shares	2.8	3.0	2.3	2.6	5.8	4.6	4.3	8.4	8.8
Consumption credits	2.4	2.5	2.6	3.3	3.6	3.7	3.7	1.6	1.4
Agriculture	5.2	4.8	4.4	3.5	2.6	2.2	2.1	2.0	2.1
Other	10.7	11.3	11.6	8.0	13.9	14.3	15.0	15.6	20.3
Total	100.0	100.0	100.0	100.0	100.0	100.0	100.0	100.0	100.0
Commercial bank loans (US$ billion)	29.9	35.7	40.6	43.4	52.4	68.9	86.2	74.5[a]	71.1[b]
Commercial bank loans/GDP (%)	69.8	73.4	71.2	71.0	70.5	80.0	87.2	104.5	n.a.

Notes: [a] at RM 3.8883 = US$1.00; [b] at RM 4.1750 = US$ 1.00

Source: Ong (1999, 151).

89

Table 3.6 Malaysia: external loans, 1991–98 (RM million)

		Loans from Nonresidents	Loans to Nonresidents
1991		3,436	477
1992		9,440	648
1993		12,845	1,533
1994		19,729	3,228
1995		19,405	2,108
1996		21,856	2,403
1997	1st Quarter	5,622	586
	2nd Quarter	9,994	563
	3rd Quarter	7,485	1,338
	4th Quarter	6,070	472
1997	Total	29,172	2,958
1998	1st Quarter	5,378	637
	2nd Quarter	4,858	427
	3rd Quarter	4,343	752
	4th Quarter	6,796	1,013
1998	Total	21,375	2,829

Sources: BNM, *Monthly Statistical Bulletin*, September 1998, Table VIII.13, pp. 116–19, and April 1999, Table VII.14, p. 123.

bank loans at the end of 1997. The rapid banking credit growth was partly associated with the BNM's new two-tier regulatory system introduced in December 1994 in its efforts to consolidate Malaysian banks and in anticipation of further financial liberalization. As only bigger 'tier-1' banks were allowed to handle certain lucrative kinds of transactions denied to other banks and on the criterion used to qualify for 'tier-1' category is value of capital, many smaller commercial banks borrowed to increase their capital base. Having borrowed the capital funds, they had to lend these funds and this partly led to the rapid credit expansion prior to the crisis;

(d) Rising external indebtedness. Malaysia's medium- and long-term debt, as a percentage of net external reserves, rose dramatically from 102 percent at the end of 1994 to 176 percent by mid-1997, after declining since the mid-1980s (see table 3.6). Unlike the public sector's external borrowing in the first half of the 1980s, it was the private sector which was responsible for incurring these large foreign obligations.

Malaysia was incurring a current account deficit of RM14.8 billion in 1994, which rose significantly to RM21.7 billion in 1995 before falling to RM12.2 billion in 1996. While running a current account deficit *per se* is not necessarily problematic, nevertheless given Malaysia's worsening export position (growing by only 6.5 percent in 1996 as compared to over 20 percent per annum during the 1993–95 period) and its declining efficiency, the current account deficit was perceived to be a cause for concern. More worrying to foreign investors was the fact that the current account deficit has been largely financed by foreign savings as Malaysia continued to face an escalating savings–investment gap, rising to 10.5 percent of the GNP in 1995 (see table 3.1). The earlier report by the Bank of International Settlements, which shows that the bulk of Malaysia's foreign loans were short term – 56 percent of the total as of 30 June 1997 which was rather volatile in nature and not sustainable in the long run, added further concern. However, according to the BNM, even including intercompany borrowings, the correct figure for short-term external borrowing for Malaysia should be 30 percent. Even including the medium- and long-term debt with one year or less remaining to maturity, the ratio would not exceed 39 percent of the foreign debt. However, the earlier figure could have put additional pressure on the ringgit when the crisis started (Ong, 1999, p. 161).

Hence the combination of these factors generated contagion effects for Malaysia where common risk factors were perceived to be present by speculators and genuine investors alike. Furthermore, with the sharp and sudden depreciation of the ringgit, coupled with the reduction of the foreign reserves in initial anti-speculation attempts (estimated to be about US$3.5 billion), the burden of debt servicing rose correspondingly in terms of the local-currency amount required for loan repayment. The fact that a rather significant proportion of the foreign loans were short term became an additional problem. This was followed by the short-term foreign funds starting to pull out sharply, causing reserves to fall further.

Hence, despite its relatively stronger initial conditions as compared with other regional economies, Malaysia was not spared from the contagion effect of the crisis.

3.   NATIONAL POLICY RESPONSES

The Malaysian government's response to the crisis changed at various stages, reflecting the different assessment and policy orientations. During the initial stage of the crisis, the monetary and regulatory authorities attempted to stabilize the ringgit by intervening in the foreign exchange markets and raising domestic interest rates. The government also introduced selective administrative measures to curb speculation in the currency and stock markets. According to the *Economic Report 1997/98*, issued by the Ministry of Finance, among measures introduced to boost market confidence included:

(a) Declaring all the 100 component stocks of the Composite Index of the KLSE as 'designated securities' – that is, requiring actual presentation of share script at the moment of transaction (rather than a few days later, as was the normal practice) – on 28 August 1997, ostensibly to check 'short selling';

(b) Announcing a RM60 billion standby facility to stabilize the stock market on September 3 1997; and

(c) Freezing new share issues and corporate restructuring.

However, intervention in the foreign exchange markets became very costly as it led to the depletion of the country's foreign exchange reserves. Subsequently, the BNM abandoned its defense of the ringgit and allowed it to move in response to market forces. Similarly, the raising of domestic interest rates had the negative effect of exacerbating the economic downturn and contributing to the drastic fall in the stock market. Administrative measures to stabilize the stock market also did not produce the desired result. Instead, these measures and the various contrarian statements of Malaysia's Prime Minister (including his tough speech at the joint World Bank–IMF annual meeting in Hong Kong on September 20 1997) appeared to have adversely affected investors' confidence and contributed to a further fall of the ringgit and the share prices at the KLSE.

After the failure of its initial measures to stem the steep decline in the ringgit and the share prices, the government sought a more comprehensive solution. The second phase of the response was characterized by efforts to improve domestic fundamentals including enhancing the soundness of the banking system and addressing the various structural weaknesses in the economy. Unlike its neighbor, Malaysia refused to seek the IMF bailout package. None the less, it implemented an IMF-style adjustment which included efforts to maintain fiscal discipline, reduce the current account deficit, and improve the country's resource position as well as restraining credit growth and strengthening the banking system.

Accordingly, a set of austerity measures was announced in early September 1997 to further reduce the level of aggregate demand and contain the current account deficit. These measures included a 2 percent cut across the board in government spending; rationalization of the purchase of imported goods by public agencies (including the armed forces); and deferment of several large privatized projects (BNM, 1998). These measures were further reinforced with additional measures in the 1998 budget announced in October 1997. However, as the crisis persisted into the last two months of 1997, the Malaysian government introduced a stronger and more comprehensive package of policies to address the situation. Among the measures taken were a sharp cutback in federal government expenditure by 18 percent in 1998; the deferment of selected projects, including privatized projects amounting to RM65.6 billion; the intensive promotion of exports, tourism, and the usage of locally produced goods. To counter the country's overdependence on imported intermediate goods, the development of the small- and medium-scale industries (SMIs) was being accelerated. Measures to increase exports include the introduction of various tax incentives to boost the manufacturing, agriculture, and services sector. In addition, the government also imposed a freeze on its reverse investment which amounted to RM10.5 billion (including retained earnings overseas) in 1996.

Measures were also instituted to further strengthen prudential standards of the banking system. These measures included the recognition of a loan as non-performing when its servicing has been in arrears for three months instead of six; increasing the minimum general provision from 1 percent to 1.5 percent and greater disclosure in financial statements. To achieve the objectives of reducing overall credit growth and exposure to the less productive sector, the financial institutions were advised to voluntarily undertake efforts to reduce overall credit growth in stages, that is to 25 percent by end-1997, 20 percent by end-March 1998 and 15 percent by end-1998. Concurrently, the banking institutions had to ensure that in allocating credit, priority would be given to borrowers engaged in productive and export-oriented activities. Measures were also taken to address the concerns about the high leverage of corporations (BNM, 1998).

However, as the country's GDP declined sharply in the first quarter of 1998, the government launched a countercyclical move in an attempt to head off an impending recession. Among the measures introduced is the injection of RM7 billion into the economy via the creation of a number of projects in productive sectors such as agriculture, low- and medium-cost housing, schools, expansion of skills training centers and institutions of higher learning, clinics, bridges and rural roads, water supply system, and infrastructure. As the crisis worsened, the National Economic Recovery Plan (NERP) was introduced, aimed at promoting economic recovery in Malaysia. The NERP presents six strategic areas of action to address the financial crisis and its pervasive negative effects on the Malaysian economy. These measures were aimed at stabilising the ringgit, restoring market confidence, maintaining financial market stability, strengthening economic fundamentals, continuing the equity and socioeconomic agenda, and revitalizing affected sectors of the economy. Among the major policy decisions that have been implemented in line with the objective of the NERP was the establishment of the Pengurusan Danaharta Nasional Bhd (Danaharta) to purchase non-performing loans from the banking sector and Danamodal Nasional Bhd (Danamodal) for the purpose of recapitalization of the banking system.

In an attempt to fend off further battering of the ringgit that might result following the pending removal of the then Deputy Prime Minister, Anwar Ibrahim, which would worsen the financial and economic crisis faced by the country, the government introduced selective capital and exchange control measures on 2 September 1998 to insulate the economy from externally generated risks and vulnerabilities. The new Malaysian policy package included the official fixing of the ringgit at 3.80 to the US dollar, thus removing or greatly reducing the role of the market in determining the day-to-day level of the ringgit *vis-à-vis* the US dollar (but the ringgit value in relation to other currencies will still fluctuate according to their own rates against the dollar); measures to eliminate international trade in the ringgit by bringing back to the country ringgit-denominated financial assets such as cash and savings deposits via the non-recognition or non-acceptance of such assets in the country after a one-month deadline; the measure that non-residents purchasing local shares will not be able to withdraw from the country the proceeds from the sale of the shares for a year from the purchase date; all dealings in shares listed on the KLSE must be effected through the exchange or a stock exchange recognised by the KLSE; measures curbing the taking out or bringing in of funds with Malaysians travelling abroad are limited to carrying RM1000 and to another RM10,000 worth of foreign currency, while non-resident travellers can take out foreign currencies up to the amount they brought in (and no limit on the import of foreign currencies); and imposing conditions on the operations and transfers of funds in the external accounts. It has been stressed that foreign direct investors, who are free to repatriate their earnings, are not affected as these controls are aimed at containing the impact of short-term fund flows.

At the same time, in its continued effort to revive the economy, the 1999 budget presented in October 1998 adopted an expansionary fiscal policy. In fact, the government development expenditure was increased by about 23 percent in 1998 to RM19,378 million while the operating expenditure increased by 4.2 percent to RM46,563 million. With the expected fall of 16.2 percent in the federal government revenue, the overall federal government financial position registered a deficit of RM9.587 billion (or 3.7 percent of GNP) in 1998. Out of the additional allocation for development expenditure in 1998, RM1000 million has been allocated to social safety net projects to address and ameliorate the effects of economic crisis on the lower-income groups. However, some of the expenditure allocated were for off-budget purposes including the RM1,500 million provided to Danaharta, and the RM654 million provided to Cyberview (part of the Multimedia Super Corridor project). For 1999, the budget allowed a 1 percent increase in federal government operating expenditure to RM47.042 billion while the gross development expenditure was reduced by 9.4 percent to RM17.553 billion. As a result, the overall financial position of the Federal Government was expected to experience a larger deficit of RM16,135 million or 6.1 percent of GNP in 1999.

Although it may be too early to make the assessment of the success of Malaysia's experience with selective capital and exchange controls and the other measures to reflate the economy, the signs thus far reveal some of the intended effects. First, the ringgit's value was fixed and stable at 3.80 to the dollar from September 2, 1998 onwards. There were slight fluctuations relating to other currencies reflecting changes in their values *vis-à-vis* the US dollar. Second, the authorities lost no time in sharply reducing the interest rate. For example, the base lending rate (BLR) of commercial banks, which rose from 10.33 percent at the end of 1997 to 12.27 percent at the end of June 1998, further exacerbated the contraction of economic activities during the first half of 1998, and was reduced to a maximum rate of 8.92 percent by end the of September 1998 and to 8.05 percent as of November 10, 1998. This means that the average BLR at mid-November 1998 was below the level prevailing before the financial crisis, that is 8.93 percent at the end of June 1997. This easing of the monetary policy was done without triggering currency depreciation, thus resolving the policy dilemma involving a trade-off between lowering the interest rate and the maintenance of the ringgit level. In other words, with the introduction of capital controls, the link between the interest rate and the foreign exchange rate was cut, as the currency value was fixed, and there was greater freedom to vary the interest rate. The move has also benefited the banking institutions and private firms via enhanced liquidity and lower interest rates. Total loans extended by the banking system have begun to expand. Domestic demand, especially for passenger cars, has also picked up. Malaysia's external reserve position has strengthened and market capitalization of the KLSE has improved. The current account of the balance of payments has recorded a big surplus in 1998 (Malaysia, 1999).

4.   FROM FINANCIAL TO ECONOMIC CRISIS

The regional currency crisis that swept across the region quickly developed into a financial crisis, which later had an adverse impact on the real economy of the affected countries, and threw their economic achievements of the past decade into disarray. As in other affected countries, the depreciation of the ringgit hit the corporate sector in Malaysia in a number of ways. First, the exchange rate depreciation adversely affected firms that had taken foreign-currency loans as they had to pay much more in local currency in repaying their debts. Second, the initial attempt to prevent further depreciation of the ringgit through a tight monetary policy has resulted in the rising of the domestic interest rate and the banks became very stringent in giving new loans. This further led to the rapid fall of stock and share prices. Third, as the value of the firms' collateral dropped, their creditor banks commanded them to 'top up' the collateral or repay some of the loans, thus forcing some firms into financial difficulties and even bankruptcy. Finally, although Malaysia did not turn to the International Monetary Fund (IMF) for assistance, IMF-style policies were implemented until mid-1998, resulting in the contraction of government expenditures. After a lag of a few months, the financial crisis began to have repercussions on the real economy.

The impact of the financial crisis on Malaysian economic growth became evident towards the end of 1997 when the economy slowed down and registered negative growth beginning from the first quarter of 1998. The contraction of the real GDP – the first time since 1985 – was indeed severe and unprecedented. On a year-on-year basis, real GDP contracted by 2.8 percent in the first quarter of 1998, 6.8 percent in the second quarter, 8.6 percent in the third quarter and 8.1 percent in the fourth quarter. Consequently, overall real GDP for Malaysia contracted by 6.7 percent in 1998 (compared with 7.7 percent growth in 1997) (see table 3.7). Per capita GNP also declined by 1.8 percent to RM11,835 in 1998 (Malaysia, 1999).

However, with the easing of monetary policy and the countercyclical measures taken by the government in the second half of 1998, including the implementation of the National Economic Recovery Plan (NERP), the contraction of the economy was less severe in the first quarter of 1999. According to the latest estimate by the BNM, the Malaysian economy contracted by 1.6 percent during the first quarter of 1999. It was estimated that the economy will register a positive growth of 1 percent for the whole of 1999.

Table 3.7 Malaysia: gross domestic product (GDP) by sector, 1997 and 1998 (%)

	1997			1998ª		
	Growth	Share of GDP	Contribution to growth	Growth	Share of GDP	Contribution to growth
Agriculture, forestry and fishing*	1.3	11.9	2.2	−4.0	12.3	−0.7
Mining	1.0	6.7	0.9	0.8	7.3	0.0
Manufacturing	12.5	35.7	55.5	−10.2	34.4	−56.9
Construction	9.5	4.8	5.8	−24.5	3.9	−15.5
Services	8.0	44.9	46.5	1.5	48.8	1.2
Less Imputed bank service charges	14.6	8.2	14.6	7.5	9.4	11.4
Plus Import duties	6.7	4.1	3.6	−38.0	2.7	−16.6
GDP	7.7	100.0	100.0	−6.7	100.0	100.0

Notes: ª estimate.
* includes livestock and horticulture.
Source: Malaysia (1998: 72; 1999: 39).

By sectors, the output of the primary and secondary sectors of the economy declined in 1998, while the value added of the tertiary sector increased at a much slower rate. The manufacturing sector, which provided the main impetus to overall GDP growth for the past decade, experienced a considerable contraction of 10.2 percent in 1998 (see tables 3.7). This is due to the shrinking domestic demand and poor overseas sales orders, especially due to the financial crisis affecting East Asian economies, as well as increasing competition in the global market. Rising production costs (due to the higher price of imported components), tight liquidity, higher interest rates and the volatility of the ringgit movement before the introduction of the exchange control measures also led manufacturers to take a more cautious stance, particularly not to build up stocks in view of higher holding costs. Discouraged by weak demand and rising costs, most industries have put on hold their plans for further expansion. As a result, there has been a continuous decline in manufacturing output since February 1998, as evidenced by negative growth of the manufacturing production index (see figure 3.1). For the third quarter of 1998, the manufacturing sector continued its contraction, with a 14.3 percent decline from a year ago or by 1.2 percent from the second quarter of 1998. Value added in the construction sector declined sharply in 1998, that is by 24.5 percent, largely due to the erosion of financial wealth of the population caused by the declining stock prices, difficulty in getting end-financing and bridging finance from the banking sector and rising interest rates before September 1998. For the third quarter of 1998, the construction sector continued with the most severe decline, that is by 28.2 percent from a year ago or by 2.6 percent from the second quarter. Output in the agricultural sector also declined by 4.0 percent in 1998, largely due to lower output of various commodities such as saw-logs, cocoa, rubber, and oil palm. The sharp contraction in the secondary and primary sectors of the economy and lower real disposable income have led to declining demand for services, resulting in the tertiary sector experiencing a sharp deceleration to register a slower

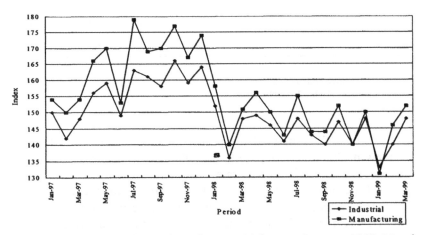

Figure 3.1 Index of industrial production, Malaysia, January 1997–March 1999

Source: Ministry of Human Resources, Malaysia, *Labor Market Report* (various issues).

growth rate of 1.5 percent in 1998 (Malaysia, 1999).

Reduced economic activities and the lower real disposable income have led to a significant reduction in private consumption expenditure and the demand for imports. Real private consumption registered a negative growth of 12.4 percent while real import declined by 18.3 percent in 1998 (Malaysia, 1999, p. 35). With import volume declining sharply against a marginal increase in export volume, the current account of the balance of payments recorded an unprecedented surplus of RM36.1 billion in 1998, the first surplus since 1989. For the whole of 1998, Malaysia recorded a trade surplus of RM69.3 billion, exceeding an earlier projection of RM35 billion (see table 3.1). Consequently, the country's external reserve position at the end of 1998 strengthened to RM99.4 billion or US$26.2 billion, which is equivalent to 5.7 months of retained imports (Malaysia, 1999).

As expected, the overall financial position of the federal government recorded a deficit of RM5.0 billion in 1998, the first deficit since 1993 (see table 3.8). This is due in part to lower revenue collection, particularly indirect taxes, as a result of reduced economic activities. At the same time, the federal government total expenditure in 1998 was actually raised to RM62.7 billion as a result of the countercyclical measures undertaken since the last quarter of 1998.

5. SOCIAL IMPACT OF THE CRISIS

As the financial and economic crisis unfolded, its consequences on the well-being of the population become increasingly more apparent. As in other affected countries, the financial and economic crisis in Malaysia exerted an adverse social impact through the following channels: the drastic changes in the labor market; rising prices; the drastic decline in the value of assets; the tight monetary policy and the contraction in government budget as implemented in the earlier phase of the crisis. This section, however, will look at the social impact of the crisis by focusing on changes in the labor market and rising prices.

5.1 Changes in the Labor Market

The contraction of the real economy has affected the pace of job creation and led to an increased incidence of structural unemployment. The cutbacks in the manufacturing sector, for example, resulted in the reduction of employment opportunities available, thus reversing the increasing employment trend in that sector. In contrast to the increase by

*Table 3.8 Federal government expenditure and financing,
Malaysia, 1995–98 (RM million)*

Item	1995	1996	1997[3]	1998
Total revenue	50954	58280	65736	56710
Direct taxes	22699	25851	30432	30016
Indirect taxes	18972	21421	23195	15320
Non-tax revenue[1]	9283	11008	12109	10833
Operating expenditure[2]	36573	43865	44665	44584
Development expenditure	14051	14628	15750	18103
Repayment	1531	2028	1305	975
Overall surplus/deficit	1861	1815	6626	−5002
(% of GNP)	0.9	0.8	2.5	−1.9
Sources of financing				
Net foreign borrowing[4]	−1635	−2177	−1681	1819
Net domestic borrowing	0	1291	−2048	11040
Change in assets & special receipts	−226	−929	−2897	−7858

Notes:
1 Includes government commercial undertakings, interest and returns on investment, licences, service fees, road tax, fines and forfeitures, rental revenue from federal territories, contributions from foreign governments and international agencies, and petroleum royalties/gas cash payments.
2 Excludes transfer to development fund.
3 Estimated actual.
4 Includes special receipts.

Sources: BNM, *Annual Report* 1998, p. 97; *Economic Report 1998/99*, Statistical Tables, p. xxxv.

an average of 7.7 percent experienced during the 1996–97 period, the employment in the manufacturing sector registered a decline of 3.6 percent in 1998. However, the largest decline was in the construction sector with negative growth of 16.9 percent (see table 3.9). Consequently, based on the latest estimate, total employment declined by about 3.0 percent to 8.537 million in 1998 and the unemployment rate increased to 3.9 percent of the labor force. The total employment dropped to its lowest level of 8.464 million in September 1998 before improving to 8.582 million by the end of 1998 (see table 3.9). The number of unemployed increased from 233,100 in 1997 to 343,200 in 1998, an increase of 110,100 (or 47.2 percent).

Table 3.9 Employment by sector, Malaysia, 1997 and 1998 ('000 persons)

Sector	1997		1998		1998	
			Mar.	June	Sept.	Dec.
Agriculture, forestry, livestock & fishing	1494.5	1433.4	1589.0	1580.0	1667.0	1622.0
Mining & quarrying	38.8	39.0	26.0	26.0	25.0	34.0
Manufacturing	2390.5	2305.3	1981.0	1909.0	1803.0	1957.0
Construction	874.2	726.7	760.0	777.0	694.0	52.0
Electricity, gas & water	75.8	77.3	52.0	43.0	51.0	738.0
Transport, storage & communication	436.2	438.4	454.0	389.0	432.0	1639.0
Wholesale & retail trade, hotels & restaurants	1447.3	1438.4	1623.0	1658.0	1549.0	403.0
Finance, insurance, real estate & business services	405.8	416.4	436.0	440.0	415.0	395.0
Government service	873.2	875.0	1807.0[a]	1814.0[a]	1828.0[a]	1742.0[a]
Other services	768.8	787.8	–	–	–	–
Total	**8805.1**	**8537.7**	**8728.0**	**8636.0**	**8464.0**	**8582.0**
Labour force	8256.8	8880.9	8989.3	8931.4	8752.8	8884.0
Unemployment	232.9	343.2	260.7	294.7	288.8	302.0
Unemployment rate (%)	2.8	3.9	2.9	3.3	3.3	3.4

Note: [a] includes community, social and personal services.

Sources: *Economic Report 1998/99, Statistical Tables*, p. 1, xi; *Monthly Statistical Bulletin*, May 1999, p.127.

Unemployment was increasing in the country partly as a result of the retrenchment of workers in the major sectors of the economy. According to official statistics released by the Ministry of Human Resources, a total of 83,865 workers were retrenched by 4,789 firms in 1998. This figure amounts to 1 percent of the total workforce, and is much higher than the number of 18,863 workers reported to be retrenched for the whole of 1997.

The urbanized states in Peninsular Malaysia had a higher number of retrenched workers, with Selangor having the highest number of 20,082 (or 23.9 percent of the total), followed by Penang (16,884 or 20.1 percent), and the federal territory of Kuala Lumpur (10,863 or 13.0 percent). By sectors, the largest retrenchment took place in the manufacturing sector, with 53.7 percent of the total retrenched workers, followed by the wholesale and retail trade, the restaurant and hotel sector (12.4 percent) and the construction sector (11.4 percent). By occupational categories, production workers constitute the biggest category with 53.8 percent, followed by professional and technical workers (14.5 percent), clerical workers (11.8 percent), and administrative and managerial workers (7.5 percent).

The paradox in the Malaysian labor market situation was that while there was retrenchment, there were also still large numbers of unfilled vacancies, and that the Human Resources Ministry claimed 'almost all the retrenched local workers have already found new jobs' (*New Straits Times*, 3 December 1998). For example, between January and December 1998, 74,610 job vacancies were available in various industries. It was also reported that between May 2, 1998 and January 7, 1999, a total of 572 workers who failed to find replacement jobs had enrolled in various courses under the Retrenched Workers' Training Scheme managed by the Human Resources Development Fund Council. From that figure, 64.8 percent were being trained at diploma level, and the rest at certificate level. A sum of RM2.52 million was set aside for this purpose.

However, while it is true that a proportion of those retrenched have found new jobs, many of the vacancies in various states could be in lower-paid categories or demanding a certain level of skill and were thus not conducive to facilitating labor mobility. Thus it was reported by the Ministry of Human Resources that out of 43,102 workers retrenched between June and 12 December 1998, 11,498 have found new jobs, 5,615 could not get new jobs, 4,120 ventured into new areas such as small trading and 21,869 could not be detected. A study among 150 retrenched workers in Ipoh conducted in October 1998 found that 45 percent of them were still unemployed (after eight months), 13.4 percent took four to seven months to get a new job, 38 percent between one to three months, and only 4 percent obtained a new job immediately. Among those who managed to get a new job, only 46 percent said the new job was suited to their experience, education and skills, while for the majority (54 percent), it was not so. Though this may not reflect the overall situation, the fact of a mismatch between the new job and the workers' work experience existed, something to be expected in a crisis situation.

A re-emerging phenomenon during the crisis was graduate unemployment. The monthly statistics released in November by the Department of Human Resources on Malaysia's job market for professionals indicated a widening gap between supply and demand. The number of graduates registered with the department for September 1998 was 4,592, virtually unchanged from the previous month's figure of 4,646, but had more than doubled from last September's 2,150. The number of vacancies for September 1998 was 73, down from 153 the previous month (more than 50 percent), and 117 for the same month in 1997. However, these figures might not reflect the true job market in the country as only an estimated 15 percent of unemployed graduates sign up, even though it is a free service (*The Sun*, 9 November 1998, p. 4).

The latest official data indicate that the labor market showed some improvement, with retrenchment slowing down from 12,335 in July 1998 to 7,395 in February 1999 (see figure 3.2). This development has been used as one of the important indicators to indicate that 'the worst is over' and that the Malaysian economy is on the road to gradual recovery. A survey of 138 companies (45 local companies and 93 multinationals) in

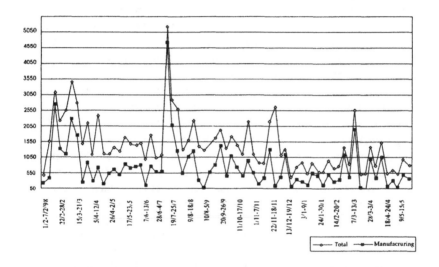

Figure 3.2 Weekly retrenchment trend, Malaysia, February 1998–May 1999

Source: Department of Statistics Malaysia, *Industrial Production Index* (various issues).

14 industries in Malaysia conducted by Watson Wyatt Worldwide, which seeks to establish the response of the private sector to the economic downturn, tends to support this assessment. According to a *New Straits Times* report (12 December 1998, p. 21), the survey found out that 17 percent of the companies were forced to retrench workers in 1998, but only three companies indicated they would do so in 1999. The survey also reported that not only was retrenchment slowing down, but the exercise was more industry-specific, mainly in the manufacturing and construction

sectors. None the less, the fourth quarter 1998 labor force survey conducted by the Statistics Department showed that the unemployment rate has yet to show a declining trend; it increased slightly to 3.4 percent compared to 3.3 percent in the third quarter (see table 3.9).

However, it is important to stress that in a crisis situation it is difficult to estimate unemployment and retrenchment figures. Therefore, allowances have to be made for those unemployed and retrenched but not captured in the official figures. Partly, a significant number of retrenched workers were foreign workers and many of them were unregistered (or illegal) workers. This was especially so in the construction sector – which is one of the most adversely affected during the 1997–8 crisis, where 80 percent of its workforce were migrant workers and a significant percentage are unregistered. According to one estimate, there were 1.7 million foreign workers in Malaysia in 1997, out of which 560,000 are unregistered workers (BNM, 1998, p. 63). During this crisis, reverse migration took place among foreign workers in Malaysia, most noticeably among illegal foreign workers, both on an organised basis (repatriation and deportation) as well as on an individual informal basis. Based on official figures, between January and August 1998, 207,946 illegal foreign workers and their dependants returned to their countries. Under an amnesty program, another 176,000 were repatriated between September 1 and November 15, 1998. In other words, based on the official reports, a total of 383,946 foreign workers and their dependants have returned to their respective countries. In addition, registered foreign workers in the manufacturing industries also faced non-renewal/termination of their contract by their employers during this crisis. At the same time, retrenchment of the locals in the informal sector was also taking place and their number most probably was not captured in official statistics. Press reports indicated a substantial number of small businesses went bankrupt as a result of falling demand and the rising cost of doing business, resulting in their employees losing their source of livelihood. Interviews with various focus groups also revealed that there was considerable underemployment, which was probably not captured in official statistics.

5.2 Falling Incomes

Some firms reacted to the crisis not by laying off their workers but by cutting wages or lowering (and sometimes freezing) pay increases. For example, in the car assembly industry, where unions existed, workers had to accept a 25 percent wage cut to avoid retrenchment. But, there were some employers who imposed excessive pay cuts of 30 to 50 percent, including on lower-paid workers. The move by firms to cut wages, together with lower or no pay increase agreed upon in collective bargaining negotiations between unions and employers as a solution to avoid retrenchment of workers, has contributed to the decline in workers' wages during 1998. This has resulted in reversing the trend of rising real wages since the early 1990s. This correction in the labour market could have contributed to lower retrenchment and unemployment figures for the country, thus lessening the adverse impact of the crisis.

In addition, a very high percentage of workers in both the private and public sectors were no longer working overtime although they were most willing to do so. In fact, in some industries, workers were underemployed (that is working less than 40 hours per week) and forced to take pay cuts.

Some companies also defaulted or delayed in paying wages and retrenchment benefits to their workers. The Human Resource Minister revealed that 43,889 retrenched workers had not been paid compensation amounting to RM56.7 million (or 23 percent of the total compensation payments) in the first seven months of 1998 (*New Straits Times*, 6 October 1998). It is believed that the delay may be due to 'technical and administrative reasons', and may have been sorted out a few months later.

This changing situation in the labour market has resulted in a big drop in workers' income, causing serious difficulties for many of them, especially those having vehicle and housing loans to settle. With the retrenchment of workers and the reduction in wages/salaries experienced by some sectors of the economy, several indicators showed moderating increases in the wage rates. The Monthly Surveys of Manufacturing Industries conducted by the Department of Statistics showed wages increasing at a slower rate of 5.6 percent in 1998, compared with 10.2 percent in 1997 (BNM, 1999, p. 78). Based on the estimate provided by the *Economic Report 1998/99*, real wages per worker declined by 9.9 percent during the first seven months of 1998 as compared to an increase of 18.9 percent during the corresponding period in 1997 (Malaysia, 1998, pp. 73–4). The fall in real wages is higher in some of the sub-sectors (e.g. the electrical, electronics and machinery industry) of the manufacturing sector.

The survey conducted by Watson Wyatt Worldwide mentioned above also found that 68 percent of the companies were still giving pay increases in 1998, while 28 percent froze wages, and 4 percent carried out pay cuts. However, workers' wage increases for 1998 have already been halved compared with 1997's double-digit levels. The survey speculates that, for 1999, wage increases may continue falling. Lower pay increases will be accompanied by smaller bonuses as more firms opt for variable bonus or productivity-based bonus payment than for the guaranteed or contractual bonus.

Although the late 1997–98 crisis seemed to have hit hardest the urban workforce in the formal sector, those in the informal sector and some sections of the rural working population have not been spared. For example, the livelihood of taxi drivers was adversely affected by the crisis as people tended to be more cautious with their spending and travelling and there were fewer tourist arrivals. In order to cover rentals, fuel and other incidentals, and also have some income, some taxi drivers had to work long hours, sometimes up to 16 hours per day. At the same time, transportation lorry drivers were affected because they had fewer trips in sending consigned goods. In two instances, some lorry drivers were not paid their wages for three to four months, while others faced retrenchment as their employers faced serious cash flow problems. Rice farmers' and fishermen's incomes were also affected by the rising cost of production due to the increase in input prices.

The *batik* (traditional textile) industry in the east coast state of Kelantan was badly affected due to the rising price of imported white linen as well as due to a slump in domestic demand, and competition from Indonesia and Thailand. Before the crisis, at its height, there were approximately 350 *batik* entrepreneurs in Kelantan, and over 30,000 people were dependent on it directly or indirectly. A person who draws patterns on the *batik* could earn as much as RM1,000 per month. In 1998, the batik industry was in crisis, with many entrepreneurs having gone bankrupt or on the verge of bankruptcy, and many of their employees were either thrown out of work, or only worked one or two days a week. Hawkers and small traders were not spared the brunt of the crisis, experiencing a big drop in their business. Yet the informal sector provided some sort of safety net for those retrenched and others seeking more income to make ends meet, leading to an overcrowding problem. Though the informal sector was hit by the crisis, its impact was uneven, depending on the location and type of business performed.

Due to falling income, many retrenched workers had to rely on past savings to overcome budgetary deficits during the crisis. In fact, some of them had resorted to borrowing from friends and relatives; some resorted to getting loans from informal sources, which charged high interest rates. Others, especially women, had gone to pawn shops to pawn their jewellery. Those relying on their savings were worried that their savings would soon be depleted and they might also have to resort to borrowing if the crisis persisted.

Among private sector workers and government employees, not a few had to take additional jobs to supplement their reduced incomes. Some resorted to small trading in night markets or selling cakes/*nasi lemak* in their residential areas and by the roadside.

Remittances to parents in rural areas had also declined as a result of retrenchment or a big fall in the workers' income. Many workers interviewed in the rapid assessment study reported that they either had to stop sending money altogether, or to reduce the amount. This could affect the income of rural people as transfer payments (including remittances from children working in urban areas) form a substantial proportion of their income.

At the same time, due partly to their cash flow problem, the number of employers defaulting on Employment Providence Fund (EPF) contributions on behalf of their workers has increased since the crisis. For example, during the first six months of 1998, a total of 15,560 employers (or 5.4 percent of the total registered employers) failed to contribute to the EPF as compared to 13,143 for the whole of 1997. The default by employers may seriously jeopardize the workers' savings for old age.

5.3 Rising Prices of Consumer Goods

Every section of the communities in Malaysia is adversely affected by rising prices of goods and services, including basic essentials, reflecting largely the impact of ringgit depreciation on the prices of imported food as well as exportable commodities produced locally such as palm oil. The official consumer price index (CPI) recorded an increase of 5.3 percent in 1998, as compared to an increase of 2.7 percent in 1997 and 3.5 percent in 1996 (see table 3.1). However, the price increase in the number of essential commodities such as rice, flour, sugar, milk, and cooking oil is much higher and affects the monthly household expenditures. This is reflected by a significant increase of 8.9 percent for food items in 1998 as compared to 4.1 percent increase in 1997 and 5.7 percent in 1996 (see table 3.1).

It is interesting to note that changes in the Malaysian economy since independence have brought about drastic change in the degree to which individuals and households in both the urban and rural sectors are integrated with both domestic and international markets. An increasing percentage of rural households in Malaysia earn much of their income from wage labor. For example, based on the estimates from the Household Income Survey of 1989, 45.0 percent of the heads of rural households in Peninsular Malaysia are classified as 'employees', with another 37.8 percent classified under the 'self-employment' category (the majority are smallholders producing commodities such as palm oil, rubber, cocoa and coconut) (Hashim, 1998). This means that a very high percentage of the population has to buy much or all of its food and other consumer goods and is thus vulnerable to price changes. In other words, with the higher rate of inflation as one of the consequences of the recent financial and economic crisis, the different groups in both rural and urban areas in Malaysia were exposed to a rapid increase in the prices of goods and services. The burden of the rising prices of goods was heavier among some of the rural population as they too experienced a big decline in their incomes. For example, unlike the oil palm smallholders who benefited from a sharp increase in the price of oil palm, rubber smallholders' income had been badly affected by falling rubber prices. The price of coagulated rubber was reported to have dropped from RM1.60 per kg to RM0.70–RM0.80 per kg last year, resulting in many rubber smallholders earning between RM200 and RM450 per month. With rising food prices, many of them find it increasingly difficult to meet their daily basic needs, including the schooling expenses of their children.

Statistics have shown that the smaller the income per household, the greater proportion of it is spent on food. The Household Expenditure Survey 1992/3 shows that households earning less than RM500 per month spent 46 percent of their income on food. A micro-level study of the rubber estates in Ipoh and Semenyih also reveals that among estate workers who earn RM300 to RM500 a month, 60 to 70 percent of their income is spent on food. Hence, with higher increases in the prices of food items, the poor and lower-income groups are most affected by the phenomenon of rising prices of consumer goods.

To cope with rising prices and falling income, consumers had to adjust their consumption pattern, for example, by reducing the purchase of 'quality food' (such as meat, chicken, eggs and milk), thus affecting their dietary requirements, especially for growing children. This phenomenon is reported by respondents from all groups covered by the rapid assessment study. A number of respondents interviewed reported that some households had to reduce the number of their meals from three to two per day, while in badly stricken areas (for example, among displaced *batik* workers in Pantai Cahaya Bulan in Kelantan), one or two families are said to be able to have only one proper meal a day on certain days.

5.4 Impact on Certain Vulnerable Groups

The crisis appeared to have more serious adverse impacts on certain vulnerable groups in Malaysia. For example, it was evident that women felt the burden more acutely than men. While on the whole women workers formed 42.3 percent of the total retrenched workers in 1998, they formed a higher percentage of retrenched workers in the manufacturing sector as women workers constituted a higher proportion of the total workforce in various sub-sectors in manufacturing. Furthermore, being mainly responsible for domestic budgeting, women also face a tough time juggling reduced income and the rising prices in their effort to feed their husbands and children, and keep up a normal family life. This task is not only physically taxing, more so for working mothers, but also a mental and psychological burden. As a result, women workers today have less time to spend with their children and husbands and to enjoy a family life. The findings of a pilot study on 50 households conducted by Expert Research Group 21 of Universiti Sains Malaysia on the consequences of the economic crisis on women in Penang (see Wazir Karim 1998) also tend to confirm this observation. The study reveals that there was a sharp drop in the income of workers and a drift towards the informal sector (particularly vendoring, food catering and direct selling). With increasing pressure to supplement family income, parents (fathers and mothers) tended to spend less time on child-minding and parenting.

In addition, the falling income faced by single mothers and female-headed households seriously affected their well-being, especially if they were old and sickly, or they had many young dependent children. They constituted a segment of the new poor.

Rubber estate workers not only received low wages, but also did not enjoy proper medical and health facilities in some of the estates. According to the Consumer Association of Penang (CAP), rubber estate workers found it hard to make ends meet during the crisis. They not only had to contribute to the Employment Providence Fund, the Social Security Organization (SOCSO), and union membership, but also had to pay for basic foodstuffs which were generally higher in price in estates than in towns. Given the low income of rubber estate families and increased living costs due to the economic crisis, the malnutrition problem of their children might worsen, and this would affect their education. It was probable that this would increase the already high drop-out rates among estate school-going children who mainly attend Tamil schools. The high failure rates in Tamil schools and the high drop-out rates would seriously affect chances of social mobility through education for estate children, a problem compounded by the economic crisis.

Underprivileged children and orphans live on the margin of society, and are very vulnerable. Financing charitable homes for these children was a tough job during the crisis, because of declining donations from the public, though they received a certain amount of government financial support. As a result, some voluntary organizations running charitable homes faced great difficulty in continuing their programs.

The Orang Asli (the aboriginal people) is one of the most poor and marginalized groups in the country. To understand the impact of the economic crisis on the Orang Asli, it is important to have an understanding of their general situation in the context of their poverty. Official statistics revealed that 80.8 percent of the Orang Asli live below the poverty line (compared to 8.5 percent nationally), of which 49.9 percent are among the very poor (compared to 2.5 percent nationally). The crisis impacted most severely those in 'fringe' areas (that is, with less access to forest resources, or whose forest has been destroyed or lost to others), and had to depend on some sort of regular cash income, while those practicing a higher level of subsistence living were able to ride out the crisis better as they were less dependent on the cash economy for their subsistence needs.

As mentioned above, during the 1997–98 crisis, many foreign migrant workers were retrenched and sent home. Many in the construction sector did not receive their wages because of their contractors' cash flow problems. Due to reduced income, foreign workers who were still employed could only remit half the amount they used to. Of the sub-sectors in which foreign workers were employed – construction, plantation, services, and manufacturing – only the plantation sub-sector was short of workers, while construction had been severely hit. While some immigrant workers were still retained in their jobs in the construction sector, their main problem was that they had not been paid their wages, many for as long as five consecutive months. According to one estimate provided by a non-governmental organization, about 25 percent of Indonesian construction workers and 8 percent of service workers were facing this problem. The contractors could only advance RM10 to RM15 per day per worker (which was less than half the daily pay) to help tide them over their difficulties.

6. IMPACT ON POVERTY AND INCOME DISTRIBUTION

As the financial and economic crisis was affecting households adversely through increasing unemployment, falling income and rising prices, it is therefore pertinent to investigate what the impact of such developments is on poverty and income inequality in the country. In particular, we have to address the following questions:

(a) Is the crisis and the policy response from the government particularly harsh on the poor?
(b) Is the nature of the crisis and structural reforms inherently equitable or inequitable?

According to the Ministry of Rural Development, there were 417,200 households or 9.6 percent of all households throughout Malaysia living below the official poverty line in 1995. The government defines poor households in Peninsular Malaysia in 1995 as those earning RM425 or less per month (for a household size of 4.6). The poverty line income (PLI) for Sarawak in the same year is RM516 per month (for a household size of 4.8) and RM601 for Sabah (for a household size of 4.9). The PLI for Peninsular Malaysia has been determined since the mid-1970s and adjusted over the years for price changes as reflected in changes in the consumer price index.

According to the Mid-Term Review of the Seventh Malaysia Plan 1996–2000, the percentage of total households living below the poverty line fell to 6.7 in 1997 (see table 3.10 for incidence of poverty by states in that year). However, in October 1998, the Deputy Minister of the Ministry of Rural Development reported to Parliament that the incidence of poverty in the country was expected to increase to 8 percent by the end

Table 3.10 Incidence of poverty by state, Malaysia, 1976, 1990, 1995 and 1997 (%)

State	1976	1990	1995	1997
Johor	29.0	10.1	3.2	1.6
Kedah	61.0	30.0	12.1	11.5
Kelantan	67.1	29.9	23.4	19.5
Melaka	32.4	12.4	5.2	3.6
Negeri Sembilan	33.0	9.5	4.8	4.5
Pahang	38.9	10.3	6.8	4.1
Perak	32.4	8.9	9.1	4.5
Perlis	43.0	19.3	12.7	10.6
Pulau Pinang	59.8	17.2	4.1	1.6
Sabah[1]	58.3	34.3	26.2	22.1
Sarawak	56.5	21.0	10.0	7.5
Selangor	22.9	7.8	2.5	1.3
Terengganu	60.3	31.2	23.4	17.3
Wilayah Persekutuan Kuala Lumpur	9.0	3.8	0.7	0.1
Malaysia	42.4	17.1	9.6	6.8

Note: [1] Includes Wilayah Persekutuan Labuan.

Source: Malaysia (1999).

of 1998. In absolute terms, the number of poor households was expected to increase by 22 percent from 346,000 in 1997 to 422,100 in 1998 (*Business Times*, 30 October 1998). The incidence of hard-core poverty was also expected to increase from 1.2 percent in 1997 to 1.7 percent in 1998.

However, the Economic Planning Unit of the Prime Minister's Department argued that the poverty incidence of 8 percent for 1998 could be an overestimation as the estimate was made based on the expected price increase of between 7 and 8 percent. It is true that the CPI increased at the rate of 5.3 percent in 1998. However, the price index for food items in the overall CPI increased by 8.9 percent. While the weighting for the food component for the overall CPI is 33 percent, it is important to reiterate that the food component in the poor household's expenditure is always much higher, with a percentage as high as 50 percent. Hence, taken together with the fact of the emergence of new poor groups due to the adverse effect of the crisis, the 1998 poverty figures cited above may not be overstated. Instead, it is quite likely that the poverty incidence in the country was higher than has been officially announced.

Furthermore, as shown by experiences of many developing countries in Latin America, it is not easy for a country suffering from such a severe crisis to pull its way out within a short period of time. Even if Malaysia managed to do so, the impact of the crisis and the various structural adjustment programs on the poor and low-income groups most probably will last longer.

What will be impact of the crisis on income distribution in Malaysia? Unfortunately, a lack of household income data for 1998 does not allow us to answer the question empirically. However, *The Mid-Term Review of the Seventh Malaysia Plan 1996–2000* seems to be quite optimistic that the urban–rural income imbalances and the overall income inequality improved slightly in 1998, thereby lessening the extent of the widening gap during 1991–97. It is argued that this development could be attributed to the slight fall in the mean income of the urban households as well as those in the richest 20 percent group in 1998. At the same time, the income of households involved in the agricultural sector grew at a slightly faster rate than in 1997, owing to higher prices for palm oil and the increased production of food crops in response to the higher costs of imports. It is also argued that the mean income of the bottom 40 percent of households, especially those in the rural areas, remained stable owing to their ability to diversify their sources of income which helped to cushion the full impact of the economic slowdown. If this argument is true, the impact on income distribution during the 1997–98 crisis seems similar to the one experienced during the economic recession of the

1985–86 period. Based on available data, it was found that the mean incomes in real terms of the richest 20 percent of both the urban and rural households declined on average by 3.1 percent and 0.4 percent per annum respectively during the 1985–87 period. Only the mean real incomes of the middle 40 percent and the bottom 40 percent of the rural households enjoyed a slight average increase of 0.8 and 2.4 percent per annum respectively during the same period.

However, the pattern of income distribution in Malaysia could be adversely affected by the crisis in various other ways. First, an increase in unemployment will generate little or zero labor income in many households, thus worsening the overall size distribution of income. Second, the decline in workers' wages, especially among the production workers whose numbers are increasing rapidly with rapid industrialization in the country, is likely to push down the income share of those at the lower end, thus increasing the income gap between wage earners and asset holders and worsening income inequality. Third, factors that had contributed to increasing differentials between skilled and unskilled workers, and thus contributed to greater income inequality during the 1991–97 period, still prevail during the current crisis. As argued in Shari (1998), one of the factors contributing to growing income inequality has been the sharp wage differentials between skilled and unskilled categories as the government works towards technological deepening in the manufacturing sector. Due to a mismatch between demand and supply of skilled and unskilled labor, unskilled wages lag behind, and the bottom of the income distribution suffers, and hence the worsening of income inequalities. This problem appears to persist in spite of the current crisis. According to the *Mid-Term Review of the Seventh Malaysia Plan 1996–2000*, although the total number of workers in the skilled and semi-skilled categories increased from 895,803 in 1995 to 1,044,301 in 1998, there is still a shortage of those categories of workers in the manufacturing sector, especially in the electronic and IT-related industries, due to the progression of industries towards technology- and capital-intensive production activities. Consequently, wage inequality in the manufacturing sector, as well as the overall income distribution, is likely to worsen, thus extending the trend of widening income inequalities experienced during the 1991–97 period.

7. HUMAN DEVELOPMENT

It seems clear that the evolving social impact of the crisis in Malaysia, as in other affected countries, is both widespread and may be long-lasting.

This is partly due to the fact that it may take some time to overcome the financial and economic crisis. In the meantime, the crisis continued to have a negative impact on household investments in human development, particularly in education, health, and nutrition, and fertility for several reasons. First, although social services are subsidized, households still incur direct or associated costs in trying to get access to these services. With reduced income and higher prices, including medicines and schooling expenses, the poor and low-income households tend to consume less than is individually and socially optimal. Second, human capital investment takes time, which becomes scarcer as household members work longer hours to cope with falling incomes. Third, the quality and quantity of certain public services are likely to be affected owing to budget constraints and big shifts of clients from private to public providers. Fourth, as households try to maintain current levels of consumption, they are most likely to reduce human capital investment or even deplete existing stocks. It is therefore important also to investigate the crisis-induced welfare declines as well as falling investment in human development. Here again we are faced with a data limitation and the ·discussion will be limited to certain issues.

The initial tight fiscal policy measures implemented by the Malaysian government, among other things, were affecting some programs for the poor in some parts of the country. Although the big budget cut had been compensated by an additional allocation of RM3.7 billion made available as assistance to vulnerable groups adversely affected by the crisis and government expanding programmes to improve the livelihood of the poorest households, some state government-supported NGOs had to reduce their activities significantly, thus affecting their programs to help the poor and the vulnerable groups. For example, due to the reduction in the Sabah State Government allocation, the number of loans given by the Yayasan Usahamaju (YUM) to poor households had to be reduced quite substantially.

As regards allocation for public health and medical services, although the 1999 budget increased the allocation from RM3.494 billion in 1998 to RM4.51 billion in 1999, Malaysia's national health expenditure as a percentage of GNP continues to show a declining trend (see table 3.11). Furthermore, it is much less than the WHO recommendation of 5 percent for a middle-income country like Malaysia. There is also increasing concern as to whether the government would continue to bear the heavy burden of providing healthcare because of the rising cost of healthcare in Malaysia. As it is, available data show that the total government expenditure for social services (including education, health, housing and others) as a percentage of GNP has been declining since the mid-1980s (see table 3.12).

Table 3.11 Operating and development budget for Ministry of Health, 1965–98 (RM million)

Year	Total (RM million)	% to national budget	% to GNP
1965	140	5.95	1.92
1970	183	5.64	1.51
1980	895	5.27	3.53
1985	1255	4.30	2.14
1990	1840	5.5	1.68
1991	2166	5.7	1.80
1992	2352	5.4	1.70
1993	2482	5.62	1.56
1994	2390	5.07	1.36
1997	3727	6.17	1.43
1998	3672	5.57	1.40

Sources: Economic Report 1986–87, Economic Report 1995–96 and Economic Report 1988–99.

Table 3.12 Federal government expenditure on social services, Malaysia, 1971–98 (RM million)

Year	Social services expenditure (RM million)	Total expenditure (RM million)	Percentage to total expenditure (%)	Percentage to GNP (%)
1971	924	3,483	26.5	7.9
1975	1,973	7,051	28.0	9.1
1977	2,919	10,615	27.5	9.4
1980	4,477	21,080	21.2	9.1
1981	6,523	27,044	24.1	11.7
1985	7,131	27,208	26.2	9.9
1986	7,963	27,634	28.8	12.0
1991	10,427	37,861	27.5	8.5
1995	15,654	50,624	30.9	7.5
1997[1]	19,970	60,415	33.1	7.6
1998[2]	18,813	65,941	28.5	7.2

Due to the rising cost of imported medicine since the ringgit depreciation, many patients who patronized private clinics have turned to government hospitals, leading to overcrowding in the latter, thus increasing the workload of doctors and other hospital staff. This issue was critical because there was a smaller number of doctors in government hospitals than in private practice (based on 1997 figures, there were 4,719 government doctors to 6,051 private practitioners). None the less, it is important to point out that during the crisis, the health ministry has devised specific strategies to ensure the provision of quality care to the people. Among the strategies undertaken were the optimization of resources, rationing and providing options, innovation and alternatives for care provision. As a compensatory measure arising from the increased cost of drugs, expensive drugs were being replaced with alternative drugs which are claimed to be of equal efficacy and effectiveness. Public health care continues to be provided at highly subsidized rates, with the poor given free treatment at the point of service delivery. As such, the government feels that the quality of health is not compromised.

The fall in the value of the ringgit and the rising cost of overseas education have resulted in a reduction in the number of students sent overseas. For example, the number of Malaysian students doing tertiary education in Britain dropped by about 44 percent, from 18,000 in 1997 to 10,000 in 1998. The pressure on local institutions of higher learning to accept more students is greater. However, given the limited resources available, not all students could receive tertiary education. For example, in 1998, from a total of 112,000 high school students who applied to enter public tertiary education, only 40,220 or 35.9 percent managed to secure a place in public tertiary institutions. Some of them managed to join private universities and colleges. However, while students who secure places in state and private universities can apply for government study loans, those joining private colleges have to depend on their own resources, or some private funding institutions/foundations. Though private college education is about two-thirds cheaper than going overseas, the fees are still high, and well beyond the reach of students from most middle- and lower-income groups. In 1999, the number of applicants for tertiary education was expected to be higher. At the same time, due to various reasons, universities had to increase the fees for their post-graduate programs, thus creating a disincentive to potential applicants. These trends, if unchecked, will eventually affect the ability of the country to produce the needed manpower for R&D activities to propel the economy forward in the future.

Another concern among parents in late 1998 was the move by the Education Ministry to reduce the number of school children entitled to receive assistance under the Ministry's Text Book Loan Scheme. Many parents were dissatisfied, and wanted to launch a protest. As a result, the Cabinet agreed to increase the eligibility ceiling to parents earning between RM1,001 and RM1,500 per month. While the RM1,000 ceiling applies to all national primary and secondary schools, the extension of the eligibility ceiling only applies to children in national primary and public religious secondary schools. The changed conditions would cost the government RM72.58 million in 1999, an additional RM4.59 million from the RM67.99 million allocation in 1998.

8.   SOCIAL CAPITAL

In dealing with the social impact of the current financial and economic crisis, it is important to pay attention to some emerging social issues, which are related directly or indirectly to the crisis. These issues matter significantly in the development of social capital, that is, the informal norms and established relationships that enable people to pursue objectives and act in concert for common benefit. In Malaysia, some of these issues include: increases in crime, domestic violence and child abuse; the rise of drug addiction and prostitution; school drop-outs and child labour.

Official statistics and observations show that petty theft, housebreaking, pickpocketing, kidnapping, robbery, and robbery-related murder were on the increase. Police statistics show that there was an increase in cases of domestic violence in 1998. As of June 1998, 3,578 cases of domestic violence were reported nation-wide, and police expect the statistics to top the 1997 figure of 5,799. Cases of child abuse, abandoned babies, rape, and outraged modesty were also expected to increase. Whether these cases were related to the economic crisis is difficult to establish. However, based on micro-level interviews and press reports, there were indications that the crisis helped fuel domestic conflicts and violence, especially between husbands and wives, and between parents and children in some households over financial matters.

Drug trafficking, addiction, and abuse are some of the biggest problems Malaysia has to tackle. With a view to promoting human development, the government has embarked on an ambitious new 25-year plan to produce a generation free from drug abuse by the year 2023. However, there were unconfirmed reports that the crisis has forced some people, as a means to obtain income, to resort to pushing drugs, or even cough mixture. Also, drug addicts were believed to be behind some of the petty thefts, burglaries, and snatching activities to get money to purchase drugs. Drug abuse, taken intravenously through sharing of needles, has been identified as the major transmitter of HIV.

Available statistics show that AIDS and HIV cases are on the increase. One worrying factor is that the overwhelming majority of the cases are young people below the age of 40. While it is difficult to establish that the economic crisis is a contributory factor in the increase in AIDS, HIV cases and other sexually transmitted diseases, it is believed that prostitution, at least among foreign prostitutes from Indonesia, Thailand, and Burma, is on the rise since the crisis. But data on prostitution are difficult to come by, and whatever data are available are only based on estimates and conjectures. It is also believed that prostitutes, both foreign and local, previously operating in high class-hotels, had come down to lower-grade hotels and joints because of declining business from their rich clients. Thus, there would probably be greater exposure of AIDS and other sexually transmitted diseases since the circle of clients had probably now probably widened to include the non-affluent groups.

Though it is difficult at this juncture to come up with hard evidence, it is believed that school drop-outs are emerging as a problem, though not very serious, except perhaps among the hard-core poor. Focus group interviews, especially with rubber estate workers, retrenched workers, and those in some badly affected areas, revealed that some of them and their neighbors had to stop their children's schooling for financial reasons, or would have to do so if the crisis were prolonged. In addition, while the phenomenon of delinquents from the formal system was not serious, attention must also be focused on the issue of the drop-out of children from, and non-participation in, the informal educational system (that is private tuition, kindergarten and pre-schooling). It has also been observed that even before the crisis, a number of children of low-income parents had been doing part-time work helping parents, who were hawkers, night stall holders or doing other jobs. Sometimes they did so during school holidays. With the crisis, this situation is expected to be on the increase.

Another problem being thrown into sharp focus during the crisis relates to the phenomenon of Malaysia's ageing population. Although the proportion of the elderly in Malaysia is relatively small compared to Western countries, this number is increasing steadily. As a result, while the general dependency ratio for Malaysia has declined, the elderly dependency ratio has remained constant. Among the additional number of the elderly, the majority are found in rural areas. What is becoming a cause for concern to the Malaysian government is the number of elderly being sent to old people's homes, which has been on the increase. As of September 1998, there were 1,711 senior citizens were are poor, destitute or neglected in nine institutional service centers or old people's homes, run by the Welfare Department of the Ministry of National Unity and Social Development in Peninsular Malaysia, and this number is expected to increase.

It is perhaps premature to conclude that the current economic crisis has become a contributing factor in an increasing number of old people being sent to these homes. But the crisis was certainly putting greater pressure on hard-pressed families with dependent elderly parents. Another pressing issue, especially since the economic crisis, is healthcare for the elderly. With government hospitals being far away for some, and the over-crowding of these hospitals, elderly people were concerned that health facilities would not be easily accessible to them. It is reported that some basic needs of the elderly were not met, for example, some were unable to afford basic aids such as glasses, hearing aids, and dentures – all of which had become more expensive since the crisis.

9. LESSONS FROM THE CRISIS AND FUTURE RESEARCH AGENDA

The currency and financial crisis in Malaysia was preceded by financial liberalization that had not been accompanied by strengthening of the regulatory and supervisory framework. In a globalized world, such development, coupled with efforts to promote the securities market, has led to a big inflow of foreign capital (particularly portfolio investment) and sharp expansion in lending by both banks and non-banks largely to non-productive sectors. Hence, after the devaluation of the Thai baht in July 1997, the financial contagion spread to other countries in the region including Malaysia. This was partly due to the perception that the Malaysian economy was suffering from the same weaknesses as the Thai economy, namely broadly pegged exchange rates, sluggish export earnings, banks with overexposure in the property and share markets, and a lack of 'transparency' and regulation in the financial market. It was also partly due to fears of Malaysia's declining competitiveness against Thai and other economies with already devalued currencies. This has led to a large outflow of foreign funds resulting in the depreciation of the ringgit and a rapid and steep fall of share prices on the KLSE. The move by local firms to buy US dollars and transfer funds overseas worsened the situation. Hence, the crisis highlighted how external financial liberalization has made a small economy such as Malaysia much more vulnerable to both external shocks as well as capital flight, and rendered the tasks of managing exchange rate and monetary policies more difficult. It also pointed to the need to base financial liberalization on strengthened macroeconomic policies and institutional – legal, regulatory and supervisory – structures. In other words, Malaysia should have been more prudent in reforming its financial sector so as better to face the challenges of further liberalization.

The major findings on the social impact of the financial and economic crisis in Malaysia – though still tentative – tend to suggest that the intensity of its negative impact is relatively less severe compared to that experienced by other affected countries. Several macro reasons can be adduced for this. First, the relatively less severe social impact in the country could be attributed to the government's relatively high social expenditure and pro-poor programs since 1970. In its efforts to redress ethnic imbalances in particular, Malaysia has adopted a strategy of allocating substantial budgetary resources for poverty reduction programs as well as for social services to ensure that various groups have an opportunity and the means to participate in the growth process. The government, for example, has devised programs to protect certain vulnerable groups, particularly income-tested programs targeted at the hard-core poor. The government maintained and continues to maintain a high percentage of its budget spending on health and education to improve the quality of human resources. In addition to its long-term objective of preserving and building on the country's social progress, the government introduced measures to mitigate short-term adverse effects of the economic slowdown on vulnerable groups in Malaysian society. Thus the government ensured that budget shares for social services, particularly health and education, in 1998 remained approximately at their 1997 levels and maintained the public expenditure on major anti-poverty programs despite the reduction of its total development expenditure. The programs of support for key social sector services include: the construction of additional classrooms for primary and secondary school in rural areas and upgrading of rural school facilities (RM100 million); expansion of education facilities for skill development (RM100 million), retraining and enhancement of skills among retrenched workers, and increases in the Higher Education Loan Fund to enhance accessibility to higher education, especially among low-income groups (RM200 million); Construction and equipping of health clinics, particularly in rural areas, and the provision of adequate funds for medicine and other essentials in public health services to cater to the needs of the population (RM100 million).

Second, the tightness of the Malaysian labor market before the crisis played a fairly important role. With an unemployment rate of 2.6 percent and the presence of more than one million foreign workers in the country, the impact of the crisis on employment opportunities has been relatively moderate. At the same time, the restrained attitude of the unions and workers, who were willing to suffer a decline in real wages rather than face retrenchment, also contributed to this situation. Furthermore, the strict enforcement of legal provisions protecting workers' interests during the present crisis and insistence that any retrenchment exercise is undertaken in accordance with the law is also a very important factor. According to the Employment Act 1955 (Section 69), retrenched workers must be paid lay-off benefits or compensation. Although there are firms which have yet to pay such lay-off benefits, a labor report ending October 3, 1998 showed that 81 percent of the severance pay and retrenchment benefits were already paid to the affected workers by then. The informal sector in Malaysia also provides alternative employment opportunities for the retrenched workers. This helps to cushion the adverse impact of the crisis on the latter and ameliorate their conditions.

Third, the decision to reverse the tight monetary and fiscal policy has helped to reduce the interest rate and enabled many firms to have access to cheaper loans. This development, together with an increase in domestic demand, has helped many firms from going bankrupt, thus putting a brake on further retrenchment.

Although the adverse social impact of the crisis was less severe in Malaysia, it is still important to take stock of the whole impact of the crisis and devise comprehensive strategies so that the country is more prepared to face them when a similar crisis occurs again in the future. The evolving social impact of the crisis in Malaysia — though, in the main, an urban and peninsular phenomenon — may actually have a deeper and wider impact than appears and may be more long-lasting especially on the poor and vulnerable groups. This is partly because existing safety net mechanisms at their disposal are still inadequate and sometimes too weak and unreliable. In the past, steady economic growth provided the underpinnings of the livelihood of the poor, and substituted for a formal social safety net. Today such underpinnings have gone or have been seriously eroded. Although the economy is on the road to recovery, it may take some time to overcome its adverse social consequences. Based on the study of selected target groups among the poor and vulnerable groups, it becomes obvious that personal savings — whether voluntary or compulsory — are inadequate and can easily be depleted.

Based on the preliminary findings presented in this chapter, a few issues may deserve consideration for purposes of reflection and generating hypotheses for further research. First, there is no doubt that the ultimate solution to the poverty problem and the problem of vulnerable groups will depend largely on the ability of the government to put the Malaysian economy on a sustainable moderately high growth path. However, as the economy will most likely experience more regular downturn in the future, the need to develop cost-effective social safety net programs to help those adversely affected by the crisis becomes more urgent. It is a truism that reducing the social cost of the crisis is critical to ensure political and social stability in the country, which is an important prerequisite for a sustainable and relatively rapid expansion of the Malaysian economy in the future. Furthermore, for such cost-effective social safety net programmes to be successful, it is vital that the social partners be fully involved in this reform process. The crisis reveals that when trade unions—which throughout the crisis exercised restraint in their wage claims—played an effective role in the negotiating process with employers and the government, the affected workers obtained a better deal. This tripartite mechanism appears to be useful and therefore needs to be further developed and strengthened to ensure workers' welfare. The unions' restrained attitude, to be matched with humane consideration and understanding by employers, is an asset in such a process. This process will go a long way towards winning the understanding and support of the affected population and their organizations, which is a critical ingredient in ensuring the success of any reform plan. In this context, there is a need to design new cost-effective social protection programs, which can cope with such sudden changed situations. In this context, the Malaysian Trade Union Congress's proposal for the setting up of a Retrenchment Fund – though containing some shortcomings – merits more careful consideration.

Second, as mentioned above, the crisis has brought many of the economically active labor force into the informal sector. However, those who find employment in the informal sector enjoy little or no social protection. In this respect, the suggestion by the International Labor Organisation (ILO) (1998) for governments to promote self-help grassroots mutual insurance schemes, and gradually to extend compulsory coverage and improve the level of compliance as well as to provide adequate public health services for them may be worth considering.

Third, the crisis affects women, migrant, and older workers as well as indigenous people in particular ways. Women workers, for example, may face not only reduced opportunities in formal employment as a result of the crisis, but also difficulties due to the overcrowding effect in the informal sector and the attendant implications of the crisis on family life. Migrant workers face particular difficulties as retrenchment and downturn put them in a more vulnerable position with much weakened bargaining power. Older workers may face greater difficulties in finding new jobs as a result of crisis-driven restructuring and may be disadvantaged in terms of access to relief measures. The *Orang Asli* experience the crisis unevenly, with the more urbanized households experiencing the impact more seriously than those in remote areas. Furthermore, given Malaysia's commitment to building a caring society and developing the family as a social institution to shoulder the welfare of its members, including children and the elderly, the impact of the crisis on this basic social institution needs be studied more carefully. During the crisis, some household heads/members may be working longer hours juggling between multiple odd jobs to earn sufficient income for the household, while some other household heads/members may be unemployed or underemployed. It is not clear to what extent the crisis contributes to family conflicts and effects on physical and mental health, but these effects should not be discounted. The immediate and long-term implications of this situation on the quality of family life, on the relations between husband and wife and between parents and children requires careful study and reflection.

Fourth, since Malaysia is committed to develop a strong human resource base for long-term economic growth, global competition, and the equitable distribution of income, the education and training of technical labor will increasingly become a major source of continuing its industrialization process in the future, and thereby contributing towards poverty reduction efforts. During the current crisis, due to the available social policy, school drop-out is not a serious problem, except perhaps among some of the poor households. Nevertheless, while the phenomenon of drop-out from the formal system is not serious, we need to take into account the drop-out from and non-participation in the informal educational system, that is, private tuition, kindergarten and pre-schooling. Given the keen competition to succeed, private tuition has become a 'must' to obtain good grades in school. The key question is, while the rich can afford to have their children in both the formal and informal systems, there is a high degree of non-participation in the non-formal system among the lower-income groups and poor households. This may put them at a disadvantage in competition, especially for higher education, which has been the main channel of upward social mobility for many Malaysians, particularly those from rural areas, and from lower-income groups.

Last but not least, the crisis has eroded some of the progress achieved in social development over the last few decades, though its exact extent has yet to be assessed. There are indications that with the emergence of some new poor groups, the number of poor and hard-core households in the country may be increasing, particularly in urban areas and among female-headed households. This suggests that there may be a need to re-examine the new realities and their implications for social development, particularly issues related to social exclusion. Moreover, while there is a strong basis to give priority to immediate measures to overcome the adverse social consequences of the crisis, it is also important to keep in mind the long-term solution to the problems. One fundamental challenge that needs to be addressed is how to restore growth. Moderately rapid growth will ensure that the unemployment problem, and the many social ills which stem from the loss of income and the sense of exclusion and disillusionment, can be tackled more effectively. Preparing a strong human resource base for long-term economic growth, global competition, and equitable distribution of income as suggested above is necessary for this purpose. Education, including the training of technical labor, will become increasingly a major source of continuing the industrialization process in Malaysia in the future and thereby contributing efforts to poverty reduction. To minimize market and government failures, maybe it is worth studying the Korean and Taiwanese experience of planning, which involves public and private organizations and firms, so that educational and training institutions can anticipate future demand for skilled and professional labor more effectively. The transformation of the labor force in this way will also help raise the competitiveness of firms operating in Malaysia, and should narrow wage differentials and income inequalities more generally. In addition, broader multi-skilling, cross-skilling and institutionalization of the work process, including union participation in worker training to strengthen effective tripartism, may be needed. Such flexible work practices can also lower income inequalities. Technological development is essential to sustain the success of such a model. To ensure continued real wage rises, it is pertinent to ensure growth, which should be part of the responsibility of all parties within the national system of innovation.

REFERENCES

Ariff, Mohamed, Mohammad Haflah Piei, Diana Wong and Syarisa Yanti Abubakar (1998), *Responding to the Economic Crisis in Malaysia. A Pro-Human Development Perspective*. Report prepared for the United Nations Development Program/Regional Bureau for Asia and the Pacific (UNDP/RBAP) in Kuala Lumpur.

Bank Negara Malaysia (1998), *Quarterly Bulletin*, Third Quarter 1998, 13 (3). Kuala Lumpur.

Bank Negara Malaysia (1999), *Annual Report 1998*. Kuala Lumpur.

Department of Statistics, Malaysia (1999), *Monthly Statistical Bulletin, Malaysia. Mei*. Kuala Lumpur: Jabatan Perangkaan Malaysia.

Chu, Ke-Young and Sanjeev Gupta (1998), Social Safety Nets: Issues and Recent Experiences. Washington: International Monetary Fund.

Hashim, Shireen Mardziah (1997), *Income inequality and poverty in*

Malaysia. Lanham: Rowman and Littlefield.

International Labour Organization (ILO) (1998), 'The Social Impact of the Asian Financial Crisis'. Technical report for discussion at the High-Level Tripartite Meeting on Social Responses to the Financial Crisis in East and Southeast Countries, Bangkok, 22–24 April.

Jomo, K.S. *et al.* (1997), *Southeast Asia's Misunderstood Miracle: Industrial Policy and Economic Development in Thailand, Malaysia and Indonesia*. Boulder: Westview Press.

Jomo, K.S. (ed.) (1998), *Tigers in Trouble: Financial Governance, Liberalisation and Crises in East Asia*. London: Zed Press.

Karim, Wazir Jahan (1998), Malaysian Women In and Out of the Crisis in Malaysia, mimeo.

Khor, Martin (1998), 'The economic crisis in East Asia: Causes, Effects, Lessons'. Paper presented at the conference on 'The engagement of civil society in the APEC process', Penang.

Malaysia (1991a), *The Second Outline Perspective Plan 1970–1990*, Kuala Lumpur: Percetakan Nasional Malaysia Berhad.

Malaysia (1991b), *The Sixth Malaysia Plan, 1991–1995*. Kuala Lumpur: Percetakan Nasional Malaysia Berhad.

Malaysia (1996), *The Seventh Malaysia Plan 1996–2000*. Kuala Lumpur: Percetakan Nasional Malaysia Berhad.

Malaysia (1998a), *Economic Report 1998/99*. Kuala Lumpur: Ministry of Finance.

Malaysia (1998b), *Social Statistics Bulletin, Malaysia*. Kuala Lumpur: Department of Statistics.

Malaysia (1999), *Laporan Pasaran Buruh 1998*. Kuala Lumpur: Ministry of Human Resources.

Malaysia (1999), *Mid-Term Review of the Seventh Malaysia Plan 1996–2000*. Kuala Lumpur: Percetakan Nasional Malaysia Berhad.

Marshall, Katherine (1998), 'The Asian Crisis: Social Implications and the Agenda Ahead'. Paper presented at the Regional Conference on 'Social Implications of the Asian Financial Crisis', Seoul, 29–31 July

Montes, Manuel F. (1998), *The Currency Crisis in Southeast Asia*, Singapore: Institute of Southeast Asian Studies.

National Economic Action Council (NEAC) (1998), *National Economic Recovery Plan: Agenda for Action*. Kuala Lumpur: Percetakan Nasional Malaysia.

Nelson, Joan M. (1992), 'Poverty, Equity and the Politics of Adjustment'. In Stephan Haggard and Robert R. Kaufman (eds), *The Politics of Economic Adjustment: International Conflicts and the State*. Princeton, New Jersey: Princeton University Press.

Ong Hong Cheong (1998), 'Coping with Capital Flows and the Role of

Monetary Policy: The Malaysian Experience, 1990–95', in C.H. Kwan, D. Vandenbrink and S.Y. Chia (eds), *Coping with Capital Flow in East Asia*, Singapore: Institute of Southeast Asian Studies and Nomura Research Institute.

Ong Hong Cheong (1999), 'Evolution of the Malaysian Financial System Beyond the Financial Crisis', in S. Masuyama, D. Vandenbrink and S.Y. Chia (eds), *East Asia's Financial Systems: Evolution & Crisis*, Singapore: Institute of Southeast Asian Studies and Nomura Research Institute.

Pernia, E.M. and J.C. Knowles (1998), *Assessing the Social Impact of the Financial Crisis in Asia*. EDRC Briefing Notes Series, No. 6.

Rhee, Jae Y. (1998), '*Social Implications of the Asian Financial Crisis*'. Executive Summary Paper prepared for UNDP, Seoul on the occasion of UNDP/KDI Regional Conference on 'Social Implications of the Asian Financial Crisis', Seoul, 29–30 July.

Robb, C. and C. Zhang (1998), '*Social Aspects of the Crisis: Perceptions of Poor Communities in Thailand*'. Paper prepared for Thailand's Social Investment Project of the World Bank, mimeo.

Shari, Ishak (1998), 'Income Inequalities in Malaysia, 1970–1995'. Paper presented at the workshop on 'Poverty and Income Distribution in Asia and the Pacific', University of New South Wales, Sydney.

Shari, Ishak and A. Rahman Embong (1998), 'Rapid Participatory Assessments of the Social Impact of the Financial Crisis in Malaysia'. Draft final report presented for UNDP Regional Bureau for Asia and the Pacific.

4. Indonesia in crisis: causes and consequences

Hal Hill

1. INTRODUCTION

Since the middle of 1997, we have witnessed momentous and tragic events in Indonesia. Momentous because nobody — from the pre-eminent Washington institutions to rating agencies and academics — foresaw the events, and we still have only an imperfect understanding of their origins and future course. And tragic because ordinary Indonesians are suffering a great deal, and many have experienced a substantial decline in their living standards. As the 1998 annual World Bank (1998a) assessment of the country soberly observed:

> Indonesia is in deep crisis. A country that achieved decades of rapid growth, stability, and poverty reduction, is now near economic collapse. ... No country in recent history, let alone one the size of Indonesia, has ever suffered such a dramatic reversal of fortune.[1]

There is a particular irony in Indonesia's case, for it has been by far the worst affected among the four East Asian 'crisis' economies (that is, along with Korea, Malaysia, and Thailand), and yet initially there was a general expectation that it would not be as adversely affected as Thailand. 'Why Indonesia is not Thailand' was a widely held topic over the period June–August 1997.

The purpose of this chapter is to describe and analyze Indonesia's most serious economic crisis against the general backdrop of economic decline in Southeast Asia. We first look at the events leading up to the crisis (section 2), followed by a charting of its course from July 1997 to March 1999 (section 3). Section 4 assesses the socioeconomic impacts, while section 5 attempts to explain the crisis, both at the onset and in its subsequent developments. The final section looks forward, and considers Indonesia's immediate and medium-term policy challenges.

127

2. PRELUDE TO THE CRISIS

Four features of pre-crisis Indonesia stand out. These center around the absence of any 'early warning' indicators of impending collapse, and they set the stage for our subsequent analysis.

First, economic growth was strong, and all available evidence suggested that the benefits continued to be broad-based. The country's statistical agency, BPS, estimated that the percentage of the population in poverty continued to decline in the 1990s, from 15.1 percent in 1990 to 13.7 percent in 1993 and 11.3 percent in 1996. A declining incidence of poverty was found over this period in all 27 provinces, for both rural and urban areas. Interpersonal inequality remained low, and the Gini ratios showed no upward trend. Real wages were growing in every sector for which good quality data were available (Manning, 1998). Other social indicators, such as educational enrolments, nutritional intake and various indicators of health status, also continued to improve over the decade prior to the crisis. International comparisons (for example, World Bank, 1998b, p. 75) confirmed these good results, while also underlining the conclusion that, by East Asian standards, some of Indonesia's social indicators continued to lag somewhat.

It is easy to quibble with these social indicators. Indonesia's national poverty line is extremely conservative, and the poverty estimates are very sensitive to where the line is drawn. The inequality indices are considered less reliable than the poverty figures. The sample sizes in the smaller provinces are such that the regional poverty figures are at best approximate. Other social indicators, especially quality-based statistics (for example, educational standards), need to be interpreted with caution. It is of course true that some of the wealthy and well-connected grew very rich (obscenely so in the case of the Soeharto family) over this period. But it is important not to lose sight of the big picture. There is certainly no evidence of growing and widespread inequality or immiserization in the period leading up to the crisis. Life was almost certainly improving for the vast majority of Indonesian citizens.

Secondly, economic growth appeared to be robust. Indonesian economic development was no 'myth' in the Krugman (1994) sense of growth being driven almost entirely by factor augmentation rather than total factor productivity (TFP). Among the various TFP estimates, Singapore, not Indonesia, was most commonly singled out as the prime example of 'perspiration-led' growth in East Asia. Various estimates placed Indonesia in the mid-range of TFP growth since the 1960s (Chen, 1997). Detailed research focused on the country's industrial sector confirmed these results. Moreover, in examining the trends over time,

TFP growth appeared to be rising over time, with slower growth during the oil-financed import substitution era of the 1970s giving way to higher increases in the period of deregulation in the 1980s. Aswicahyono (1998), for example, concluded that non-oil manufacturing TFP grew by 1.1 percent per annum in 1976–80, but 5.5 percent and 6.0 percent during 1984–88 and 1989–93 respectively.

Thirdly, there was growing political turbulence and uncertainty over this period, but until the middle of 1997 there was no discernible impact on the economy or on any major financial indicators. The years 1996–97 were arguably the most unstable politically since 1967 (Forrester and May, 1998). In 1996, the mildly oppositionist Indonesian Democratic Party (PDI) was the subject of ruthless and violent manipulation to ensure that its leader was to the liking of the Soeharto. Younger and more radical opponents of the regime were given long jail sentences. In late 1996 and early 1997 a series of nasty incidents with unpleasant ethnic overtones occurred in several mid-sized Javanese cities. The unrest escalated in the first half of 1997 in West Kalimantan, with extremely violent ethnic conflicts between the indigenous Dayak people and immigrant Madurese (and which occurred again on an even more gruesome scale in March 1999). In May 1997 the election campaign and voting for Parliament took place, also against a backdrop of unprecedented violence. Then, by the middle of the year, the region's worst ever forest fires occurred, owing to a combination of indiscriminate forest clearing, an unusually long dry season, and lax regulatory supervision. The haze engulfed much of Sumatra and Kalimantan, and also seriously disrupted parts of Malaysia and Singapore.

Nevertheless, these political events had no discernible impact on the economy through to mid-1997. Capital inflows remained buoyant. The stock market was rising. The rupiah continued to bump against the lower limit of the intervention band, and on each occasion the latter was widened the currency quickly appreciated to the new, lower limit. Despite the simmering discontent, the widespread disgust at the business antics of the Soeharto children, and frustration that the much vaunted *keterbukaan* (political openness) of the early 1990s had not materialized, the political protests seemed to abate following the general elections. By July, Soeharto again appeared to be in supreme control.

Finally, almost all available economic and financial indicators looked either buoyant or reasonably comfortable pre-crisis. This is the subject of more detailed analysis in section 5 below.

3. COURSE OF THE CRISIS

Figure 4.1 provides a summary of the flow of events from the middle of 1997, while figure 4.2 shows trends in exchange rates which, in an era of floating regimes, have proven to be a highly sensitive financial and political barometer. At the risk of oversimplification, and recognizing differences among countries, it is possible to identify eight principal sub-phases in the evolution of the crisis.

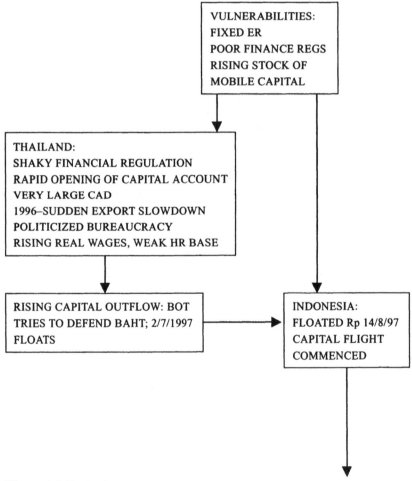

Figure 4.1 Beginnings

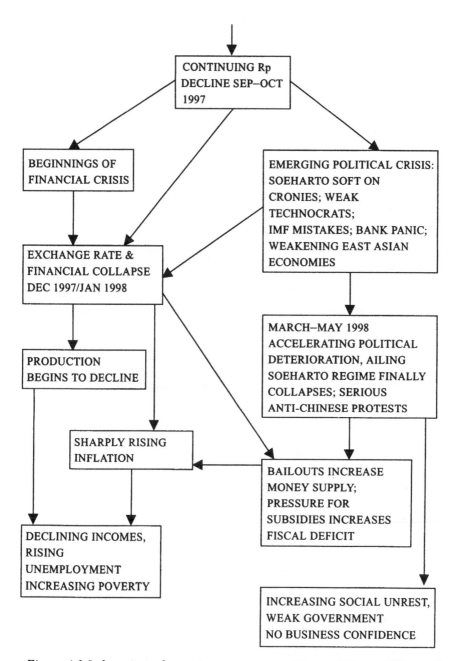

Figure 4.2 Indonesia in deep crisis

(i) *January–July 1997, beginnings — concern in Thailand* In discussing the course of the crisis, it is useful to distinguish between triggers and fundamental causes. In East Asia the trigger was clearly Thailand. Initially, Indonesia appeared much more robust. 'Why Indonesia is not Thailand' (in the words of Tubagus, 1997) was a widely held view in mid-1997, and one to which this author was attracted. Around August–September 1997, Indonesia looked better because:

- its authoritarian political system looked better able than Thailand's shaky coalition politics to deliver a clear response to the crisis;
- Bank Indonesia had not squandered its international reserves trying to fight the foreign exchange market;
- its exchange rate regime had not been so rigid;
- it had invited the IMF in advance for 'consultation';
- its geo-strategic significance is such that no major country could afford not to participate in a rescue package (in the way that the US had not signed up to the first Thai package).

(ii) *August–October 1997, a wake-up call for the region* The Indonesian government initially seemed to be moving promptly and decisively over most of this period, and at least through until the first half of October 1997 there was still no real indication of what was in store. The rupiah came under sustained selling pressure about three weeks after the baht was floated. The government moved quite quickly, floating the rupiah in mid-August, and introducing minor reform packages in September. It invited the IMF in for 'consultation', and by the end of October it had signed up to a package.

(iii) *November 1997–January 1998, serious problems evident, Indonesia parts company*
November–December: But just as the crisis was not accurately foreseen, so too did this early assessment prove to be excessively sanguine. One might date the really serious beginnings of the crisis — that is, when it was apparent that we had more than a passing 'blip' on our hands — from November and December. Over this period, Indonesia's economic and political situation deteriorated sharply. The bank closures of 1 November triggered widespread uncertainty; backtracking on key reforms to preserve the Soeharto family interests was evident; Korea also joined the casualty list in November; and Soeharto was very ill for a week in early December (at one stage rumours of his death began to circulate). Indonesia then began to part company with the other East Asian crisis economies, as its currency and stock market plummeted to new lows and

its financial system virtually ceased to function. The government also began to lose control of the money supply, and hence inflationary pressures quickly surfaced.

January 1998 was a dreadful month, with another round of seriously adverse events: an implausible budget, widening rifts with the IMF, and a clear indication that Habibie was set to be elevated to the vice-presidency. At one point the rupiah was pushed to as low as 17,000, that is, one-seventh of its pre-crisis level.

(iv) *February–April 1998, mixed trends* In the next three months of 1998 there were mixed trends. The policy and political uncertainty continued in Indonesia throughout February, as President Soeharto toyed with the highly controversial currency board system (CBS), and then dismissed his respected central bank governor. By now, four critical months had been lost, and there was still no sense of a coherent response to the crisis.

In March and April, a modicum of optimism returned to the region. Exchange rates and stock markets began to pick up a little, especially in Thailand and Malaysia, and even a little in Indonesia. Indonesia's new Cabinet was seriously flawed, with the inclusion of Soeharto's eldest daughter, Tutut, and one of his principal cronies, Bob Hasan. But the new economic policy team offered at least a glimmer of hope. Finally, international institutions appeared to be slowly coming to grips with the enormity of the East Asian challenge, and seemed willing to offer assistance in a more flexible and effective manner than was initially the case.

(v) *May 1998, The end of the 'New Order' —Soeharto toppled* May 1998 will be recorded as a watershed in Indonesian history – the demise of the once seemingly impregnable Soeharto regime. Fuel price increases in early May resulted in a wave of protests. Amid the mounting demonstrations, some students at Jakarta's Trisakti University were shot. This in turn led to a student occupation of the Parliament, a general breakdown in civil order, an exodus of many expatriates and ethnic Chinese, and diminished support for Soeharto among the armed forces and the Cabinet. On 21 May these events culminated surprisingly swiftly in the end of the 32-year Soeharto era and the installation of Vice-President B.J. Habibie as the Republic's third president.

(vi) *June–August 1998, Habibie's shaky beginnings, deepening pessimism* The Habibie administration got off to a shaky start. In the wake of the traumatic events of May, the government was in some respects immobilized and all significant business decisions were put on hold. The

Sino-Indonesian community was especially apprehensive following the outbreaks of violence specifically targeting its members. Capital flight continued, and the foreign exchange and stock markets were in the doldrums.

(vii) *September–December 1998, renewed, cautious optimism* By late September, a modicum of optimism was again returning to the region, based principally on a perception that the worst might have passed. In Indonesia, the Habibie Administration survived its first 100 days, and most of the new political actors were displaying a sense of pragmatism on economic policy issues. The rupiah strengthened to below 7,500 for the first time in more than six months, and thus appeared to be entering a range broadly considered to be 'manageable'. The international donor pledges in late July were deemed to have given the country's fiscal position much-needed credibility. Inflation in September fell to 3.75 percent, which was well down on the previous four months. A good crop was bringing rice prices down. Non-oil exports were holding up reasonably well.

(viii) *January–April 1999, mixed trends again* The hopeful signs emerging in late 1998 continued into 1999. In the first quarter of 1999, Indonesia again returned – unexpectedly – to positive economic growth, and inflation was slightly negative in March and April. Nevertheless, the country's immediate prospects were clouded by uncertainty. Export performance continued to be very poor. The commercial climate was dominated by a perception that all major economic policy decisions were on hold until after the general and presidential elections. Continuing ethnic and religious violence also deterred investors. Moreover, it was not clear that the regional crisis was definitely over. Japan in particular was still poised precariously.

4.   SOCIOECONOMIC IMPACTS

Owing to the frustratingly slow release of relevant data, it is still too early to be precise about the social impacts of the crisis. But economic and financial statistics are readily available, and the broad social picture is clear enough. We consider each of these in turn.

4.1 Economic Indicators

Indonesia is by far the worst affected Southeast Asian economy. Its economy contracted by 13.6 percent in 1998, about double that of Malaysia and Thailand (table 4.1). It was also the only economy to experience serious inflation in 1998. Its current account adjustment in 1997–98 was very large, equivalent to over 8 percentage points of GDP. However, since it was running a smaller deficit pre-crisis than either Malaysia or Thailand, the magnitude of the adjustment in the latter two countries was actually larger. The change in Indonesia's fiscal policy stance was similar to that of its neighbors. As the country deepest in crisis, it is not surprising that it is running the largest fiscal deficit.

As would be expected, the sectoral effects of the crisis have been very uneven, and the aggregate figure masks large inter-sectoral differences

Table 4.1 Southeast Asian economic indicators, 1991–98 (%)

	Ind	Mal	Phil	Sing	Thai	VN
GDP growth:						
1991–95	7.8	8.7	2.2	8.5	8.6	8.2
1996	8.0	8.6	5.5	6.9	5.5	9.4
1997	4.7	8.0	5.1	7.8	−0.4	9.0
1998	−13.6	−6.7	0	1.3	−6.5	5.0
Inflation:						
1991–95	8.9	3.6	10.5	2.6	4.8	23.4
1996	6.5	3.5	8.4	1.4	5.8	4.5
1997	11.6	2.6	5.1	2.0	5.6	4.0
1998	65.0	5.4	9.0	−0.2	8.1	5.0
Current account/GDP:						
1991–95	−2.4	−7.0	−3.6	12.9	−6.2	−5.5
1996	−3.3	−4.9	−4.5	15.0	−7.9	−16.2
1997	−2.9	−5.2	−5.2	15.4	−2.0	−8.6
1998	5.4	7.5	1.2	17.8	8.1	
Govt balance/GDP:						
1991–95	−0.2	0.3	−1.6	12.4	2.8	−3.5
1996	1.2	1.1	−0.4	13.9	2.4	−0.4
1997	1.2	5.5	−1.8	6.0	−0.9	
1998	−5.5	−1.0	−3.6	−1.0	−4.5	

Sources: Asia Pacific Economics Group, *Asia Pacific Profiles 1998*, Canberra, 1998; IMF *World Economic Outlook*; JP Morgan, *World Financial Markets*, First Quarter 1999; press reports.

(see table 4.2). In particular, agricultural output has been virtually constant, whereas the decline in the construction and finance sectors has been quite dramatic. A number of factors have contributed to the relatively buoyant situation in agriculture from about the middle of 1998. The breaking of the El Niño-induced drought mid-year produced good dry-season food crops; but for the drought, agricultural output would have been more strongly positive. The gradual removal of food subsidies and price controls increased returns to farmers. The export-oriented cash crop sector benefited from the rupiah depreciation, which more than outweighed low international prices. Other major sectors have fallen between the extremes of agriculture and construction. Manufacturing has contracted at about the economy-wide average, but with major differences between export-oriented and local market activities. The export-oriented mining sector has been affected by low international commodity prices. The decline in the government sector highlights the fact that fiscal policy has been only weakly countercyclical.

Table 4.2 GDP growth by sector, 1995–98 (%)

	1995	1996	1997	1998
Agriculture	4.2	1.9	0.7	0.2
Mining & quarrying	6.6	7.1	1.7	−4.2
Manufacturing	6.7	11.0	6.4	−12.9
Utilities	15.5	12.6	12.8	3.7
Construction	12.9	12.4	6.4	−39.7
Trade, hotel, restaurant	7.7	7.6	5.8	−19.0
Transport & communication	9.4	8.6	8.3	−12.8
Finance	13.6	9.9	7.2	−37.6
Accommodation	5.5	6.8	5.0	−20.7
Public administration	1.3	1.3	1.2	−7.0
Other services	9.3	8.8	5.7	−0.9
GDP	8.2	7.8	4.9	−13.7

Note: 1998 data are preliminary.
Source: BPS.

As the world's largest archipelagic state, Indonesia's regional dynamics have altered significantly during the crisis. At the time of writing, no new regional accounts data had been released, but the broad picture is clear enough. This has been a crisis first and foremost of the modern, urban economy of Java. Greater Jakarta (Jabotabek), with its reliance on formal sector manufacturing, modern services, a large construction industry, and the public sector, is experiencing a painful contraction. By contrast, many of the hitherto poor and neglected provinces east of Bali are doing quite well. The distant province of North Sulawesi, for example, with its strong cash crop sector and good human capital base, is said to be one of the few provinces which may have experienced positive growth in 1998. Bali, the fastest growing province during the Soeharto era, has been affected by the downturn in tourism, but it is unlikely to have declined as sharply as Java.

There have been even more pronounced variations among the major expenditure groups. The decline in household consumption was quite modest, for a number of reasons related to various survival strategies. The dramatic wealth losses associated with the demise of the stock market had little impact on personal consumption, presumably because stock holdings are still limited mainly to a small urban elite. By contrast, the crisis hit investment and inventories very hard, and both collapsed. Government consumption declined at about the same rate as the economy as a whole, and underlines again the absence of a fiscal stimulus. Exports rose modestly, while imports contracted, though not as much as might have been expected. Since both are foreign currency denominated, allowance must be made for the large rupiah depreciation in 1998.

These figures provide a number of clues about the welfare effects of the crisis. Agriculture is still by far the largest jobs provider, and thus the welfare of this largest single group in the community has not been adversely affected *directly*. 'Other services' contains much of the informal sector activities, and here the decline has been slight. The modest fall in household consumption also suggests that, in aggregate, community living standards fell much less than implied by the decline in GDP. Export growth rose, to the benefit of those deriving income from this sector. This varied outlook is important in assessing social impacts, an issue we address shortly.

We can trace the monetary impacts of the crisis by observing monthly data on money supply, inflation and interest rates over the period 1996–98. The origins of the sudden bout of inflation are clearly evident in the base money data, which suddenly increased sharply (by 36 percent on a month-on-month basis) in December 1997 and January 1998 (22 percent); in May 1998 it rose a further 11 percent. All three months coincided with bank bailouts or runs. From May 1998 onwards, the government regained control of the money supply, and it rose by just 7.5 percent over the next six months.

Inflation followed these trends very closely, with a lag. The first appreciable increase was December 1997 (3 percent), jumping quickly to 7 percent and 13 percent respectively in January and February 1998. From March to September, inflation was high, though around a gradually declining trend. It then flattened out quite suddenly, and in the seven months from October Indonesia was suddenly almost inflation-free, the CPI rising just 5.2 percent. The prospect of hyper-inflation receded swiftly — monetary orthodoxy works quickly! Interest rates also began to respond promptly, albeit with a lag. SBIs almost trebled in January–April 1998, and rose a further 50 percent to July, before declining quite sharply in November. Time deposits moved in the same direction, but with a further lag.

The balance of payments provides an additional dimension to this picture of economic collapse. As noted, the current account turned from deficit to surplus quickly, primarily owing to the collapse of imports, which fell by about $15 billion compared to pre-crisis levels. One of the disappointing features of the crisis has been the poor performance of exports, which in dollar terms actually declined in 1998/99. Some 60 percent of this decline occurred in the oil/gas sector, and was beyond the country's control as it reflected historically low international prices. But non-oil exports also declined, and here too Indonesia's record was inferior to that of its neighbors. The capital account mirrors in part these trends in the current account. It turned negative in the first crisis year, 1997–98 because private capital movements changed so dramatically, from a net inflow of $13.5 billion to an outflow of $11.8 billion, and because official inflows obviously could not respond with the same speed. By 1998–99, the capital account is estimated to have turned positive again, thanks to large official flows, grossing $19.2 billion.

4.2 Financial Indicators

Stock markets and exchange rates have fallen sharply in the crisis economies, and here also Indonesia has fared much worse than its neighbors since mid-1997, and especially since about November of that year. Whereas some of the other countries' currencies began to recover in the first half of 1998 from their initial overshooting, Indonesia's market continued to be very low until the last quarter of 1998. As table 4.3 documents, from July 1, 1997 to the beginning of 1998 and to the first quarter of 1999 the rupiah fell much further against the US dollar than any other internationally traded East Asian currency. By March 31, 1999, its nominal value was just 28 percent of that in mid-1997, less than half that of the region-wide average and any other crisis economy. The data

Table 4.3 Comparative financial data, 1997–99

(a) Exchange rate (/$) (indexed at 30/6/97=100)	1/1/97	30/6/97	1/1/98	31/3/99
China	100	100	100	100
India	100	100	90	84
Indonesia	103	100	30	28
Korea	105	100	51	73
Malaysia	100	100	56	66
Philippines	100	100	58	68
Singapore	102	100	82	83
Taiwan	101	100	81	84
Thailand	102	100	48	67
(b) REERs (1990 =100, period averages)	1996	1997	1998	12/1998
India	75	82	80	77
Indonesia	104	95	46	71
Korea	89	83	66	71
Malaysia	111	108	83	82
Philippines	115	109	91	96
Singapore	115	117	113	109
Taiwan	89	90	87	92
Thailand	106	97	88	99
(c) Stock market index (in local currency; indexed at 30/6/97=100)	1/1/97	30/6/97	1/1/98	31/3/99
China	70	100	97	91
India	80	100	90	90
Indonesia	89	100	55	55
Korea	92	100	58	88
Malaysia	116	100	49	47
Philippines	112	100	62	71
Singapore	110	100	68	75
Taiwan	77	100	87	77
Thailand	168	100	75	73
(d) Stock market index (in $; indexed at 30/6/97=100)	1/1/97	30/6/97	1/1/98	31/3/99
China	70	100	97	91
India	80	100	81	76
Indonesia	92	100	17	15
Korea	97	100	29	64
Malaysia	115	100	27	31
Philippines	113	100	36	49
Singapore	112	100	56	62
Taiwan	79	100	71	65
Thailand	165	100	36	49

Notes: Stock market and nominal exchange rate data refer to the nearest weekly closing figures for the date indicated. Upward movements in exchange rate series refer to appreciation.

Sources: *The Economist*, various issues, for stock market and nominal exchange rate data; JP Morgan for real effective exchange rates.

also illustrate that Indonesia's currency has been much slower to rebound from the lows of early 1998 than that of its neighbors. These exchange rate movements initially translated into a much sharper real depreciation than in the other crisis economies, and for 1998 as a whole. But by the end of the year, the nominal appreciation in the last quarter, combined with the country's much higher inflation, had eroded a good deal of these gains in competitiveness. The decline in Indonesia's stock market in local currency terms was initially broadly similar to the crisis economies, but it displayed very little recovery through to early 1999, a feature it shares (for different reasons) with both Malaysia and Thailand. Owing principally to currency movements, Indonesia's stock market decline in US dollar terms has been by far the greatest over this period. By March 31 1999 its stock market index was still just 15 percent of that in mid-1997.

4.3 Social Indicators

Assessments of the social impact of the crisis vary wildly. At one extreme is an alarmist estimate by a major international agency that about one-half of the population is now in poverty (ILO, 1998); at the other are upbeat assessments suggesting the 'rebirth' of a newly invigourated people's economy. Jellinek and Rustanto (1999, pp. 1–2) provide an example of the latter:

> Indonesia's informal sector has picked up the slack and seems to be experiencing an economic boom. ... Small enterprises, killed off during 20 years of economic boom of the New Order, are being revived. Old traditions of artisanship and trade are being rediscovered. Rich and middle class consumers who formerly bought from the formal sector are now buying from traditional markets. ... In contrast to the economic crash depicted in the official, national and international media, we are witnessing an unprecedented economic boom in the small-scale sector.

Both these conclusions are misleading in important respects, the former because the estimation procedures were flawed, the latter because a return to activities characterized by low productivity and incomes hardly constitutes good news. In fact, all available evidence suggests that social outcomes have been between these two extremes. Many people have obviously been hurt by the crisis, but the severity of the social impacts has been overstated.

These disagreements have arisen in part because, in contrast to the economic–financial data, which provide a reasonably accurate picture of the crisis, social trends are much more difficult to estimate with any precision. And, as important as the overall figures, there needs to be an analytical understanding of the adaptive and survival strategies of the poor and 'near-poor'. This includes their capacity to adjust consumption patterns (for example deferring the purchase of consumer durable goods, switching to nutritionally more cost-effective food sources); to draw on savings, remittances, and extended family networks; and also their ability to shift to new employment opportunities either sectorally or spatially. In addition, many middle-class households have had some dollar-denominated assets. Beneath the aggregate poverty figures, there is known to be considerable 'turnover' in poverty incidence, as people move in and out of poverty. This is especially so during the current crisis, with its highly uneven sectoral and spatial impacts. Finally, in a new, highly politicized environment, one does not have to be excessively cynical to observe that powerful vested interests exist with a stake in either overstating or understating the seriousness of the situation.

An assessment of social trends is also sensitive to selection of time periods and to the impact of unrelated, non-crisis phenomena. Through until early 1998, the rural poor were affected much more by the drought, which resulted in below-average agricultural growth in 1997 (table 4.2). The government maintained food subsidies, partly through rice imports at a special exchange rate of Rp 5,000, for several months into 1998. In addition there were subsidies for fuel, electricity and some other 'essentials. Moreover, many firms made an effort to maintain their workforce during the first 6–9 months of the crisis, at least until the end of the fasting month in late January 1998.

It is perhaps not surprising, therefore, that the estimates of poverty incidence vary so widely, and why general social assessments range from the alarmist to the cautiously optimistic. One's approach depends in part on which particular socioeconomic 'snippets' are being more intensively observed. The export-oriented cash crop farmer in Sulawesi and the displaced Jakarta construction worker will present a very different picture.

The labor force data provide one reasonably clear indication of social impacts, although one must be cautious in drawing strong inferences from just two, point-to-point observations. Early reports suggested that the unemployment rate was rising sharply, from less than 5 percent to over 20 percent, with underemployment rising equally rapidly. However, in an economy like Indonesia, labor market adjustments invariably take the form of transfers to informal sector activities and reduced earnings, rather than open unemployment (Manning, 1999). The Sakernas labor force survey data conducted in August 1997 (essentially pre-crisis) and 1998 (well into the crisis) reported very little change in either open unemployment or underemployment (table 4.4). These figures appear

Table 4.4 Labor market adjustment, 1997–98

	1997	1998
% unemployed	4.7	5.5
% underemployed	12.0	9.3
Workforce by sector (% of total):		
agriculture	40.7	45.0
mining	1.0	0.8
manufacturing	12.9	11.3
construction	4.9	4.0
trade & tourism	19.9	19.2
transport & communication	4.8	4.7
finance & accommodation	0.8	0.7
govt & private services	14.7	14.1
Labor productivity (major sectors, Rp '000, 1993 prices):		
all sectors	5083	3966
agriculture	1848	1635
manufacturing	9885	9544
construction	8373	5996
trade & tourism	4336	3543
transport & communication	7798	6753
finance & accommodation	58977	45924
govt & private services	2994	2894
Contribution to employment expansion, 1997–98 (percent of total):		
agriculture	204	
mining	−8.9	
manufacturing	−47.4	
utilities	−3.8	
construction	−29.3	
trade & tourism	−6.1	
transport & communications	1.2	
finance & accommodation	−1.7	
govt & private services	−8.0	
(absolute expansion = 2,266.9 thousand)		

Note: Underemployment is defined as those in the workforce working less than 35 hours per week, and seeking additional employment.

Source: Badan Pusat Statistik, Sakernas, August 1997 and 1998.

implausibly low, especially the suggested decline in underemployment, but they do at least correct the earlier, more sensational conjectures. The employment data also suggest substantial sectoral mobility one year into the crisis. Agriculture's share is reported to have risen 10 percent (or more than 4 percentage points), and it accommodated more than double the increment to the workforce over these 12 months. Every other sector shed labor, with the biggest decline occurring in manufacturing.

Various estimates of real wages suggest a significant decline, but one which varies according to region and sector, and is sensitive to the choice of deflator (Manning, 1999). Those in rice agriculture on Java fell by about 30–50 percent during 1998. Non-agricultural activities were generally worse affected, particularly sectors such as construction and import-substituting manufacturing. By contrast, the decline in agriculture off-Java was probably less, and in some buoyant sectors (for example, cash-crop agriculture) it is possible that they were roughly constant. In the case of the latter, the benefits of increased international competitiveness accrued directly to plantation owners and small-holders, and so will not necessarily be reflected in the wage data.

As noted, the poverty estimates are the most controversial, but the most plausible set of estimates suggest a modest increase. Immediately before the crisis, about 11 percent of the population was estimated to be below the official poverty line. A priori, if per capita incomes have fallen back to about 1994 levels, the starting point in the analysis would be to assume that poverty incidence would resemble the figure for that year, or some 13 percent of the population. In fact, it might even be expected to be slightly lower than this. Poverty estimates are generally expenditure-based, and the decline in real per capita household consumption in 1998 was very similar to the increase in the previous year, suggesting that perhaps 1996 might be the relevant benchmark guesstimate. These are averages for the whole country. One might also hypothesize that income and expenditure inequality fell somewhat during the crisis, since the better off are more likely to derive their income from the modern urban economy, which has registered the sharpest decline (not to mention the collapse on the stock market and in 'top-end' real estate), whereas the poor are more likely to work in the relatively resilient agricultural and informal sectors. Thus it is even conceivable that the increase in poverty could be less still. All this is very approximate, of course, and, pending the arrival of better data, must remain speculative. But, as with unemployment, if nothing else, this back-of-the-envelope reasoning demonstrates that some of the early alarmist estimates are quite unreliable.

Three major sets of poverty estimates for 1998 and 1999 had been prepared by early 1999, and their results vary wildly (table 4.5). The most reliable and rigorous are those prepared by Poppele, Sumarto and Pritchett (1999). They base their findings on three data sources, covering the months August–September 1997 and 1998: the ongoing Indonesian

Family Life Survey (IFLS) collected by Rand and the University of Indonesia's Demographic Institute; a '100-village survey' undertaken by BPS and UNICEF; and a qualitative Kecamatan Crisis Impact Survey, also conducted by BPS. A resample of the first data base, involving almost 2,000 households in seven provinces, constitutes their main source of information.

Table 4.5 Estimates of poverty incidence (percent of population)

		Urban	Rural	Total
BPS	1993	13.4	13.8	13.7
	1996	9.7	12.3	11.3
	1998 (June)	28.8	45.6	39.1
ILO	1998 (Dec.)	39.1	53.2	48.2
	1999 (Dec.)	56.6	71.7	66.3
Poppele et al.	1998 (A)	12.0	15.2	13.8
	1998 (B)	15.8	23.0	19.9

Sources: ILO (1998), Poppele et al. (1999), and unpublished data from BPS.

The authors' findings of a small rise in poverty incidence are generally consistent with the expectations adumbrated above. The study also concluded that between 1997 and 1998 there was a strong inverse correlation between education levels and the rise in poverty. That is, those with little or no formal education, although registering the highest poverty incidence, experienced very little increase in poverty. The percentage increase in poverty then rises for each completed education level (primary, secondary, tertiary). Such a finding lends additional support to the *prima facie* hypothesis that interpersonal inequality has declined during the crisis.

All three sources are at best approximate, but the earlier estimates prepared by the ILO and BPS greatly overstate the incidence of poverty.[2] The ILO figures are the most flawed methodologically, since they were based on an inflation rate of 80 percent (fairly close to the mark) but allowed for no rise in nominal incomes. In fact, nominal wages rose appreciably in all sectors, and real agricultural earnings may have actually increased through the year: in the case of food crops when the drought broke and rice prices were lifted to international levels, and in the case of export-oriented cash crops as the exchange rate depreciation began to feed through to producers. BPS estimates apparently allowed for some increase in nominal wages, but assumed incorrectly that poorer groups would be most affected by the crisis.

Education indicators present a mixed picture. Enrolment ratios fell slightly in 1998, by about 1.6 percent in both primary and junior secondary schools (MOEC/World Bank, 1999). In the case of the latter, urban enrolments fell more sharply, confirming the impression that the urban economy has been hardest hit. Private school figures appear to be worse affected than government schools, reflecting the relative costs of the two systems, and also the partial success of the government's campaign to abolish entry fees (but not the many other informal levies) at these two levels. Thus the data suggest that the educational impacts of the crisis have been largely contained, but more comprehensive data are obviously required to confirm such a conclusion.

There are as yet no comprehensive data on other social indicators, which are in any case even more difficult to monitor. Nation-wide, quick-release health data are not available. Unpublished UNICEF data, based on hospital surveys, suggest some increase in infant and maternal mortality, and in the incidence of diarrhoeal diseases. It is reasonable to surmise that rising costs in the modern health sector have put these services beyond the reach of many. But this sector catered mainly to the urban middle class anyway, and so the effects are probably limited. Modern pharmaceuticals have risen in price, since their manufacture is highly import-intensive, but the increases have been cushioned owing to subsidies and a switch to generic products. Similarly, the reported incidence of malnutrition has been rising, but by how much is not yet clear. It is arguably the case that the drought had a more serious impact on food availability than the financial crisis, certainly in rural areas, and that the good rains since mid-1998 have alleviated these pressures. The principal challenge here too relates to the those in the urban economy who have experienced a sharp fall in real incomes, and who have only limited access to traditional support mechanisms in rural areas.

In addition to these quantifiable indicators, there are frequent media and anecdotal reports of dislocation, hardship, and violence among local communities and families. The state of law and order certainly appears to have deteriorated markedly. Crime is reported to be rising sharply. 'Jakarta: City of Fear' was the perhaps overly dramatic headline of a *Jakarta Post* edition in January 1999. Looting of containers in the ports, factories and shops is souring the commercial environment. Attempts have been made partially to appropriate some private plantations in Sulawesi. There are frequent reports about disputes over land, while government offices at all tiers of the administration have been attacked. The dominant ethnic Chinese business community continues to be a prime target, but it is by no means the only one. No doubt rising poverty and unemployment have been a factor in all this. Political paybacks have been another factor in the equation, as those who felt mistreated by officialdom during the Soeharto era have sought to level the score. In addition, the widely reviled police force (as distinct from the armed forces, which continue to command somewhat more respect) has been unable to preserve local order in a number of locations.

5.   CAUSES OF THE CRISIS

This obviously is the big question of our time: why and how could high growth and seemingly well-managed economies suddenly fall so far and so fast in the space of just 6–12 months? The question has special relevance to Indonesia, since it has been by far the worst affected of the crisis economies, and its recovery path will almost certainly be the slowest and the most difficult.

The major argument in this section is that it was the conjunction of many factors which caused the crisis: political, social and economic; longer-term and structural, and immediate and short-term; and domestic and international. It is also necessary — though empirically not easy — to distinguish between the factors leading up to the crisis, and the government's management of it. The former is concerned with a range of precipitating and vulnerability factors up to mid-1997, while the latter focuses on the domestic and international response once the crisis hit.[3] It is no exaggeration to state that in Indonesia practically *everything* went wrong at once over the period 1997–98. Some may find such a broad and eclectic approach rather frustrating — nothing satisfies more than a single grand theory! However, the pieces of the jig-saw puzzle comprise such disparate parts that I doubt whether such an approach will ever really work.

As background to the analysis, it is useful to consider a range of comparative 'crisis' and 'vulnerability' indicators for Indonesia and its ASEAN neighbours (table 4.6), which we will refer to in the subsequent analysis. Most of these indicators reinforce the argument that there was little forewarning of the catastrophic events which engulfed the country from late 1997.

(a) *Macroeconomic policy*
   • Fiscal policy, conventionally defined, was conservative; the budget

Table 4.6 *Southeast Asia: pre-crisis indicators (all %, and for the years 1994–96, unless otherwise indicated)*

INDICATOR	Ind	Mal	Phils	Sing	Thai	VN
GDS/GDP	25.0	40.2	17.3	50.6	35.4	17.2
Fiscal/GDP	0.2	1.3	0.7	13.1	1.9	–2.8
Inflation	8.1	3.5	8.6	2.1	5.4	10.5
CAD/GDP	2.8	6.9	4.0	+13.5	7.2	11.0
Debt/GDP	54	n.a.	51	n.a.	48	35
ST/Total debt	26	n.a.	17	n.a.	48	n.a.
REER, 1996 (1990=100)	104	111	115	115	106	115
Internat. reserves (months of imports)	6.0	4.7	4.0	7.1	5.7	2.1
ST debt/internat. reserves, 1997	1.9	0.8	0.9	n.a.	1.7	n.a.
Euromoney rating (Sept. 1996; 0–100)	71	80	62	96	77	52
Non-performing loans as % of total assets, 1997	12	8	6	2	15	n.a.

Sources: Asia Pacific Economics Group, *Asia Pacific Profiles 1998*, Canberra, 1998; Asian Development Bank, *Asian Development Outlook 1998*, Manila, 1998; World Bank, *World Development Indicators 1997*, Washington DC, 1997; JP Morgan for REERs (increase indicates appreciation).

was broadly in balance, as it had been for some 30 years.
- Inflation was (just) single-digit.

(b) *Current account and debt*
- The current account deficit appeared manageable, and as a percentage of GDP was less than half that of Thailand in the immediate pre-crisis period.
- The external debt to GDP ratio, while quite high, was gradually declining and was appreciably lower than during the difficult adjustment period of the mid-1980s.

(c) *Business/efficiency indicators*
- Investment and savings were buoyant.

- Indonesia's ICOR was broadly stable in the 1990s and did not register the sharp increase in some of the other crisis economies. (For example, it almost doubled in Thailand and Korea in the course of the decade — see World Bank, 1998b.)
- Unlike Thailand, in late 1996 and the first half of 1997 there was no evident loss of investor enthusiasm for the rupiah or the stock market.
- Indicators of corporate health appeared broadly satisfactory.
- The construction industry and the urban real-estate markets were growing vigorously, but there was no evidence of a major asset price 'bubble'.
- All major financial ratings exercises for Indonesia continued to be positive, and generally improving. International comparisons (such as the World Competitiveness Report) ranked Indonesia rather low compared to the OECD economies, but among emerging markets it assumed an intermediate position, and one which was improving substantially over time. International development agencies as always emphasized the need for further reforms, but their public and semi-official statements gave little hint of an impending crisis.
- There was no generalized wage explosion; real wages in most sectors were rising gradually. Although sharper increases were evident in some high-level international-quality services, the numbers employed were small in aggregate.

(d) *Microeconomic/financial reform*

- International trade and investment barriers were steadily declining, although the forward momentum had declined since the late 1980s, and several egregious exceptions were much commented upon.
- The process of financial deepening appeared to be progressing steadily, as new financial instruments were introduced; similarly Bank Indonesia's capacity for prudential regulation seemed to be improving.

(e) *Balance of payments*

- Also unlike Thailand, exchange rate policy was gradually being relaxed, as Bank Indonesia widened its intervention band; there did not appear to be any serious exchange rate misalignment.
- International reserves, both in absolute terms and in months of merchandise imports, were comfortable and rising.
- Export growth showed considerable year-to-year fluctuation in the 1990s, but there was no sudden drop in 1995 and 1996 (World Bank, 1998b, p. 20ff).
- Among major East Asian economies, Indonesia was the least exposed to the electronics sector, which appeared to be a significant

factor in much of this regional export slowdown. (In its merchandise trade Indonesia was, however, the most exposed to Japan.)

We consider the major arguments commonly advanced to explain the East Asian crisis, distinguishing between pre-crisis vulnerability factors and the management of the crisis from mid-1997 onwards.

5.1 Pre-Crisis Vulnerability Factors

(i) *External debt and capital mobility?* There can be no doubting the rapid build-up, and volatility, of private capital flows immediately prior to, and during the onset of, the crisis. For example, in Indonesia net private capital inflows in FY 1996/97 (that is, in the year through to March 31 1997) totalled $13.5 billion, followed by net outflows of $11.8 billion a year later (and an estimated additional outflow of $10.8 billion in 1998/99). Of special note is the behavior of the various components of the capital account. The switch in portfolio and debt flows was particularly pronounced.

To make the case that international capital markets were a problem, one has to examine both the flows in aggregate and their composition. Depending on the measure used, it is possible to discern a potential crisis in the making. First, Indonesia's external debt as a percentage of GDP was broadly stable pre-crisis, at approximately 54 percent. By the end of 1998, it totalled $142 billion, with the private sector owing slightly more than the public (table 4.7). Pre-crisis the public debt to GDP ratio was declining, as indeed was the absolute total in some years, as a result of cautious fiscal policy and some pre-payments of existing debts. Thus, for example, the share of public debt in total debt declined from 75 percent in 1991 to 42 percent in 1997. If Indonesia's external debt is seen as being a key factor in the crisis, then this was very much a private sector phenomenon.

Much more problematic are the various estimates of short-term debt, and on this crucial variable we lack reliable time series data. The Bank of Indonesia data on short-term debt (defined as one-year maturity or less) suggest, implausibly, that there was virtually no increase over the period 1991–95. It then doubled between 1995 and 1997. Alternative estimates of short-term debt suggest a much faster build-up. For example, according to the World Bank, *World Development Indicators*, it almost trebled in 1990–96, from $11.1 billion (16 percent of the total) to $32.2 billion (25 percent).

Although hardly at stratospheric levels, here was one significant early warning indicator. Indonesia's external debt was sizeable well before the

Table 4.7 Indonesia's external debt, 1998 ($ billion, 30 September)

PUBLIC		68.6
Government		58.8
SOEs		9.8
banks	4.5	
corporations	5.3	
PRIVATE		73.3
Banks		6.5
Corporations		66.8
TOTAL		141.9
Memo items		
(a) Corporate debt		72.1
composition:		
SOEs	5.3	
Foreign-owned	31.9	
Domestic private firms	31.1	
Domestic securities	3.8	
(b) Banking sector		11.0
composition:		
State banks	4.4	
Private (foreign & domestic)	6.5	
Domestic securities	0.2	

Note: Domestic securities are those owned by non-residents.
Source: Bank Indonesia.

crisis, much of it accumulated during the 1980s when it had successfully negotiated the collapse in oil prices. The rapid increase in private debt — particularly that (unknown) portion which could quickly leave the country — was a new phenomenon for Indonesia, and one which the government was not well equipped to handle. One obvious implication of this rising short-term debt is that the conventional way of viewing international reserves was flawed. Instead of viewing the reserves in a current account context, in terms of months of imports, a capital account yardstick has become more relevant. As table 4.6 demonstrates, estimates of the ratio of short-term debt to international reserves indicate that Indonesia was the most vulnerable country in Southeast Asia, with a short-term debt almost double the level of reserves.

Of course, what constitutes 'mobile capital' is a matter of debate. External debt is only part of the story. Portfolio investment can also leave the country at short notice, and Indonesia received large quantities of this capital when the stock market was deregulated in late 1988. Adding the stock of portfolio investment to the short-term debt produces a still higher figure. Ultimately, almost all financial assets — foreign and domestic — might be regarded as internationally mobile if, as in Indonesia, there is an open capital account and there is a total loss of confidence in a regime. Indeed, crises invariably commence with *domestic* capital flight, since this group of investors generally has a superior understanding of domestic economics and politics. On this basis, the most appropriate ratio might be broad money (M2) to reserves. Alternative estimates (see for example Athukorala and Warr, 1999 and World Bank, 1998b) report broadly similar rankings, with Indonesia consistently among the more vulnerable economies both in terms of levels and rates of increase.

(ii) *Poor macroeconomic management?* As was emphasized above, this was definitely not an old-style macroeconomic crisis. Indonesia had experienced nearly three decades of conventionally sound macroeconomic management. First, budget deficits were broadly in balance, had rarely exceeded 2 percent of GDP in any year, and were tending recently towards a modest surplus. Secondly, inflation had been under control since the late 1960s. Thirdly, there did not appear to be any serious exchange rate misalignment. The government had been basically targeting a constant rupiah–dollar rate in real terms (that is, with nominal depreciations of a magnitude similar to the two countries' inflation differential). Moreover, a policy of more flexible exchange rate management was being pursued, through a widening of the intervention band. And on each occasion the band was widened — five times in 1994–97 — the market pushed the rate to the bottom limit (that is, the maximum possible appreciation).

However, while on the surface there appeared to be no looming crisis, here too problems were emerging. The principal one, *à la* Mundell-Fleming, was the attempt to set monetary policy targets and to run a quasi-fixed exchange rate with an open capital account, which facilitated rapidly rising capital inflows. A particular issue was the attempt to use one instrument (monetary policy) for two objectives, that is, one internal (inflation) and the other external (competitiveness). Through the 1990s the government resorted to tighter monetary policy to counteract perceptions of an overheated economy. But the resultant higher interest rates actually attracted more capital inflows, which in turn fueled a further monetary expansion (McLeod, 1997). As long as capital inflows were modest, and took the form primarily of public sector borrowings and foreign direct investment, the fundamental flaw in this strategy was contained. But rising private flows of the 1990s, which were not amenable to any of the government's policy levers then in use, progressively undermined exchange rate and monetary policy settings.

Moreover, the government had maintained its real exchange rate target since the last major nominal depreciation of September 1986, and its evident commitment to this strategy convinced borrowers and creditors alike that there would be no deviation. As a result, only a small proportion (estimated to be less than 30 percent) of the country's private external debt was hedged. For most of the 1990s, the differential between rupiah and foreign currency lending rates was in the range 10–15 percentage points. Thus the attraction of foreign borrowings, supplied by international financial institutions only too keen to participate in Indonesia's booming economy, was irresistible. The gap in lending rates far outweighed the likely modest depreciation of the rupiah. The government's quite explicit exchange rate commitments and, especially for the well connected, bailouts for troubled debtors underpinned the massive unhedged borrowings. The magnitude of the problem became quickly evident only when, in the face of large-scale capital flight from August 1997, the government's commitment to a targeted normal exchange rate collapsed.[4]

(iii) *Poor financial regulation?* Poor financial regulation, political interference in commercial bank lending, premature and hasty financial liberalization and an open international capital account are widely regarded as key factors explaining East Asia's crisis. These were indeed central to Indonesia, but the story is complex and not amenable to some of the sweeping generalizations that have been offered over the past two years.

Some early warning indicators were present, but a full assessment pre-crisis was hampered by data deficiencies – some intentional, others reflecting bureaucratic weaknesses. Comparative estimates of the incidence of non-performing loans placed Indonesia somewhat higher than most of its neighbours (table 4.6). However, they were below Thailand, and hardly in the precarious range. Moreover, Bank Indonesia data on non-performing (NPLs) and bad loans showed no obvious build-up of a problem. In fact, these ratios were actually reported to be trending downwards slightly. Moreover, the external debt of Indonesia's commercial banks never reached the levels of most of its neighbors, partly owing to the restrictions placed on the activities of the still-large SOEs: the banks accounted for just 8 percent of the country's external debt. Most government and corporate borrowing abroad did not go through the country's banks. Finally, Indonesia did not appear to experience such a 'bubble' in asset prices as Thailand in the mid-1990s, and Japan earlier in the decade, and corporate commercial performance indicators generally appeared quite satisfactory.

There were of course serious problems. Indonesia's financial sector, *à la* Krugman, was indeed 'under-regulated and over-guaranteed' and these problems did contribute to the unfolding crisis. The 'over-guaranteed' part of the equation was arguably more important, especially through its connection to the next causal factor to be examined, that of the Soeharto family businesses. The banking sector had been expanding recklessly, and with little substantial regulation, since the major liberalization of October 1988, and in the context of a very open international capital account. In addition, domestic credit was expanding. Over the years 1991–96, the credit/GDP ratio grew at about 5 percent per annum in Indonesia and by 1996 it was about 0.5.

Nevertheless, the evidence points to this factor as a contributing variable, rather than the key explanator. The pre-crisis data were admittedly quite inadequate, but Indonesia's financial vulnerability indicators (for example, the ratio of outstanding bank credit to GDP) were only moderately high, and the financial sector was a relative small direct player in the country's external debt.

(iv) *Corruption and governance*? It is empirically difficult to invoke corruption, which we use here as shorthand for the 'KKN' (*Korupsi, Kolusi*, Nepotism) phenomenon, as a key, *pre-crisis*, causal factor. Corruption was extremely widespread in Soeharto's Indonesia. Various estimates place Indonesia very high in comparative assessments. One widely quoted estimate, prepared annually by Transparency International, ranked Indonesia at 80 out of 85 countries in 1998. Most other surveys also clearly placed it towards the top. There can also be no doubting that the extraordinary concentration of power and privilege around Soeharto, and the dramatic expansion in his family's business empire, from a scale which was trivial in the 1970s and still quite modest in the mid-1980s. The expansion of his children's conglomerates was particularly remarkable. Nobody outside the family — or perhaps even in it — has a clear picture of the family fortune. According to one highly publicized estimate (*Time*, 24 May 1999), the figure may amount to about $15 billion.[5]

However, these arguments do not demonstrate conclusively that corruption was a major causal variable. Other countries — China, India, Vietnam — also rank highly in these corruption comparisons but have not (yet) succumbed to the crisis. Moreover, one also has to explain how corrupt countries like Indonesia, and many others, could have grown so fast for so long with corruption an ever-present variable. More plausible is the thesis that the particular forms corruption, and the political system in general, had assumed by the 1990s rendered the Soeharto government unwilling — indeed unable — to move decisively and swiftly once the crisis had hit. Our argument, to be developed shortly, is that corruption deserves great emphasis at this stage of the process, rather than as an initial precipitating factor.

5.2 Management of the Crisis

Thus far our examination of Indonesia pre-crisis suggests an economy moderately vulnerable to a crisis, but no more so than several of its neighbors. How, therefore, is one to explain the catastrophic events of 1997–98, which saw Indonesia plunge far more deeply? The explanation has to lie in the management of the crisis, which in turn was embedded in the fragile political system and escalating social and ethnic tensions.

(i) *A chronicle of policy errors* Serious problems began to emerge in Indonesia by late October 1997 and the real damage was done over the next seven months, to May 1998. The first major policy mistake was the sudden closure of 16 banks on November 1, 1997. This event was mishandled (by both the IMF and the Indonesian government) since it immediately undermined confidence in the entire financial system. It marked the beginning of a series of bank runs, and also the loss of monetary policy control as ever-increasing amounts of liquidity were injected into the system to cover these runs. The second set of problems related to the growing perception that President Soeharto was intent on protecting his family's commercial interests at all costs, a sentiment that quickly snowballed into a general loss of confidence in the regime's economic management credentials. The government began to backtrack almost immediately on the first IMF agreement (of 31 October), particularly in protecting family business interests. In early January the annual budget was delivered, with key macroeconomic assumptions which were hardly credible. Shortly afterwards, the rift with the IMF became very public. By then the rupiah had really crashed, and was trading at just one-seventh of its pre-crisis dollar exchange rate.

The problems continued unabated. In February, Soeharto toyed with the establishment of a currency board system, in the process dismissing his highly regarded central bank governor, and deepening the dispute with the IMF and bilateral donors. For a period, IMF support was suspended. The presidential and vice-presidential elections proceeded according to script in March, followed by the appointment of a contentious new Cabinet. Mounting political protests in May stymied the short-lived reform efforts, eventually tipping out Soeharto following persistent street protests and the loss of over 1,000 lives.

Having chronicled the major policy mistakes and lost opportunities in the first nine months of the crisis, it is useful to look again more closely at the two major actors, the Soeharto regime and the IMF.

(ii) *KKN again* If it is difficult to mount a case for corruption precipitating the crisis, the argument that it incapacitated the Soeharto regime once the crisis had hit is much more compelling. The distinguishing feature of the regime had been the immense and increasing power centred around Soeharto (MacIntyre, 1999). In consequence, as noted above, corruption too became ever more centralized around the palace. Meanwhile, the influence of the technocrats was diminishing. The 1993 Cabinet marked a watershed in this respect, for it ended the era of the so-called 'Berkeley Mafia', the gifted economists who had guided economic policy since 1967. At the same time, a number of key Habibie allies (the so-called 'technologs'), with views opposed to the technocrats' economic orthodoxy, were included in the Cabinet.

At the onset of the crisis, the three key economists in this Cabinet, while technically able and widely admired for their professionalism, were in various ways incapacitated. For example, the Finance Minister continued to run tight fiscal policy. But he reportedly rarely conferred directly with Soeharto, nor did he communicate with the foreign financial press. Lines of communication between Soeharto and the central bank governor broke down over the issue of a currency board, and the governor was later dismissed. Over this period, also, the Coordinating Economics Minister was occasionally quite ill and required hospitalization.

Thus, partly be design, partly by accident, the key economics portfolios were weakened just when they were most needed. The late 1980s financial liberalization urgently required comprehensive follow-up regulation and supervision, yet the technocrats were sidelined. Indonesia's political system rested so absolutely on this one supremely powerful individual that it quickly began to crumble when Soeharto himself faltered from late 1997 (MacIntyre, 1999). There were no institutional checks on his authority, and conversely no safeguards in the event of his failure in a crisis. The political crisis which developed so suddenly over this period had its roots in the early stages of the foreign exchange and financial crisis, but its origins were much deeper, in the political and social problems, and they quickly drove the economic collapse to new lows. It is in this sense that 'corruption' contributed decisively to Indonesia's crisis. It was not simply a matter of an insatiably greedy first family, but also a political system which had lost its capacity to act decisively in a crisis, and thereby lacked credibility in the eyes of both domestic and foreign investors.

(iii) *The role of the IMF* Should the IMF also be cast in the role of a villain? This is a large and complex issue, on which professional opinion divides sharply, and one on which inevitably outsiders cannot be fully informed. It would be a mistake to attribute primary responsibility to this institution, but equally one cannot escape the conclusion that it mishandled the situation. There is no evidence that it was any better (or worse) than anyone else in foreseeing the crisis. There is certainly not a hint of deep concern in the Fund's public statements. The Fund's early approach to the problem also appeared to constitute mis-diagnosis. A one-size-fits-all prescription of a fiscal surplus was seemingly based on the premise of profligate public sectors and high inflation, neither of which was accurate. The sudden bank closures of 1 November, which precipitated the general loss of confidence in the banking system, were certainly conducted under Fund tutelage, if not direction.

The Fund's reform programs have been excessively ambitious and comprehensive. Rather than focusing on the key variables required for the restoration of market confidence, a 'scatter-gun' approach seems to have been adopted. The Fund seems to have taken the decision early on that this was the opportunity it had long been waiting for, to push through practically every conceivable item on its Indonesian reform agenda. Most of these were highly desirable, it should be added, if implemented at the right time, and by a government able to deliver. But in the circumstances of late 1997 and early 1998, failure was inevitable: an overloaded, weak and demoralized bureaucracy was not even remotely capable of implementing such an ambitious agenda; those reforms requiring fundamental legal and institutional change will take years to implement effectively.

One lesson from the crisis is that the IMF should have focused its attention much more on the core problems associated with the financial and foreign exchange collapse. This does not preclude wider forays into the realm of microeconomic reform. But priorities do matter, given the

Fund has limited technical resources, and also a limited capacity to influence government policy. Ensuring a well-functioning and regulated financial sector is overwhelmingly more important than efforts to dismantle a national clove monopoly or a national car program, outrageous though the latter two interventions (both in support of Tommy Soeharto's business empire) were. In the Fund's major evaluation of its activities in Indonesia, Korea, and Thailand (Lane et al., 1999), 'Governance and Competition Policy' gets two pages and the 'overload' thesis just one paragraph in a 147-page report. Yet these programs feature centrally, explicitly or implicitly, in the Indonesian program.[6]

(iv) *Additional adverse factors* To complete this story of 'everything going wrong at once', four additional factors should be mentioned. First, and most important, the regional economic environment, Japan in particular,[7] was subdued. This is a major difference in the comparison between East Asia 1997–98 and Mexico 1994–95. A second problem was that the El Niño phenomenon had caused a very serious drought in Indonesia, resulting in declining food crop production of as much as 8 percent per capita in 1997–98, and necessitating the first large-scale rice imports in over a decade, just as the country was experiencing a balance of payments crisis. Thirdly, international oil prices were at a historic low throughout the period, so there was an additional problem caused by declining terms of trade.

Finally, related partly to the political turbulence, and uniquely in East Asia, Indonesia's social fabric came under severe stress. The role of the small Chinese community, numbering about 3 percent of the population and controlling perhaps up to 40 percent of the economy, has always been a sensitive issue. The breakdown in civil order in May 1998, and the systematic attacks on this community, deeply traumatized many ethnic Chinese (Wanandi, 1999). Some left the country temporarily or permanently. Many took their money out. In addition to its key domestic commercial role, this community has provided a crucial conduit to the international business community, and particularly investors from Singapore, Hong Kong, and Taiwan. Subsequent localized violence, with nasty religious or ethnic overtones, in Ambon, West Kalimantan, Aceh, and East Timor, further contributed to the perception that the central government could not guarantee stability and security.

6.   LOOKING TO THE FUTURE

What of the short- to medium-run prospects? It is possible to identify at least three alternative scenarios for Indonesia over the next few years. These are:

- 'Mexico': a quick return to positive growth, in which in retrospect 1997–98 recedes as a passing aberration.
- 'Aquino': a 'muddle through' period, which halts the economic decline and arguably lays the foundation for a more durable recovery, but in which political instability and lack of economic policy coherence deny the country a quick return to strong and sustained growth.
- 'Burma': an awful scenario in which Indonesia closes itself off from the world, both politically and commercially, and which results in declining living standards, political brutality, and possibly ethnic and geographic fragmentation.

It is already clear that Indonesia will not be able immediately to replicate the Mexican record. Nor, fortunately, does the third scenario look all that likely. Mexico returned to positive growth within six quarters and it regained its pre-crisis per capita GDP (though not personal income) within nine quarters (see OECD, 1998). As noted, the key to its recovery was exceptionally strong export growth (60 percent in volume terms in the first year after the crisis), and a swift Washington-orchestrated bail-out. Indonesia's crisis has been deeper, and its recovery almost certainly will be slower, notwithstanding the hopeful signs to emerge in the first quarter of 1999 (1.34 percent growth, quarter on quarter; growth of 1–2 percent and inflation of 10 percent projected for FY 1999/2000).

Something like the Aquino scenario appears much more likely. But political, social, and economic factors are currently so fluid in Indonesia that it is impossible to make forecasts with any confidence. Instead, a more useful approach is to identify some of the major parameters which hold the key to recovery and which will determine how quickly Indonesia returns to positive economic growth.[8] A crucial source of uncertainty will be the domestic political system and its capacity to deliver effective economic policy-making. It is as yet not clear what sort of economic policy will emerge, but already several features of this new political economy environment stand out:

- No one political leader or party is likely to have a clear parliamentary majority. Thus coalitions, in the running of Parliament and in the election of the president, will be the order of the day.
- These coalitions are likely, at least initially and probably in the

longer term, to be pragmatic, opportunistic, and personality-based.

- Independent of any coalition arrangements, Parliament is likely to behave in an unpredictable and assertive fashion. (Conversely, it may be that, once passed, legislation will be more 'legitimate' and receive wider community acceptance.)
- By contrast, the bureaucracy is likely to be much weaker than it was during the Soeharto era. It will also be much more subservient to the Parliament in important respects, and it will be under sustained public scrutiny, not least from a reinvigorated press.
- It will take a long time for effective, independent and credible institutions to develop. This applies particularly to the legal system. Thus reform packages which emphasize primarily the making of new laws rather than their implementation will produce uncertain — and probably unintended — results.
- There will be great pressure for increased regional autonomy, so that many of the new policy debates — and possibly quite a bit of the power — will shift to the provinces.

Underlying these changing political parameters is the challenge of how to handle the Soeharto family. Soeharto's presence will inevitably continue to divide the nation, not least owing to allegations that he commands resources on such a scale that his supporters are able to destabilize the political system, its institutions, and its processes. There is also mounting pressure for the state to sequester his assets, and to prosecute him for corruption. As in the case of Marcos, this is likely to be a long and tedious process, with low and uncertain pay-offs, and it would be unfortunate if the new government gets sidetracked by the politics of revenge. Still, something needs to be done. One practical step which commends itself is that family members' outstanding debts to the state banking system be called in and, in the event of non-compliance, they then be subject to bankruptcy proceedings. Such proceedings have already begun on a very minor scale as they affect one son (Tommy), but they could easily and quickly be extended to the entire family.

6.1 Monetary and Exchange Rate Policy

Indonesia's new macroeconomic framework is precarious, but probably working as well as possible in the circumstances. Essentially the government has shifted from an awkward combination of a money supply target, loosely defined, and a nominal exchange rate anchor (keeping the real rate against the dollar approximately constant), to a tighter money supply targeting and a floating exchange rate (albeit with some central bank 'smoothing' intervention). By April 1999, six months of low inflation had been achieved. Thus the looming fear of hyper-inflation, and with it a rise in entrenched inflationary expectations, has abated. The exchange rate seems to have settled in the range 7,000–10,000, despite very serious social disturbances in February and March 1999. There is now a good chance that Indonesia has locked in its current, very competitive exchange rate, to the great benefit of its export industries.

However, both these monetary and exchange rate variables could be easily derailed. A sudden loss of international confidence in Indonesia's social stability, political system, or the government's capacity to manage the recovery, could see renewed capital flight, especially as trading on the foreign exchange market remains thin, and IMF support is winding down. As long as fiscal deficits are primarily foreign financed, the money supply goals are more easily managed. But while a short-term Keynesian fiscal stimulus is surely justified over the difficult period 1998–99, beyond the immediate crisis period, if the new political system generates irresistible demands for government expenditure, this fragile monetary stability could easily be jeopardized. Moreover, the process of bank recapitalization, and financial reform more generally, has barely begun. Renewed bank runs, pressure from the politically powerful for preferential assistance, and the sheer cost of recapitalization could all lead to a blow-out in money supply, and hence renewed inflation.

There will continue to be a constant clamor for a more stable exchange rate and for partial closure of the international capital account. The appeal of greater exchange rate stability in the wake of the turmoil since mid-1997 is understandably powerful. Similarly, one can readily understand the capital account argument: countries with restrictions have not been as devastated as Indonesia (for example, China, India), there is the moderately successful Malaysian experiment nearby, and the intellectual argument for it is quite respectable. However, while there may be a case for some curbs on the inflow of 'hot' money in good times, in the current environment any attempt to impose capital barriers would almost certainly backfire.

6.2 Fiscal Policy

Here the analytical options are more straightforward, but the devil is in the detail. There is a strong case for a short-run fiscal stimulus (see Corden, 1998 for a clear statement of the principles). Private demand, especially investment, has collapsed, and thus a fiscal stimulus is necessary to avoid an even deeper contraction. The usual objections to deficit financing are not so important in the crisis context: a large proportion of the deficit is being financed by donors; there is no danger of the deficit 'crowding out' the private sector; and the markets are unlikely to see a deficit as a dangerous loss of fiscal discipline, providing the government presents it as a temporary measure and as part of an analytically robust framework (for which an IMF blessing makes a positive contribution). Complex practical matters do intrude immediately, however. Theory provides very little guidance on how large the deficit ought to be, whether for example it should be 8.5 percent of GDP (the earlier target for FY 1998–99), or half that figure (close to the actual outcome). The issue of how to spend the deficit is of secondary importance in the first instance, but it quickly becomes the dominant consideration, as the government needs to avoid programs which lock it into future commitments, and to select programs which meet some sort of efficiency and/or equity test, and which are not overtaken by corruption.

6.3 Banking Reform and Corporate Debt Restructuring

Progress has been slow. Indonesia's external debt is very large, its bureaucracy and institutions are not well prepared for dealing with the problem, and the international financial community – both existing creditors and potential new buyers – are holding back pending clearly established rules of the game. There have been few tangible signs of a quick resolution in Indonesia. Foreign investor interest remains negligible. It will almost certainly remain so until after the general and presidential elections, and the composition of Indonesia's first post-Soeharto democratic government is clear, and until the serious social tensions and anti-Chinese sentiments abate. Some mergers and acquisitions are beginning to take place, but in aggregate the amounts are still small. Also, by April 1999 capital inflows began to push the Jakarta Stock Exchange up sharply. The privatization program was basically stalled until late 1998, and there is pressure for a sizeable portion of the proceeds to be handed over to cooperatives. However, activity did at least pick up in the second quarter of 1999. The Bankruptcy Law was finally promulgated in late 1998, but thus far its operations have disappointed the financial community, in particular as its findings appear consistently to favor debtors over creditors. After missing an earlier target, the government finally announced in mid-March its plans for financial recapitalization, which represents a start, but the hard work lies ahead.

6.4 Microeconomic and Sectoral Reform

Microeconomic reform under the Habibie administration, and probably beyond, represents a case study in stark contrast. On the one hand, Indonesia has been moving steadily forward in achieving a cleaner and more transparent trade regime, and its external commitments – to the IMF, APEC, and AFTA – will likely ensure no significant backtracking. Conversely, as in most countries, the sectors are typically the domain of more intense rent-seeking pressures: government projects have to be allocated, distributional considerations intrude, and line ministries are more vulnerable to capture.

Much of the debate now centers around the concept *ekonomi rakyat* (people's economy) which, under the active sponsorship of Minister Adi Sasono, entails support for small–medium enterprises and cooperatives. Implicitly, and sometimes explicitly, this translates into support for *pribumi* enterprises. In principle, the goals here are laudable, but it is doubtful that subsidized credits and cooperatives are the best tools to tackle this problem, and the risk of corruption is very high.

The issue of privatization also provides an illustration of the complex interaction between ethnic tension, local-level pressures in the new political environment, and bureaucratic inertia and resistance. Indonesia has a large, poorly performing SOE sector, but one which has been sustained by resentment at non-*pribumi* and foreign commercial dominance, and by the government's ambitious industrialization objectives. Privatization was a key item in the IMF program. It is important as a means of raising efficiency, attracting foreign capital, and bolstering the government's short-term fiscal position. However, progress was initially very slow. In FY 1998–99, the government projected assets sales of $1.5 billion, but actual receipts were less than one-third of this figure. However, as the regional economic outlook has improved, and the government has become more experienced in SOE disposal, the pace has accelerated.

6.5 Social Policy

The difficulties of devising and implementing social safety net (SSN) programs should not be underestimated. First, the affected groups need to be identified, both in aggregate and by location. Second, it is not obvious which programs are the most cost-effective and quick-impacting. The government has adopted four main approaches: food security, including subsidies (the latter also extends to non-food items such as fuel); labor-intensive public works; social protection, including enhanced access to basic education and health services; and promotion of the *ekonomi rakyat*, especially cooperatives and SMEs. Each of these approaches has strengths and weaknesses. For example, subsidies are a blunt instrument, which may encourage corruption, including export smuggling. If there are price controls, they act as a production disincentive for farmers; if budget support is used, then there is concern about fiscal sustainability, and possibly the adverse effects of inflation on the poor.

Public works programs have a record of quite successful implementation in Indonesia, having been initiated in the early Soeharto era as a means of quickly recycling the windfall oil revenues into rural areas. However, some dubious investment projects appear to have been selected, and monitoring the disbursement of funds is no easy task. Perhaps unexpectedly, in view of the range of potential obstacles, social protection programs are thought to be working quite well. In the case of the scholarship schemes, for example, local educational authorities are presumably well placed to identify those in need, and there is also pressure on these officials to disburse the funds cleanly.

NOTES

1. Papers analyzing the Indonesian crisis include McLeod (1998), Manning (1999), World Bank (1998a) and the 'Survey of Recent Developments' in *BIES*. Assessments by prominent Indonesian economists include Sadli (1999), Simandjuntak (1999) and Tubagus (1998). For the onset and early stages of the crisis, see in particular Soesastro and Basri (1998) and Johnson (1998).

2. See Booth (1999), Cameron (1999) and Poppele et al. (1999) for discussion of data and methodological estimates associated with these estimates.

3. As the World Bank (1998b, pp. 54–5) argued: 'It is clear that while a crisis was building quickly in Thailand, and to some extent in Korea, other countries — Malaysia, Indonesia and the Philippines — seem to have been affected by the crisis through contagion.'

4. It should be noted in passing that there continues to be some conjecture over pre-crisis trends in the real effective exchange rate (REER). It is no simple matter to measure the REER accurately, and alternative series produce different numbers, both in magnitude and even trends.

5. Backman (1999) estimated that, at the time of resignation, Soeharto's family had significant shares in at least 1,251 companies. These holdings were spread over an extraordinarily diverse group of activities, including huge and widely publicized investments in satellites and telecommunications, toll roads, luxury hotels and tourism complexes, petrochemicals, an airline, shopping complexes, plantations, and mining.

6. Until the signing of IMF III (10 April 1998) there was a cumulative total of 117 policy commitments, across the following areas: fiscal policy (17); monetary and banking policy (17); bank restructuring (24); foreign trade (16); investment and deregulation (15); privatization (13); social safety net (2); environment (6);

other (7). Most of these were desirable in some short or long-run sense.

7. Japan is Indonesia's largest commercial creditor by a large margin. According to Bank for International Settlements data, as at 30 June 1998, Japanese creditors account for 38 percent of this debt; the next largest creditor is Germany, with 12 percent. There seems little doubt that the reluctance of Japanese financial institutions to accept write-downs, owing to their own perilous circumstances, has complicated and delayed the debt resolution process.

8. The key document in this context is the report of the 'Canberra Conference', involving a group of senior economists from Indonesia, Australia, Japan, and the USA, and held at the Australian National University, 23–25 November 1998. Its 'Report of a Conference on Indonesia's Economic Crisis' was published bilingually in January 1999 by the Fakultas Ekonomi, Universitas Indonesia. See in particular Manning (1999), who presents the Report and places it in a broader analytical and political-economy context.

REFERENCES

·(Note: *BIES* refers to the *Bulletin of Indonesian Economic Studies*.)

Arndt, H.W. and H. Hill (eds) (1999), *Southeast Asia's Economic Crisis: Origins, Lessons, and the Way Forward*, Institute of Southeast Asian Studies, Singapore; Allen & Unwin, Sydney; St Martin's Press, New York.

Aswicahyono, H.H. (1998), 'Total Factor Productivity in Indonesian Manufacturing, 1975–93', unpublished PhD thesis, Australian National University, Canberra.

Athukorala, P.C. and P. Warr (1999), 'Vulnerability to a Currency Crisis: Lessons from the East Asian Experience', forthcoming working paper, Australian National University, Canberra.

Backman, M. (1999), *Asian Eclipse: Exposing the Dark Side of Business in Asia*, John Wiley & Sons, Singapore.

Booth, A. (1999), 'The Impact of the Crisis on Poverty and Equity', in Arndt and Hill (eds), pp. 128–41.

Cameron, L. (1999), 'Survey of Recent Developments', *BIES*, 35 (1), pp. 3–54.

Chen, E.K.Y. (1997), 'The Total Factor Productivity Debate: Determinants of Economic Growth in East Asia', *Asian-Pacific Economic Literature*, 11 (1), pp. 18–38.

Corden, W. M. (1998), *The Asian Crisis: Is There a Way Out?*, Institute of Southeast Asian Studies, Singapore.

Forrester, G. and R. May (eds) (1998), *The Fall of Soeharto*, Crawfurd Press, Bathurst.

ILO (1998) (International Labour Organization), *Employment Challenges of the Indonesian Economic Crisis*, Jakarta.

Jellinek, L. and Bambang Rustanto (1999), 'Survival Strategies of the Javanese during the Economic Crisis', unpublished paper, Jakarta.

Johnson, C. (1998), 'Survey of Recent Developments', *BIES*, 34 (2), pp. 3–60.

Krugman, P. (1994), 'The Myth of Asia's Miracle', *Foreign Affairs*, 73 (6), pp. 62–78.

Lane, T. et al. (1999), 'IMF-Supported Programs in Indonesia, Korea and Thailand: A Preliminary Assessment', International Monetary Fund, Washington DC.

MacIntyre, A. (1999), 'Political Institutions and the Economic Crisis in Thailand and Indonesia', in Arndt and Hill (eds), pp. 142–57.

Manning, C. (1998), *Indonesian Labour in Transition: An East Asian Success Story?*, Cambridge University Press, Cambridge.

Manning, C. (1999), 'Indonesia's Economic Collapse and Path to Recovery: Can (and Should) the Leopard Change its Spots?', *Development Studies Papers*, Asia-Pacific School of Economics and Management, Australian National University, Canberra.

McLeod, R. (1997), 'Explaining Chronic Inflation in Indonesia', *Journal of Development Studies*, 33 (2), pp. 392–410.

McLeod, R. (1998), 'Indonesia', in R. McLeod and R. Garnaut (eds), *East Asia in Crisis: From Being a Miracle to Needing One?*, Routledge, London, pp. 31–48.

MOEC/World Bank (1999), *The Impact of Indonesia's Economic Crisis on Education: Findings from a Survey of Schools*, Office of Research and Development, Ministry of Education and Culture, Jakarta.

OECD (Organization for Economic Cooperation and Development) (1998), *OECD Economic Surveys 1997–98: Mexico*, Paris.

Poppele, J., Sudarno Sumarto and L. Pritchett (1999), 'Social Impacts of the Indonesian Crisis: New Data and Policy Implications', unpublished paper, SMERU (Social Monitoring and Early Response Unit), Jakarta.

Sadli, M. (1999), 'The Indonesian Crisis', in Arndt and Hill (eds), pp. 16–27.

Simandjuntak, D.S. (1999), 'An Inquiry into the Nature, Causes and Consequences of the Indonesian Crisis', *Journal of Asia-Pacific Economy*, 4 (1), pp. 171–92.

Soesastro, H. and M.C. Basri (1998), 'Survey of Recent Developments', *BIES*, 34 (1), pp. 3–54.

Tubagus Feridhanusetyawan (1997), 'Survey of Recent Developments', *BIES*, 33 (2), pp. 3–39.

Tubagus Feridhanusetyawan (1998), 'Social Impacts of the Indonesian

Crisis', *Indonesian Quarterly*, 26 (4), pp. 325–64.

Wanandi, S. (1999), 'The Post-Soehato Business Environment', in G. Forrester (ed.), *Post Soeharto Indonesia: Renewal or Chaos*, Institute of Southeast Asian Studies, Signapore, pp. 120–34.

World Bank (1998a), *Indonesia in Crisis: A Macroeconomic Update*, Washington DC.

World Bank (1998b), *East Asia: The Road to Recovery*, Washington DC.

5. Socioeconomic dimension of the Asian crisis: impact and household response in the Philippines

Arsenio M. Balisacan and Rosemarie G. Edillon

1. INTRODUCTION

While the macroeconomic impact of the Asian crisis is now fairly obvious, its full impact on various social and economic groups remains to be felt. Beyond impact, even less is known about the channels through which the crisis has affected the economic and social well-being of various groups of Philippine society. To be sure, numerous papers have been written – and policy forums undertaken – in recent months, describing the social dimension of the crisis. Casual reference, for example, has been made to its adverse impact on employment, consumer prices, and public spending on social and economic services, especially those directly benefiting the poor. Elsewhere in Asia, recent work has also described children, pregnant and lactating women, and old-age persons as major groups that have taken the brunt of the crisis.

Past discussions have, however, been limited by the lack (or inadequacy) of nationwide household data that could be used to describe the changes in the economic well-being of various household groups: their economic conditions before the crisis, changes in these conditions during the crisis, their responses to it, and the impact of government policies and programs implemented to address the crisis.[1] Related to this is the virtual absence of efforts systematically to explore what makes some households more vulnerable than others to macroeconomic shocks, such as the Asian economic crisis.

Needless to say, efficient delivery of economic and social services to the poor requires not only cost-effective identification of the poor (their location and circumstances, dimension of their poverty, etc.) but also an understanding of the factors contributing to their vulnerability to macroeconomic shocks. Are women, for example, likely to be more vulnerable than men to loss of employment during macroeconomic shocks *à la* Asian financial crisis? If so, why? And to what extent is this an outcome of government policies and programs? What safety nets can be put in place to mitigate conditions leading to poverty traps?

Our aim in this chapter is twofold: (i) to characterize changes in employment status for various economic and social groups during the Asian crisis; and (ii) to assess the importance of certain location and household characteristics in explaining differences in unemployment 'duration' or spell. To achieve this, we construct a panel data set from nationwide household surveys covering 1997 (pre-crisis period) and 1998 (crisis period). To our knowledge, this is the first time in the Philippines that such data have been employed to inform the discussion on the impact of, and household responses to, macroeconomic shocks such as the Asian crisis.

In the section that follows, we provide an overview of the Asian crisis in the context of the Philippine experience. We then describe the data set. The section following characterizes changes in employment status for various population subgroups, their responses to the crisis, and factors accounting for the variation in employment spells. Finally, in the last section, we provide concluding remarks.

2. THE ASIAN CRISIS IN PHILIPPINE PERSPECTIVE: AN OVERVIEW

The Philippine economic performance over the past several decades can be described as a series of boom-and-bust cycles. The decade of the 1990s began with a contraction of the economy. GDP declined by about 1 percent while GNP managed to grow slightly (0.5 percent), propped up only by the positive growth in overseas remittances. The years following saw the country initially recovering lost ground (0.3 percent in 1992), then gaining momentum (2.1 percent in 1993) and eventually sustaining growth (over 4 percent in 1994–97), seemingly in the fashion of the East Asian miracle.

There were other positive indications. On the demand side, growth seemed to have been fueled by the rise in investments (except possibly in 1995) and exports. Export growth averaged 16 percent per annum from 1994 to 1997. On the production side, output growth was highest in the industry sector. Note that these were the very factors responsible for the spectacular growth experienced by the newly industrialized economies of East Asia. Meanwhile, the national government managed to post fiscal surpluses beginning in 1994 (1.1 percent of GDP). And despite the expansion in economic activity, the inflation rate was kept in single digits (averaging 8.0 percent from 1994 to 1997) and always at less than half its level in 1991, which stood at 18.7 percent. Also, beginning 1994, growth in output outstripped growth in population, implying an improvement in per capita incomes. Official estimates show a 5-percentage-point reduction in poverty incidence, from about 40 percent in 1991 to 35 percent in 1994 and 32 percent in 1997.

There were warning signs as well. The deficit on the current account was close to, if not more than, 5 percent of GDP from 1993 even up to 1997. Gross domestic savings remained low, at 15 percent of aggregate output, and this implies that investments were financed largely from foreign savings. High domestic interest rates, coupled with signals from monetary authorities that a devaluation in the near future was anything but far-fetched, attracted portfolio investment which was considered 'hot' money and therefore unstable. The influx of foreign money led to a real appreciation of the peso. In fact, in 1994 and 1995, the local currency even appreciated in nominal terms by 2.6 percent and 2.7 percent, respectively. Other developments, however, overshadowed these warning signs. For instance, the deficit on the current account arose from high investment spending and not consumption spending and this was necessary to achieve output growth. Meanwhile, the real appreciation of the peso was not perceived as a real threat especially considering that exports were growing at all-time highs. The influx of foreign investments, even portfolio investments, was seen as an indication that the rest of the world was optimistic and confident about the country's macroeconomic fundamentals and potential for growth. In fact, the increase in foreign portfolio investments improved the capitalization of the stock market and provided opportunities for capital gains even for the domestic players. It also encouraged listed companies to expand capacity and some to venture to other investments. Moreover, the influx of foreign money enabled monetary authorities to beef up its international reserves, thereby increasing its capacity to ward off speculative attacks on the currency.

The Asian crisis began as a crisis of confidence in the financial sector. During the initial stages of the crisis, some analysts remained confident that the Philippines would be spared. After all, compared to Thailand, where the crisis started, the country's banking sector had stronger fundamentals. In 1996, non-performing assets were 3.3 percent of total assets; past due loans were 3.8 percent of total loan portfolio; tier one capital adequacy ratio stood at 17 percent, comparable to Hong Kong's

17.5 percent and definitely better than Thailand's 9.6 percent and Korea's 9 percent. Nevertheless, the contagion spread to all of East Asia, including the Philippines.

The crisis of confidence was worst among foreign portfolio investors. To start with, these portfolio investors had been attracted to the equity market because of the potential for capital gains, made even more attractive if accompanied by an appreciation of the domestic currency. With an expectation of depreciation or devaluation, the prospects for capital gains become slimmer and the objective therefore is to be the first one out. In 1997, these negative expectations were fueled by concerns that the country's financial sector was almost like Thailand's and that the corporate sector, including the largest banks, was as familial, and therefore probably unprofessional as well, as those in Thailand, Korea, and probably the rest of Asia. The greatest concern, though, was the perceived overvaluation of the peso and the anticipation of an imminent correction.

A reversal of capital flows ensued. The stock market index fell to 2,021 in August of 1997, down from 3,221 a year before. By the end of 1997, the index fell to 1,869, roughly 60 percent its value a year before. The capital outflow weighed heavily on the peso. Efforts by monetary authorities to stem the depreciation proved futile. By the end of July 1997, gross international reserves dropped to US$9.8 billion from its end of June level of US$11.3 billion. Consequently, the currency was allowed to be traded within a wider margin. As an added precaution, foreign banks were disallowed from participating in the currency market. Nevertheless, as expected, the currency depreciated, losing about 40 percent its value by end of 1997 compared to a year before.

The peso depreciation resulted in loan defaults by companies who incurred foreign debts early on before the crisis struck. These companies had been attracted to incur foreign-denominated loans even though they did not earn foreign currency because of the lower interest rates on foreign loans and the seeming stability of the peso. Some of these companies even divested into the property sector, again because the overvalued currency unduly favored the non-tradable sector. The peso depreciation meant that these companies had to pay more pesos for every dollar of their loan.

The rise in loan defaults made banks even more timid in extending loans. Average bank lending rates rose to 15.5 percent in July 1997, then rose again to 18.6 percent in August, then rose continuously, reaching a peak of 22.5 percent in March 1998. Initially, the increases were in response to repeated increases in overnight lending rates and upward adjustments in the required reserve ratios imposed by the central bank in order to stem the currency depreciation. But even after the monetary restrictions had been eased, bank lending rates remained high. The defaults by big companies like EYCO, Triple-V and PAL did not help at all, for it meant that default risks, even among prime clients, were very high indeed.

In 1998, conditions turned for the worse. The stock market slump resulted in the closure of many investment houses. The real-property sector was also badly hit, which adversely affected the construction sector as well. Although the effect was moderated somewhat by the infrastructure works that proceeded despite the crisis, gross value added of the construction sector still declined by more than 8 percent. The agriculture sector also performed poorly, contracting by 6.6 percent largely because of the El Niño phenomenon. Investments decreased by more than 17 percent. And despite the currency depreciation, exports declined to 10.4 percent, possibly because of low external demand, high valuation of imported raw materials and the volatility of the exchange rate. Gross domestic product decreased by almost half a percent.

Real per capita incomes in 1998 decreased by 2.1 percent. Of more concern than the aggregate impact is that over distributional impact. Who was hit by the crisis? Was there a distributional bias? Was there a so-called vulnerable group? What are their defining characteristics? While not claiming to be able to provide categorical answers, the present chapter is a modest attempt to shed light on these matters.

3. CONSTRUCTION OF PANEL DATA SET

One of the analytical advantages of using panel or longitudinal data to examine the impact of (and responses to) macroeconomic shocks is that it allows measurement of changes in employment and poverty status of the *same* individuals or households over time. With panel data it is possible, for example, to trace the movement of individuals into and out of poverty. It also permits evaluation of the impact of government programs since observations on changes in outcomes at two points in time are available.

This study uses three nationwide household surveys to construct the panel data set: the *1997 Family Income and Expenditures Survey* (FIES), the 1998 *Annual Poverty Indicator Survey* (APIS), and the quarterly *Labor Force Survey* (LFS), all of which are conducted by the National Statistics Office. The FIES is the main survey employed in the generation of poverty and income distribution statistics on the Philippines. Conducted every three years, the 1997 survey covers a sample of 39,520 households and uses urban and rural areas of each province as principal domains. This makes these data valid for economic welfare comparisons among provinces, between urban and rural areas, and among socioeconomic groups.

The APIS, on the other hand, covers variables other than incomes and expenditures, thereby providing more comprehensive indicators of poverty status than income- or expenditure-based poverty indicators that could be generated from FIES. It contains information about the demographic and economic characteristics of individual household members, as well as items related to health, education, family planning, and family access to housing, water and sanitation, and credit. Intended to be run every year beginning in 1998, the survey does not, however, provide consumption and expenditure data as detailed and robust as the FIES. The 1998 APIS covered 38,710 sample households and had as reference periods the second and third quarters; the sample households came from the same sampling frame as that of the FIES. Both surveys (1997 FIES and 1998 APIS) have a sample overlap of about 58 percent; that is over one half of the sample households interviewed for both surveys can be formed into panel data.

The quarterly LFS is the main source of labor statistics on the country. Every survey round, one quarter of the sample households is dropped and replaced by a newly drawn sample of households. This results in a 75 percent overlap between quarters and zero overlap between years, if the rotation is done as scheduled. However, for the third and fourth quarters of 1998, no sample replacement was made, effectively maintaining a panel of households of about 50 percent of the total sample used in the first quarter survey.

The panel formed from the above surveys consists of 5,890 households, representing 15 percent of the total sample households in the 1997 FIES. Although the full panel consists of 6,563 households, we excluded from the analysis those households whose heads were unemployed in 1997 and were not part of the labor force for the whole of 1998. We obtain employment status from the FIES for 1997 and LFS for the four quarters of 1998. The data cover information on employment status for the same households over the four quarters of 1998 (crisis period) and the second semester of 1997 (pre-crisis period). We use the APIS to obtain household responses to the Asian crisis.

A limitation of the panel data is that the three surveys (FIES, APIS, and LFS) on which it is based allow a matching of household heads over time, but not of individual household members. Thus it is not possible to extract from the panel data movement of individual family members into and out of employment.

4.   WHO WAS HURT DURING THE CRISIS?

Using the panel data, we describe below the changes in the employment status of various population subgroups during the four quarters of 1998. First, we traced their employment status throughout 1998 for the entire panel, but figures have been computed separately for those who were employed in 1997 (a pre-crisis period) and those who were not. The subsequent analyses focus on panel households who were employed in 1997. The last subsection exploits the availability of subjective information on the impact of, and household responses to, the crisis and explores whether impact and responses vary systematically across income groups.

4.1 What Income Groups were Hurt the Most?

In table 5.1, we have ordered household heads based on their 1997 income (adjusted for family size) and traced their employment status in each of the four quarters of 1998. The figures in the last four columns of the table correspond to 'unemployment rate', defined here as the ratio of unemployed workers, including those dropping out of the labor market, in 1998 to the total in 1997.[2] The figures are computed separately for those employed and those unemployed in 1997.

The unemployment rate was higher among household heads who were already unemployed in 1997. This is an expected result during crisis periods when the job-finding rate falls.

Considering only the household heads who were previously employed in 1997, we find no discernible pattern in the distribution of the unemployed across income deciles during the first quarter. However, during the second quarter, the upper 50 percent of the panel households had substantially higher unemployment rates than the lower 50 percent (with the exception of the third decile). By the third and fourth quarters, the third to fourth deciles also joined the ranks of high unemployment rates. It is also clear from table 5.1 that all but the first, fifth, and sixth deciles exhibited rising unemployment rates as the economy navigated the crisis in 1998.

Focusing only on household heads who were unemployed in 1997, we observe a declining trend for the poorest decile where the unemployment rate dropped from 56 percent in the first quarter to 20 percent in the fourth quarter of 1998. However, for the other groups, there is no obvious trend in the unemployment rates over time.

Table 5.1 What income groups were hurt?

Income decile	Households in panel	Unemployed in 1998* (% of employed in 1997)			
		1st quarter	2nd quarter	3rd quarter	4th quarter
A. Employed household head in 1997					
First (Poorest)	564	5.3	5.7	4.1	5.8
Second	561	4.3	4.6	5.0	5.9
Third	552	8.0	7.1	8.0	8.0
Fourth	555	7.6	4.9	7.2	8.8
Fifth	545	5.9	4.8	7.3	6.1
Sixth	555	6.5	7.0	6.1	6.8
Seventh	545	5.1	5.9	6.8	8.4
Eighth	543	6.6	6.8	8.3	9.4
Ninth	546	7.3	6.4	7.1	8.1
Tenth (Richest)	542	4.4	6.8	7.2	8.7
Overall	5,508	6.1	6.0	6.7	7.6
B. Unemployed household head in 1997					
First (Poorest)	25	56.0	36.0	24.0	20.0
Second	28	39.3	39.3	32.1	39.3
Third	37	51.4	62.2	35.1	59.5
Fourth	34	47.1	52.9	52.9	55.9
Fifth	44	61.4	52.3	36.4	36.4
Sixth	34	52.9	41.2	44.1	41.2
Seventh	44	50.0	52.3	36.4	25.0
Eighth	46	47.8	50.0	34.8	37.0
Ninth	43	55.8	48.8	37.2	48.8
Tenth (Richest)	47	44.7	44.7	34.0	36.2
Overall	382	50.8	48.7	36.9	40.0

*Including those not in the labor force in 1998.

Sources: Panel data constructed from the 1997 Family Income and Expenditures Survey and 1998 Labor Force Survey.

4.2 Did Urban Poor Households Fare Worse than Rural Poor Households?

The urban poor households appear to have fared worse than the rural poor households. Suppose we consider only the households coming from the lowest four deciles (poorest 40 percent of the panel households) whose heads were employed in 1997. The lowest four deciles make up 2,203 households, of which 1,000 are from the rural areas and 1,203 are from urban areas (table 5.2).

Table 5.2 Did urban poor households fare worse than rural poor households?

Employed household head in 1997		Unemployed in 1998* (% of employed in 1997)			
Poorest 4 deciles	Households in panel	1st quarter	2nd quarter	3rd quarter	4th quarter
Rural	1,000	6.4	5.3	5.5	6.5
Urban	1,203	6.1	5.8	6.7	7.7

*Including those not in the labor force in 1998.

Sources: Panel data constructed from the 1997 Family Income and Expenditures Survey and 1998 Labor Force Survey.

We note that for both groups, the unemployment rate for the first quarter was greater than 6 percent. The profile improved during the second quarter, especially for those coming from the rural areas. The improvement, however, turned out to be short-lived as the rates worsened during the last two quarters, which is reflective of the worsening of both the financial and weather crises at the time. Note further that the rates among those in the urban areas deteriorated the most. This means that rural poor households were more able to transfer to other sectors of employment than the urban poor households.

4.3 To What Economic Sectors and Occupation Groups did Those Hurt Belong?

For the first quarter of 1998, those in the agriculture and construction sectors appear to have suffered the most (table 5.3). The unemployment rate among those initially employed in the construction sector even increased up to the last quarter. This trend is consistent with the slump in the property sector, which is also manifested in the construction sector. Household heads initially employed in the mining and quarrying sectors seem to be the least affected. Also, those working in the electricity, gas and water supply services seem to have been re-employed towards year-end.

Table 5.3 To what economic sectors did those hurt belong?

Employed household head in 1997		Unemployed in 1998* (% of employed in 1997)			
Sector of employment	Households in panel	1st quarter	2nd quarter	3rd quarter	4th quarter
Agriculture	983	9.0	6.9	7.4	8.2
Mining	66	3.0	1.5	3.0	1.5
Manufacturing	645	5.0	5.2	6.3	6.7
Electricity, gas & water	67	7.5	3.0	1.5	3.0
Construction	682	8.9	9.6	8.5	11.1
Trade	810	5.6	6.3	8.1	8.6
Transportation & communication	806	4.1	4.8	5.6	6.6
Finance & real estate	175	4.5	7.4	8.0	6.8
Other services	1,274	4.8	4.6	5.4	6.2

*Including those not in the labor force in 1998.

Sources: Panel data constructed from the 1997 Family Income and Expenditures Survey and 1998 Labor Force Survey.

The profile of unemployment among those initially employed in the finance sector does not seem to be any worse than for those in the trade sector. A closer look, however, reveals that the finance sector had the lowest proportion of retained workers from its end-1997 roster. This implies that many who were originally from the finance sector had to move to other sectors of employment.

Table 5.4 shows the unemployment rate per quarter of 1998 among those initially employed in 1997 according to class of worker. Those who worked for private households in 1997 seem to be the hardest hit during the 1998 crisis. Likewise, the negative effect of the crisis seems to have persisted and even worsened for own-account workers with no employees and the wage and salary workers in private establishments. Meanwhile, wage and salary workers in government appear to be the least vulnerable to the shock.

Table 5.4 To what class of worker did those hurt belong?

Employed household head in 1997		Unemployed in 1998[*] (% of employed in 1997)			
Class of worker	Households in panel	1st quarter	2nd quarter	3rd quarter	4th quarter
Workers in private households	197	11.7	9.1	11.1	9.6
Wage & salary workers (private)	2,387	5.5	6.2	6.3	7.7
Wage & salary workers(gov't)	709	3.8	2.6	3.6	4.4
Own-account workers (no employees)	1,917	7.0	6.9	8.0	9.0
Own-account workers (with employees)	247	6.1	4.8	6.5	4.4
Paid family workers	9	0	0	0	0
Unpaid family workers	42	11.9	7.1	7.2	7.1

[*]Including those not in the labor force in 1998.

Sources: Panel data constructed from the 1997 Family Income and Expenditures Survey and 1998 Labor Force Survey.

Table 5.5 Did education matter?

Employed household head in 1997		Unemployed in 1998[*] (% of employed in 1997)			
Educational attainment	Households in panel	1st quarter	2nd quarter	3rd quarter	4th quarter
No grade	84	13.1	10.7	15.5	14.3
Under elementary	789	10.9	8.4	10.0	10.4
Elementary	1,141	6.3	7.4	6.8	7.7
Under HS	713	4.9	3.8	5.0	6.0
High school	1,235	5.3	6.1	6.1	7.2
Under college	850	3.9	4.4	5.5	7.3
College	696	4.7	4.5	5.9	6.0

[*]Including those not in the labor force in 1998.

Sources: Panel data constructed from the 1997 Family Income and Expenditures Survey and 1998 Labor Force Survey.

4.4 Did Education Matter?

Household heads with no education were the hardest hit in 1998, if we consider opting out of the labor force as a negative impact (table 5.5).
We also note an increasing trend in the unemployment rate among those who have at least a secondary education degree. Among high-school graduates, the rate worsened from 5.3 percent unemployment during the first quarter to 7.2 percent. The deterioration was worst among those who attended college but did not finish, from 3.9 percent to 7.3 percent.

4.5 Was there an Age and Gender Dimension to the Macroeconomic Shock?

Table 5.6 shows the unemployment rate among household heads who were employed in 1997 according to gender. It would seem that the impact of the crisis was more severe among male household heads. However, we note in table 5.6 that there were more female household heads who opted out of the labor force in 1998 than their male counterparts. This group probably included female heads of households who opted to manage their household personally instead of hiring

Table 5.6 Did age and gender matter?

Employed household head in 1997			Unemployed in 1998* (% of employed in 1997)			
Age	Sex	Households in panel	1st quarter	2nd quarter	3rd quarter	4th quarter
<25	Male	151	3.3	2.0	2.0	4.0
	Female	*5*	*40.0*	*40.0*	*60.0*	*100.0*
26–35	Male	1213	3.0	2.3	2.6	3.5
	Female	*49*	*38.8*	*32.7*	*44.9*	*51.0*
36–45	Male	1597	2.6	2.4	2.3	2.8
	Female	*139*	*18.0*	*25.2*	*29.5*	*28.1*
46–55	Male	1118	2.0	2.6	2.9	1.7
	Female	*146*	*27.4*	*32.9*	*37.0*	*47.3*
56–65	Male	666	2.6	2.3	1.2	1.5
	Female	*133*	*48.9*	*45.9*	*58.6*	*63.2*
>65	Male	217	0.5	0.9	1.8	0.5
	Female	*74*	*85.1*	*71.6*	*77.0*	*98.6*

*Including those not in the labor force in 1998.
Sources: Panel data constructed from the 1997 Family Income and Expenditures Survey and 1998 Labor Force Survey.

household help. Note that this observation coincides with the high unemployment rates observed among workers in private households in 1998.

Among the males, the unemployment rate was highest for those under 36 years of age, particularly those below 25 years old. For the females, the profile is confounded by the few observations in the sample under 36 years old. If we consider the older age groups, for which we have a sufficient number of observations, then unemployment was highest among females aged over 45. These observations seem to point to an employment bias against older female workers.

4.6 How did Households Respond to the Crisis?

The 1998 Annual Poverty Indicator Survey (APIS) includes two questions pertaining to the crisis. The first question inquires whether or not the household was affected by price increases, loss of jobs, reduced wages and the El Niño phenomenon. The second question inquires about the response of households and pertains only to those households affected by the crisis. Tables 5.7 and 5.8 show the percentage of households affected by the crisis and their corresponding response, respectively, distributed by income deciles based on the 1997 FIES.

The number of households affected by price increases and the El Niño phenomenon seems to vary with income deciles. There were more households coming from poorer households who were affected by price increases. Loss of jobs within the country as well as the reduction in wages seem to have affected more of the middle deciles, while loss of jobs overseas affected more of the upper-income deciles.

Most households responded to the crisis by changing their eating patterns. However, the proportion decreases as one considers households from the upper-income deciles. Increasing work hours also seem to be a major response, especially for households in the lower deciles. A disturbing trend is the greater proportion of households coming from the poorest decile who took their children out of school.

The proportion of households who received assistance from relatives and friends was more than the proportion who received assistance from the government. Interestingly, for private income transfers, responses across income deciles exhibit little variation, suggesting that recipients of such transfers are not necessarily the poorest groups in society.

5.   WHAT DETERMINES SPELLS OF UNEMPLOYMENT?

From the foregoing description of changes in employment status of

Table 5.7 Impact of crisis

Income decile (based on 1997 FIES)	Total HHs	Percentage of HH affected by				
		Price increases	Loss of job within country	Loss of job of migrant worker	Reduced wages	El Niño
1	2315	93.5	17.0	3.8	15.4	78.6
2	2315	91.5	16.6	3.2	13.9	72.7
3	2315	90.9	18.3	2.9	15.5	68.3
4	2315	91.7	18.5	4.1	17.1	64.5
5	2315	90.0	21.5	4.5	17.1	61.7
6	2315	90.2	20.5	3.8	16.8	55.0
7	2315	89.7	20.7	4.7	17.1	51.4
8	2315	89.6	19.4	4.8	15.2	45.2
9	2315	88.3	18.3	5.1	14.2	43.5
10	2315	84.7	14.7	4.8	11.2	37.8
Overall	23150	90.0	18.5	4.2	15.3	57.9

Sources: Panel data constructed from the 1997 Family Income and Expenditure Survey and the 1998 Annual Poverty Indicator Survey.

Table 5.8 Household responses to crisis

Income decile (1997 FIES)	Total HHs responding	Percentage of HH responding to crisis by					
		Changing eating pattern	Taking children out of school	Migrating to city or other countries	Receiving assistance from friends/ relatives	Receiving assistance from gov't	Increasing working hours
1	2256	56.7	12.4	7.8	16.5	10.7	37.5
2	2223	52.3	9.3	5.4	17.1	8.8	36.8
3	2211	50.7	7.3	5.4	16.3	8.4	33.6
4	2206	51.0	8.7	5.2	17.0	6.8	33.1
5	2180	47.8	7.1	4.5	17.2	5.9	29.4
6	2155	48.3	5.6	3.8	16.4	5.7	27.0
7	2138	47.0	5.0	3.7	15.0	4.5	26.1
8	2125	44.1	3.5	3.4	12.5	2.9	22.3
9	2097	41.4	3.2	3.1	13.8	3.9	23.1
10	2011	33.3	1.2	3.5	12.0	2.6	18.2
Total	21602	47.5	6.4	4.6	15.4	6.1	28.9

Sources: Panel data constructed from the 1997 Family Income and Expenditures Survey and the 1998 Annual Poverty Indicator Survey.

various subpopulation groups, it appears that spells of unemployment during an economic crisis are correlated with initial household incomes and certain household characteristics. In this section, we systematically explore the link between spells of unemployment during a crisis, on the one hand, and certain pre-crisis household characteristics, including household income (adjusted for family size), education, location and type of employment, and household demographic characteristics, on the other. The question asked is: what factors condition the unemployment spells of certain population subgroups to a macroeconomic shock *à la* Asian crisis? The main intention in this exercise is simply to assess how household characteristics before a crisis (that is, initial conditions) influence the duration of unemployment during a crisis; it is not our intention also to explain the causes of these conditions and how they could have been shaped by previous episodes of unemployment.

We employ an ordinary least squares technique, regressing unemployment spell, defined as the number of times the household head is observed to be unemployed for the four quarters of 1998, with a host of pre-crisis conditioning variables, including household income per capita, location of residence, sector and type of employment, employment status before the crisis, and demographic characteristics of the household head. The variable definitions and regression results are given in the appendices. The highlights of the regression results are summarized below.

Location. The geographic location of the household head has a significant influence on the duration or frequency of unemployment spells. Household heads in Metro Manila tend to have more frequent spells of unemployment than their counterparts elsewhere in the country, all other things remaining the same.

Demographic characteristics. The worker's gender, as well as his/her age and civil status, significantly influences frequency of unemployment spells during a macroeconomic shock. Male workers tend to have less frequent spells than female workers, all else remaining the same.

Figure 5.1, drawn from the estimation results of the unemployment-spell formation function (see appendix), shows different impact of age and previous experience on unemployment spells for male and female workers. For workers previously employed before a crisis, unemployment spells decrease with age, although at some late stage these eventually rise. For female workers, the transition from falling to rising spells tends to occur later, at age 49, than for male workers, where the transition occurs at age 38. This appears to contradict the common observation that female workers tend to be driven out of the labor market before their male counterparts during a macroeconomic crisis. For female workers previously unemployed before the crisis, unemployment spells tend to

Figure 5.1 Effect of age on spells of unemployment

remain consistently higher than for males, regardless of age. But for male workers, unemployment spells increase directly with age.

Civil status has a significant impact on spells of unemployment. Spells tend to be more frequent for married workers than for single and separated workers, all else remaining constant. Spells occur more often among widows and with greater frequency than those hitting married workers.

Education. Different levels of educational attainment have different implications for the frequency of unemployment spells. After accounting for the effects of location and other demographic characteristics, we find that the unemployment spells of workers who attended or completed only elementary education are not significantly different from those who had no education. Spells are significantly lower for those who attended (but did not complete) high school, but significantly higher for those whose educational attainment was at least high school. We illustrate this differential effect on males previously employed in 1997 in figure 5.2. The same behavior is demonstrated for females.

Note that this profile is consistent with the aggregate picture of employment. In the October rounds of the labor force surveys in 1996, 1997 and 1998, unemployment rate is observed to be highest among high-school graduates and college undergraduates. What the regression results further emphasize is that considering only the panel of household heads and controlling for the effect of other variables, the unemployment rate among those with a high-school degree is higher than average.

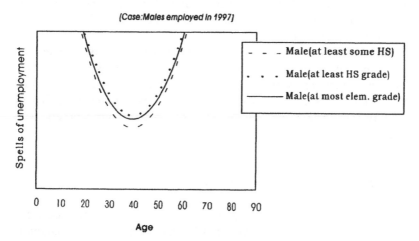

Figure 5.2 Effect of age and education on spells of unemployment

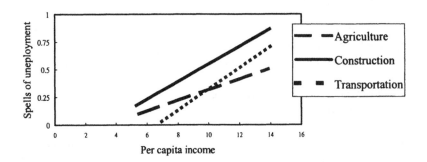

Figure 5.3 Effect of initial household income on spells of unemployment

Sector of employment. Various sectors of the economy have different impacts on the frequency of unemployment spells during a crisis. As would be expected, workers in agriculture tend to have less frequent unemployment spells than those in manufacturing. Spells tend also to be less frequent in both construction and transportation than in manufacturing. None of the other sectors of the economy have significantly different frequency of spells from that in manufacturing.

Unemployment spells rise with pre-crisis income levels, regardless of the sector of employment (see figure 5.3). However, the rise is much steeper in transportation and construction than in agriculture. This difference may reflect a much higher 'reservation wage' for workers in industry than in agriculture.

Employment in government prior to a crisis has a downward effect on employment spells during a crisis. Compared to workers in the private sector (own-account workers without employees, workers in private households), workers in government have less frequent spells of unemployment. The same can be said of own-account workers with employees.

6.   CONCLUDING REMARKS

The evidence shown in this chapter, using a nationwide panel data set, suggests that the Asian crisis has had differential effects on the economic well-being of various population subgroups. Focusing on changes in employment status of the same households, as well as their responses to the crisis, we have shown that spells of unemployment have characterized the whole range of the income distribution. However, the frequency or duration of unemployment spells appears to be systematically related to household conditions and characteristics prior to the crisis, that is, their demographic characteristics, geographic location, endowment of human capital, sector and type of employment, and employment status.

Among the key results are the following:

- Price increases during the crisis affected disproportionately more of the poorer than richer households. Loss of jobs within the country as well as the reduction in wages had greater impact on middle-income groups, while loss of jobs overseas affected more of the upper-income groups.
- A large number of households responded to the crisis by changing their eating patterns and increasing their work hours, especially for households in the lower-income groups.
- Withdrawal of children from school was a widespread response of the poorest 20 percent of the population.
- Not only the poor but also the non-poor received assistance from the government during the crisis. But, across income groups, more households received assistance from friends and relatives than from government.
- Workers in Metro Manila tend to have more frequent spells of unemployment than their counterparts elsewhere in the country. But unemployment spells also vary substantially across regions (other than NCR) of the country.
- The worker's gender, as well as his/her age and civil status, significantly influences frequency of unemployment spells during a macroeconomic shock. Male workers tend to have less frequent spells than female workers, all else remaining the same.
- For female workers previously unemployed before the crisis, unemployment spells tend to remain consistently higher than for males, regardless of age.
- The labor market pays a higher premium to experience through less frequent unemployment spells, especially for male workers, during a macroeconomic shock.
- Unemployment spells are significantly lower for workers who attended (but did not complete) high school, but significantly higher for those whose educational attainment was at least high-school grade.

- Workers in agriculture tend to have less frequent unemployment spells than those in manufacturing, construction, and transportation.

The above results support gender-sensitive policies during a macroeconomic crisis. Programs providing safety nets to female-headed households should thus form an integral component of the policy response to a crisis.

Another policy direction is to correct the external inefficiencies of education manifested in high rates of educated unemployment. What this also implies is the lack of mobility among workers with at least a high-school education. With low (private) returns expected from education investments, it should not be surprising that a number of households withdrew their student members from school to cope with the crisis. However, regardless of the inefficiencies of education, it is clear that scholarships should form part of the safety net package if only to provide members of poor households with a chance to break away from the vicious cycle of poverty–low human capital–low productivity.

It was rather unfortunate that the financial crisis coincided with the El Niño phenomenon. The timing was made even worse by the conduct of elections, where national, legislative and local positions were at stake. The latter diverted the energies of the administration away from responding to the crisis and into doing campaign rounds. There was also the effort to sustain a budget surplus, which succeeded despite the crisis. During the first three quarters of 1998, government spending declined in real terms from its level in 1997.

Although the results show that workers in government appear to have been shielded from the worst effects of the crisis, such was not the experience of the excess labor coming from the private sector who could not be absorbed elsewhere, much less by the public sector.

To be sure, government has provided assistance, albeit on a limited scale, but leakages appear to be substantial. Since the higher proportion of beneficiaries come from the lower income groups, we can assume that the intended beneficiaries were the poor. The fact that even the non-poor received assistance from the government means that government needs to strengthen its targeting mechanism. There is thus a need to identify indicators that are more sensitive to household welfare and less prone to misrepresentation. Perhaps even the delivery strategy needs to be improved.

For a public policy aimed at providing safety nets to the poorest groups during a macroeconomic crisis to succeed, it must be informed by a clear understanding of the sources of household vulnerability to shocks, the channels through which a crisis affects the economic well-being of various population subgroups, and their responses to the shock. The above results contribute to building that information, although they need to be verified and further examined for robustness.

APPENDIX

Table 5A.1 List of variables

Notation	Variable description	Mean
Demographic characteristics		
AGE	Age of household head	45.2572
AGESQ	AGE squared	2204.3240
MALE	Dummy, household head is male	0.8881
AGESEX	AGE * MALE	39.3825
MARRIED	Dummy, household head is married	0.8733
WIDOW	Dummy, household head is widow	0.0854
WIFEWK	Dummy, household head's spouse works	0.4019
Educational attainment		
COL	Dummy, household head is at least a college graduate	0.1259
HS	Dummy, household head is at least a high-school graduate	0.5017
ELEM	Dummy, HH is at least an elementary graduate	0.8367
UCOL	Dummy, HH has attended but not completed college	0.2780
UHS	Dummy, HH has attended but not completed high school	0.6302
UELEM	Dummy, HH has attended but not completed elementary	0.9839
Location of residence		
REG1	Ilocos region dummy	0.0633
REG2	Cagayan Valley dummy	0.0398
REG3	Central Luzon dummy	0.1163
REG4	Southern Tagalog dummy	0.1508
REG5	Bicol dummy	0.0570
REG6	Western Visayas dummy	0.0725
REG7	Central Visayas dummy	0.0710
REG8	Eastern Visayas dummy	0.0499
REG9	Western Mindanao dummy	0.0404
REG10	Northern Mindanao dummy	0.0418
REG11	Southern Mindanao dummy	0.0592
REG12	Central Mindanao dummy	0.0353
REG14	ARMM dummy	0.0363
REG15	CAR dummy	0.0183
REG16	CARAGA dummy	0.0423
URBAN	Dummy, HH lives in an urban area	0.6883

Table 5A.1 List of variables (Cont.)

Notation	Variable description	Mean
Sector of employment		
AGRI	Agriculture, fishery, and forestry dummy	0.1667
BANK	Banking and finance dummy	0.0297
CONS	Construction dummy	0.1158
EGW	Electricity, gas, and water dummy	0.0114
MINING	Mining and quarrying dummy	0.0112
TRADE	Trade dummy	0.1375
TRANS	Transportation and communication dummy	0.1368
Class of worker		
OWNNO	Dummy, HH is own-account worker with no employees	0.3255
OWNWT	Dummy, HH is own-account worker with employees	0.0419
WAGEG	Dummy, HH is wage/salary worker in government	0.1204
WAGEP	Dummy, HH is wage/salary worker in private establish-	
	ment	0.4053
	Household Income and Employment Status	
LNPCIN	Logarithm of per capita income (in 1997)	9.9690
LNPCIN2	LNPCIN squared	9.4360
NOWK	Dummy, HH had no work in 1997	
Other interaction terms		
INAGRI	LNPCIN * AGRI	1.6072
INBANK	LNPCIN * BANK	0.3122
INCONS	LNPCIN * CONS	1.1185
INEGW	LNPCIN * EGW	0.1174
INMIN	LNPCIN * MINING	0.1093
INTRADE	LNPCIN * TRADE	1.3885
INTRANS	LNPCIN * TRANS	1.3546
URBPCIN	LNPCIN * URBAN	6.9504
URBPCIN2	LNPCIN2 * URBAN	6.4495
NOWKAGE	AGE * NOWK	3.5922
NOWKAGE2	AGESQ * NOWK	211.2462
Dependent variable		
NWORK2	Spells of unemployment in 1998	0.3611

Table 5A.2 Regression estimates

(Dependent variable: No. of unemployment spells)

Variable	Full model		Final model	
	Coefficient	*t*-ratio	Coefficient	*t*-ratio
Constant	1.8487	5.8216	1.7544	9.2634
REG1	−0.0883	−1.7230		
REG2	−0.1539	−2.5604	−0.1139	−2.1700
REG3	−0.1313	−3.0811	−0.0944	−2.7959
REG4	−0.1622	−4.0304	−0.1249	−4.0622
REG5	−0.1308	−2.4405	−0.0931	−2.0870
REG6	−0.1427	−2.9037	−0.1031	−2.5519
REG7	−0.0030	−0.0604		
REG8	−0.1501	−2.6895	−0.1120	−2.3701
REG9	−0.1571	−2.6531	−0.1172	−2.2590
REG10	−0.1763	−3.0346	−0.1388	−2.7246
REG11	−0.1120	−2.1594	−0.0758	−1.7250
REG12	−0.0833	−1.3330		
REG14	−0.1746	−2.7772	−0.1499	−2.7568
REG15	−0.2160	−2.6730	−0.1800	−2.4131
REG16	−0.0710	−1.2094		
HDMALE	−0.8022	−5.8121	−0.7896	−5.7621
URBPCIN	−0.0003	−0.1121		
MARRIED	0.1111	1.9601	0.1158	2.0530
WIDOW	0.2081	3.2456	0.2108	3.3084
DUELEM	−0.0126	−0.1542		
DELEM	−0.0022	−0.0636		
DUHS	−0.0697	−1.9886	−0.0725	−2.2546
DHS	0.0923	2.6546	0.0856	2.7401
DUCOL	0.0055	0.1667		
DCOL	−0.0300	−0.7600		
WIFEWK	0.0783	3.5763	0.0718	3.3497
WAGEG	−0.1312	−2.2200	−0.1179	−3.6060
WAGEP	−0.0056	−0.1090		
OWNNO	−0.0479	−0.9077		
OWNWT	−0.1791	−2.5530	−0.1564	−3.1041
AGRID	−0.6043	−1.6204	−0.6046	−1.9531
CONS	−0.5949	−1.2157	−0.6116	−1.3740
MINING	0.6966	0.6332		

Table 5A.2 Regression estimates (Cont.)

(Dependent variable: No. of unemployment spells)

Variable	Full model		Final model	
	Coefficient	*t*-ratio	Coefficient	*t*-ratio
EGW	−0.0519	−0.0425		
TRADE	0.3461	−0.8481		
TRANS	−1.1487	−2.6071	−1.1847	−3.0283
BANK	−0.3228	−0.4446		
INAGRI	0.0634	1.6629	0.0613	1.9166
INMIN	−0.0757	−0.6728		
INEGW	0.0069	0.0586		
INCONS	0.0821	1.6368	0.0848	1.8475
INTRADE	−0.0342	−0.8489		
INTRANS	0.1198	2.7085	0.1233	3.1351
INBANK	0.0328	0.4744		
HDAGE	−0.0587	−9.4118	−0.0594	−9.5606
AGESQ	0.0006	11.4823	0.0006	11.6245
AGESEX	0.0107	4.0284	0.0106	4.0188
NOWKAGE	0.0628	14.8606	0.0636	16.6693
NOWKAGE2	−0.0007	−10.7389	−0.0007	−11.2271
LNPCIN	−0.0039	−0.1660		
LNPCIN2	0.0866	3.6347		
Adjusted R square		0.246	0.249	
F Sig		0.000	0.000	

NOTES

1.   Recent studies include Lim (1998), Reyes et al. (1999), and Balisacan (1999).
2.   Note that this definition of unemployment is not the same as that used in government publications on unemployment rate, in which the denominator includes the unemployed and both numerator and denominator pertain to the same time period.

REFERENCES

Balisacan, Arsenio M. (1999), 'Poverty Profile in the Philippines: An Update and Reexamination of Evidence in the Wake of the Asian Crisis', Report prepared for the World Bank.

Lim, Joseph Y. (1998), 'The Social Impact and Responses to the Current East Asian Economic and Financial Crisis: The Philippines Case', Country paper prepared for the United Nations Development Programme/Regional Bureau for Asia and the Pacific.

Reyes, Celia M., Generoso G. de Duzman, Roasario G. Manasan, and Aniceto C. Orbeta (1999), *Social Impact of the Regional Financial Crisis in the Philippines*, Makati City: Philippine Institute for Development Studies.

6. The financial crisis: Taiwan and Asia

Yun-Peng Chu

1. THE EFFECT OF THE ASIAN FINANCIAL CRISIS ON TAIWAN

The majority of economies in East and Southeast Asia had negligible or negative growth rates in the immediate aftermath of the Asian financial crisis, with Taiwan being one of the conspicuous exceptions. As a newly industrializing economy with a convertible currency and relatively open trade system, Taiwan has thus often praised and described as one of the strongholds against the contagion of the crisis. Other crisis-inflicted Asian economies, it is asserted, can learn much from Taiwan's experience.

While it is true that Taiwan's growth rate of around 5 percent for 1998 was among the highest in the world, it would be erroneous to think that Taiwan has been completely immune to the crisis. It would also be premature to believe that Taiwan's economy can independently maintain high growth rates regardless of the conditions in the rest of Asia.

Taiwan ships about half of its exports to the rest of Asia. Consequently, when these economies' demand for imports shrinks, Taiwan's exports are severely affected. At the beginning of 1998, the government's estimate of the 1998 growth rate of GDP and exports (in US$) were 6.2 and 4.0 percent respectively (Directorate-General of Budget, Accounting and Statistics or DGBAS, Taiwan, *Quarterly National Economic Trends,* No. 80). In reality, exports in the first ten months shrank by 9.0 percent, and net exports were estimated to be only US$5.5 billion for the entire year (*China Times,* 8 November 1998). Not surprisingly, the Asian market was where Taiwan's exports experienced the largest drop (by 18.8 percent) during this period in 1998 (ibid.). For an economy that exports about half of its GDP, the impact of such a weak performance is bound to be large. In fact, the 5.6 percent growth rate (of GDP) for the first half of 1998 would likely have been much lower if not for the miraculously high growth in private investment and private consumption (DGBAS).

The currency and stock markets also experienced large amounts of capital outflows. The stock market took a dive from 8,695 (Taiwan Stock Exchange Weighted Index or TAIEX, 1966=100) to 7,998 between 1 October and 16 October 1997. On 17 October 1997, the government abandoned defending the currency after spending about US$10 billion to intervene in the market in the preceding week.[1] Some Western economists have called the move to abandon the local currency a 'conspiracy', because its timing closely preceded the visit by the PRC's leader, Jiang Zemin, to the USA on 26 October 1997. And soon afterwards the Hong Kong foreign exchange market was attacked, followed by the collapse of the Korean won. It is hard to verify such an allegation. But it was obvious to observers inside Taiwan that the political pressure from a plummeting stock market was serious. It was not surprising that the government simply decided to abandon the foreign exchange market by allowing the local currency to depreciate to market levels, thus preventing the further withdrawal of funds from the stock market for transfer into US dollar purchases in the foreign exchange market.

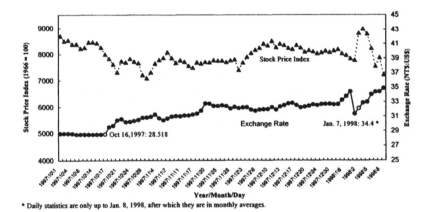

Figure 6.1 Taiwan stock price index and NT$:US$ exchange rate: October 1997–August 1998

After the abandonment of intervention, the exchange rate fell sharply from NT$28.52 per US dollar (16 October 1997) to between NT$33 and 34 per US dollar in the first half of 1998. Figure 6.1 shows the movements of the exchange rate and the index of stock prices from 1 October 1997 to August 1998. It is clear that in October and November 1997, depreciation of the local currency coincided with a fall in stock prices. This was mainly due to the market's anticipation of a depreciation, the resultant withdrawal of funds from the stock market – contributing to the fall in the TAIEX index – and then the use of these funds for the purchase of US dollars in the foreign exchange market, thus exacerbating the depreciation.

Meanwhile, the unemployment rate rose to around 3.0 percent in August 1998, the highest level since 1985, and has remained at high levels since. The government responded by adopting an expansionary fiscal policy. In July and August of 1998, it put together an NT$652.6-billion-strong expansionary package of government spending for the fiscal year ending June 1999. Of this amount, NT$541.8 billion is designated to expedite already planned projects, while the remaining NT$110.8 billion is earmarked for newly initiated projects. If successfully implemented, such fiscal stimulus was estimated to be able to boost growth by about 0.6 of a percentage point.

While the government was busy writing the expansionary fiscal package into the actual budget, the private sector in Taiwan began to show serious signs of trouble in the fourth quarter of 1998. The situation reached a semi-crisis level when in late October and November of that year quite a few big business groups' checks bounced, and prices of their stocks plummeted, amidst the eruption of incidents of large-scale defaults in stock transactions. In addition, at least two bills financing companies (a financial creation in Taiwan that is specialized in the trading of commercial paper and other short-term money market instruments) and one commercial bank were taken over by government-designated financial institutions. The bank experienced bank runs of about NT$55 billion in three days; the NT$32.1 billion run on November 25, 1998 set the record for the biggest single-day withdrawal in Taiwan's post-war financial history (*United Daily News*, 27 November 1998). These threatening developments have prompted the government to (i) announce a 'special rescue program to aid enterprises in need of funds', and to (ii) arrange public and private institutions to purchase stocks in order to bolster the stock market.[2]

It is clear then that Taiwan has by no means been immune to financial crisis, although it is too early to assess at this point whether the current round of financial trouble will soon be pacified, or whether it will deteriorate further in the future. However, as far as the growth rate for 1998 is concerned, Taiwan does perform better than most other Asian economies. Given these developments, it seems worthwhile to look into the factors that have contributed to both weaknesses and strengths in Taiwan's economy against the background of what the crisis-struck economies have experienced. To this we now turn.

2. BUBBLES

In almost all of the Asian economies that have been struck by financial crises, there had been a bubble development prior to the strike. In some economies, the development of the bubble, which was signified by the fast expansion of domestic credits and booming stock and real-estate markets, coincided with sharp rises in short-term capital inflow. Such inflow began in 1988 for Thailand, 1989 for Malaysia and the Philippines, and in 1990 for Indonesia (Bhattacharya et al., 1998). Stock prices then rose sharply — from the late 1980s to record highs in 1993 for Thailand, in 1993 (first peak) and 1997 (second peak) for Indonesia, in 1993 (first peak) and 1996 (second peak) for Malaysia and the Philippines. Real-estate capital values also rose sharply — during 1990–91, 1988–91, 1988–92, and 1988–96 in Thailand, Indonesia, Malaysia, and the Philippines respectively, followed by construction booms (ibid.).

As the bubbles increased in size, their sustainability increasingly became an issue of concern, particularly to foreign investors, who were concerned with both asset value and currency value. In Thailand, the bubble in the stock and real-estate markets began to show signs of non-sustainability as early as 1991 and 1993 respectively, but because the economic growth rate remained high, foreign capital did not evacuate.

In 1995, an attack on the Thai baht occurred after a report in the *Asian Wall Street Journal* compared Thailand with the then crisis-struck Mexico and warned of the possibility of a similar crisis arriving in Thailand. But the assault was pacified by the Thai central bank (Medhi, 1998). In early 1997, however, a trade deficit emerged much larger than expected and it cast doubts on the future value of the Thai baht. At this news, foreign investors began to flee, causing the Thai bubble to burst completely. Bubbles then also burst completely in Indonesia, Malaysia, the Philippines, Hong Kong and South Korea.[3]

In Japan, bubbles emerged much earlier, but the results were no less devastating. In the stock market, the Nikkei 225 index rose from 11,542 in December 1984 to 38,915 at the end of 1989. In the real-estate market, the index of commercial land prices for large cities rose from 38.4 in 1986 to 103.0 in 1991. In 1989 and 1990, Japan's central bank tightened monetary policy. Thereafter, the Nikkei fell to 15,951 by June 1992, and the index of commercial land price fell to 71.4 by March 1993; and so the bubbles began to burst (Johnson, 1998).

Here, even when foreign capital has not been an issue, as in Japan, the bursting of the bubble also brought casualties, which, when prolonged, could create a crisis situation. The current bad loan ratio in Japan is 15 percent of deposits according to sources cited in Schive (1998).[4] Henderson (1998) indicates that bad loans for Japan's top 20 banks amount to around 18 trillion yen. Other estimates put the amount of total bad loans at mid-year in 1998, at approximately 100 trillion yen or one-fifth of GDP (*China Times*, Taiwan, 19 June 1998).[5] The recently passed bailout package will reportedly spend about 67 trillion yen on the problem, including that spent on deposit insurance (*United Daily News*, 13 October 1998).

While it is debatable whether the bursting of the bubble is a sufficient condition for a comprehensive economic crisis, there is little doubt that it can cause severe trouble, as all the cases cited above have shown. Taiwan, which, as indicated earlier, experienced financial turmoil at the end of 1998, has also had its share of trouble with the bubble problem.

Taiwan's bubble story began in 1987. The trade surplus had reached an all-time record by 1986, constituting about one-fifth of GNP. The USA was concerned about its bilateral trade deficit with Taiwan, and opinions shifted towards the belief that Taiwan's currency was possibly under-valued. The speculative inflow of US dollars consequently began to reach the local foreign exchange market.

At first, the government resisted the pressure to appreciate the currency by purchasing large amounts of US dollars in the market. This was one of the factors contributing to Taiwan's build-up of a high level of official reserves (see, for example, Chu, 1994b). In the process, local currency flooded the market, despite a degree of sterilization. Soon afterwards, this 'hot money' entered the stock market, later penetrating the real-estate market.[6] The stock price index from 1980 to July 1998 is shown in figure 6.2, and a selected set of real-estate prices is shown in table 6.1. As can be seen from figure 6.2, the TAIEX index rose by only 46 percent between January 1980 and December 1986, from an average of 692.82 to 1,012.17 (1966=100). This changed, however, with the beginning of a spectacular climb in mid-1986, peaking at the monthly average of 11,983.46 in February 1990: a 1,084 percent increase from the December 1986 prices. The index then experienced an equally dramatic collapse, plummeting to a monthly average of 2,912.16 by October of the same year before beginning its recovery. The index has yet to recover its 1990 peak, having reached a peak of 9,890.34 in September of 1997 before succumbing to the fallout from the currency crisis.

Real-estate prices rose sharply during 1987–89: prices of residences in

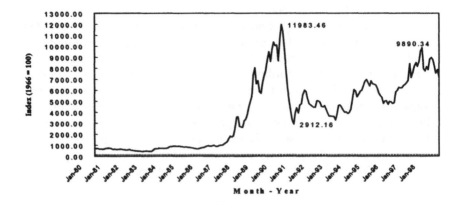

Figure 6.2 Taiwan's stock price index, January 1980–August 1998

Table 6.1 Changes in real-estate prices in Taiwan (%)

Year	Residence in Taipei City	Residence in Taipei County	Farm land in Taiwan Province
1974	−0.31		−11.63
1975	16.28		9.87
1976	−3.90		55.10
1977	−4.06		−0.14
1978	9.34		−2.32
1979	22.30		21.02
1980	12.99		7.47
1981	−2.32		12.50
1982	−10.09		13.07
1983	−3.96	3.90	−12.95
1984	−4.01	−0.19	15.21
1985	−2.39	−0.56	−1.78
1986	2.45	2.84	−4.28
1987	55.61	19.12	14.37
1988	80.75	123.77	24.31
1989	44.29	27.66	1.53
1990	−3.47	−3.67	84.51
1991	−7.43	−8.53	1.06
1992	−3.03	1.78	

Source: Lin (1995).

Taipei City and County more than tripled. Thereafter, they began to decline. Presently, while residential prices in Taipei City have remained rigidly low, those in almost all other cities and rural areas have fallen substantially. So the 'bubble' phenomenon was no less dramatic in Taiwan than it was in Japan.

And the bursting of the bubble has had its casualties in Taiwan. The credit departments of farmers' and fishermen's associations and credit cooperatives are the weakest sector in Taiwan's financial system. Many of them are controlled and abused by local politicians who try to siphon off their profits by making loans to friends and relatives. On occasion, they also underreport their amount of bad loans. When the bubble burst from the early to mid-1990s, quite a few of these institutions were in trouble and suffered from bank runs.

So the first lesson to be gained from either Taiwan's experience or that of the other Asian economies is to avoid these bubbles. Economically, there is no reason why the growth of these bubbles cannot be stopped by government action. In the ASEAN economies, the bubbles would not have developed into the actually observed sizes if measures had been taken to regulate excessive risk-taking by the financial institutions, and to cool down domestic asset inflation by, say, selective credit controls. Or at the source of fund, foreign short-term capital inflow could have been mitigated by administrative measures. In Hong Kong, the 1996–97 bubbles could have been avoided if the authorities had taken decisive contractionary action in the real-estate market. Likewise in South Korea, bubbles could have been avoided if foreign short-term capital inflow had been regulated and its business groups restrained from borrowing relentlessly from the banks.

In Japan, bubbles could have burst earlier and therefore at much smaller sizes if the authorities had applied monetary brakes earlier. In reality, according to an informative report by Werner (1997), 'window guidance' was widely practiced in the 1980s, as it was in earlier periods. Towards the end of the 1980s, when the bubble was clearly shaping up, the central bank still set high loan growth targets for the commercial banks. Some commercial banks found it increasingly difficult to find low-risk borrowers, and therefore had to lend money to riskier customers in their drive to meet the loan growth quotas handed down to them from the central bank.

Werner writes:

We conclude that it appears inappropriate for leading Bank of Japan officials to criticize the private sector for the creation of the bubble ... [B]anks merely implemented the loan growth quotas that were dictated to them by the Bank of

Japan ... [T]he evidence is that the Bank of Japan did see the speculative loans, in fact in every detail, right down to the name of the real estate speculators ... It is impossible to avoid the conclusion that the decision-makers at the Bank of Japan must have been aware that they were creating a bubble ... Our research ... casts doubt on the reliability and hence credibility of the Japanese Central Bank. (p. 24)

If these allegations are true, not only did the Japanese monetary authorities not apply brakes throughout the 1980s, they actually encouraged the bubbles to grow. One wonders why.

In Taiwan, restrictive monetary measures were taken in May 1989, after approximately three years of sharp monetary expansion (Central Bank, Taiwan, *Financial Statistics Monthly*, September 1989). In Japan, similarly restrictive actions were taken about five years after the development of the bubble.

Not only was monetary growth curbed in Taiwan, but the authorities also applied brakes by adopting selective credit controls since 1989. In the spring of 1989, the following measures were taken and conditions set: (i) all new easy-credit[7] loans to purchase land sites were banned; (ii) construction loans based on the collateral of existing land sites were now subject to a stringent upper limit; (iii) the maximum length of these loans was set at three years; (iv) the condition was set that if within one year of the approval of the construction loans construction did not begin, the loans would be withdrawn; (v) loans to purchase residential housing or offices were subject to certain limits; (vi) loans to golf course companies were subject to certain limits; (vii) the condition was set that if existing land sites in cities changed ownership more than three times within two years, those sites could not be used as collateral to apply for loans; and (viii) loans to investment companies (typically involved in the purchasing and selling of stocks and real estate) were subject to upper limits (*Economic Daily News*, 1 March 1989).

A year afterwards, the government also reduced the maximum percentage of investments on real estate by life insurance companies (out of total investment funds) from 30 percent to 25 percent (*Economic Daily News*, 27 April 1990). In addition, since most of the major banks in Taiwan were public at the time, the government, through internal controls, tried to lower the share of loans going into the real-estate market in these banks, so as to ensure that loans to the industrial sector would not be limited. As a result, the sharply rising trend of real-estate-related credit expansion was somewhat suppressed. Table 6.2, which reports the share of loans to the construction industry — an important part of the real-estate sector — shows clearly the sudden drop in this share during 1989–90.[8]

So one possible reason that Taiwan has not suffered as severely as

Table 6.2 *Sectoral shares in loans and in GDP: manufacturing vs construction* (% unless otherwise noted)

Year	Manufacturing			Construction		
	Share in loans (A)	Share in GDP (B)	C=A/B (ratio, not %)	Share in loans (D)	Share in GDP (E)	F=D/E (ratio, not %)
1978	51.35	35.6	1.44	1.93	6.1	0.32
1979	49.90	35.9	1.39	1.80	6.2	0.29
1980	48.87	36.0	1.36	1.71	6.3	0.27
1981	47.37	35.6	1.33	1.90	5.7	0.33
1982	44.07	35.2	1.25	2.08	5.0	0.42
1983	40.96	35.9	1.14	2.25	4.6	0.49
1984	38.80	37.5	1.03	2.22	4.3	0.52
1985	35.19	37.6	0.94	2.47	4.1	0.60
1986	31.13	39.4	0.79	2.74	3.8	0.72
1987	28.14	38.9	0.72	3.49	3.9	0.89
1988	25.81	37.2	0.69	4.43	4.2	1.05
1989	23.80	34.6	0.69	3.73	4.5	0.83
1990	23.21	33.3	0.70	4.02	4.7	0.86
1991	23.39	33.3	0.70	5.56	4.7	1.18
1992	22.31	31.7	0.70	7.02	5.0	1.40
1993	21.00	30.5	0.69	8.19	5.3	1.55
1994	19.17	29.0	0.66	7.97	5.3	1.50
1995	19.44	28.1	0.69	6.38	5.2	1.23
1996	17.80	27.9	0.64	5.19	4.8	1.08
1997	17.34	27.7	0.63	4.80	4.4	1.09

Notes: Loans refer to all loans made by banks. Shares in GDP are evaluated at market prices.

Sources: Data are from Central Bank, *Monthly Financial Statistics* (Sept. 1998, Jan. 1995, Jan. 1993), and Council for Economic Planning and Development (CEPD), *Taiwan Statistical Data Book*, 1998.

Japan from the bursting of its bubbles was the relatively earlier actions taken against credit expansion. Unfortunately, while these earlier actions did produce some of the expected results in the early 1990s, later on, in the mid- to late 1990s, a new round of credit expansion by many real-estate-related business groups emerged. Many of these groups are the same ones that went into difficulties at the end of 1989.

3.   THE RESCUE OPERATIONS

The wave of 'mini-crisis' in Taiwan began in July 1998, when the checks of a major business group, An Feng Steel, bounced. The head of the group belongs to one of the three well-known, politically powerful families in Kaohsiung, the second largest city in Taiwan. In addition, he was elected as City Councilman at the end of 1998. The group's line of business covers steel, fish products, publishing, cable TV, and real estate, with fast expansions both in Taiwan and overseas in recent years.

While An Feng acquired temporary relief from its creditors for several months, several other incidents took place. Tong Long Metal, another listed company, was faced with financial crisis on September 25, 1998, reportedly because its owner embezzled the company assets. On October 1, 1998, checks issued by the U-Land group (with lines of business in real estate, airline and electronics, some of which are listed) bounced, and negotiations with its creditors are ongoing. The Luo Chieh Construction group (real estate and food-processing; the latter is listed) was reported to have bounced checks in the same month, followed by defaults in stocks transactions by Chinese Automobile, a listed import car dealer, owing banks NT$40–50 billion. Chinese Automobile belongs to the Panvest group, which is also involved in real estate, electronics, convenience stores, and leasing, many of which are listed companies. This group is reported to owe the banks some NT$100 billion in total. The crisis subsequently hit the New Magnitude group, which holds lines of business in real estate, construction, electronics, and steel, owing banks a collective debt of NT$15.4 billion.[9]

Furthermore, the Central Bills and Finance Corporation was reported to be in trouble on 30 October. The Central Bills and Finance Corporation is closely related to the New Magnitude group, which held 3.96 percent of its shares and retains investments totaling NT$1 billion in group enterprises endorsed by this bills financing company (*China Times*, 3 November 1998). The bills financing company itself actually endorsed a total of NT$23 billion of commercial papers out of an equity of NT$2.7 billion (*United Daily News*, 2 and 5 November 1998). Subsequent reports on 31 October and 1 and 2 November confirmed the fear as issued checks avoided bouncing only after a last-minute infusion of funds by its banks. On the evening of 3 November, the Ministry of Finance sent approximately a dozen staff members from the Hua Nan Commercial Bank to audit the accounts of the bills financing company, but encountered resistance upon arrival at the company offices (*United Daily News*, 4 November 1998). The next day, (4 November), the government ordered a united task force, composed of the staff of Hua Nan Commercial Bank, The First Commercial Bank, and Taiwan Small and Medium Business Bank, to take control of the entire company at 8:30 in the morning with the aid of the police. All of the banks serving on the task force are under the *de facto* control of the government.

On November 5, another Hung Fu Bills Financing Company, endorsing a total of NT$29 billion of commercial papers out of an equity of NT$3.75 billion (from *China Times*, 6 November 1998), was reported to be in trouble because its creditor banks reduced the company's line of credit. The Hung Fu group, which holds interests in real estate, securities brokerage, stocks financing and banking, many of which are publicly listed, is headed by a Taipei City Councilman and Kuomintang (the ruling party in the Legislature and the dominant party in the City Council) Whip. The Ministry of Finance and the Central Bank again intervened. At their invitation, four institutions, the International Bills Financing, the International Commercial Bank of China, the Overseas Chinese Bank (the above three *de facto* controlled by the authorities) and the Shanghai Commercial Bank, negotiated a purchase of 51 percent of ownership, and sent their staff to the troubled institution for supervision and auditing (*China Times*, 10 November 1998).[10]

In response to these incidents, and apparently anticipating more to come, the Premier announced a Five-Point Rescue Plan calling for financial institutions to extend the maturity of short-term lending to enterprises in distress by six months. Meanwhile, the Central Bank announced on 5 November the release of NT$30 billion of the deposit (at the central bank) by the Postal Savings to provide emergency loans to the small and medium-sized enterprises (SMEs) in trouble, through the 'Task Force to Assist Enterprises in Need of Fund' set up by the Ministry of Finance. Also, at a meeting with major bankers on 7 November 1998, the Minister of Finance urged the banks to follow the Premier's instructions by 'moral persuasion'. He announced that bad loans directly resulting from such extension would not be counted as such in its evaluation of the banks' performance (*China Times*, 8 November 1998).

The government also attempted to stabilize the stock market. Since the liquidity problems of the Central Bills and Finance Corporation and other conglomerates occurred, the TAIEX dropped 563 points or 7.8 percent, from 7,218 points of 2 November to 6,655 points of 11 November, in seven trading days. Facing such a blow to the stock market, and expecting more listed companies to be in trouble, the Minister of Finance announced a Five-Point Rescue Plan for the Stock Market on 12 November 1998

(*Economic Daily News*, 13 November 1998). The five points are as follows: (i) establish a special unit for stabilizing the stock market and inject more than NT$200 billion into the market; (ii) permit troubled listed firms to apply for temporary trading suspension; (iii) allow securities financing companies to trade the suspended stock off the stock market under certain conditions; (iv) coordinate financial institutions to provide sufficient funds to securities financing companies; and (iv) punish individuals spreading malevolent rumors and executives of firms involved in illegal behavior.

On the second day, the central bank also announced its intention to raise the interest rate paid on the reserve B account by 0.3 percent, from 2.4 to 2.7 percent. According to the central bank's estimate, such a measure was equivalent to lowering the reserve ratio of checkable deposits by 1 percent and time deposits by 0.2 percent or the increase of high-power money by NT$60 billion. At the turn of the lunar year in February, it further reduced the business tax imposed on banks as well as lowered the required reserve rate. Both measures together were estimated to be equivalent to a subsidy of about NT$4 billion per year to the banking sector. The government hoped that the money could be used to liquidate non-performing loans, the magnitude of which has been on the rise since 1998.

With these stimulus programs in place, especially the injection of stabilization funds and the central bank's loose monetary policy, the stock market rebounded – from 13 to 19 November, the TAIEX rose 645 points, or 9.69 percent in five trading days. As of 17 November 1998, a total of seven listed companies were allowed to suspend trading on the market (*China Times*, 18 November 1998). On 19 November 1998, the governor of the central bank reportedly indicated that for those banks restraining credit to the business sector, help from the central bank would not be forthcoming in the future (*China Times*, 20 November 1998). Entering 1999, amidst the above-mentioned subsidy to banks, reinforced by the news of strong export performances and the recovering Asian economies, the stock market rose further, with the TAIEX reaching 7,400 by the end of May 1999.

Having reported the details of the episode of 'mini-crisis' in Taiwan in late 1998, we will now try to highlight the main characteristics of its development against the background of similar developments in Taiwan's history. The experience of the other Asian economies will be referred to wherever appropriate.

3.1 Swiftness

The government did not shy away from intensive intervention, but acted swiftly and decisively with the assistance of the healthy financial institutions. No doubt the fact that the government still maintains *de facto* control of the major commercial banks (despite the 'privatization' explained above) is also an important factor. Deposits at public banks, including the Postal Savings and 'private' banks where the government remains the largest share-holder, account for about 70 percent of the total as of November 1998.

The swiftness with which matters were handled might have been related to major elections on 5 December involving the legislature, city mayors, and council members. But this was more likely a learned behavior. There have been many 'bank runs' in Taiwan since 1980, involving the Asia Trust in 1982, the Tenth Credit Cooperative and Cathay Trust in 1985, the Overseas Chinese Trust in 1985, and 31 different institutions since 1990 (see table 6.3). The latter institutions mainly comprise the credit departments of the farmers' and fishermen's associations and credit cooperatives, which are the weakest components in Taiwan's financial system. In some of these incidents, the government initially adopted a wait-and-see attitude. Some scholars and the media also seemed to advocate non-intervention, promoting the idea that depositors would learn from the behavior of the market forces. However, political pressure soon mounted, and as in the case of the Fourth Credit Cooperative of Changhwa County in 1995 (NT$30 billion of deposits was lost, see *Economic Daily News*, 1 December 1998), the crisis spread to larger institutions in other areas, including the otherwise healthy ones, which were struck by rumors, prompting the government to take action.

The variety of actions taken included: (i) verbal clarification in response to rumors; (ii) emergency loans were granted and the staff of banks, designated by the authorities, were stationed at the troubled institutions to supervise transactions, to assist with the reforms, and to quell depositors' worries; (iii) cash was infused and the management was taken over by banks designated by the authorities; and subsequent mergers by healthy, bigger institutions (public or private) were also arranged by the authorities. But in all cases, depositors were protected.

This brings us to the second issue, concerning moral hazard.

3.2 Moral Hazard

If the depositors can always get their money back, why should they bother to differentiate the good banks from bad ones, or the ones with deposit

Table 6.3 Major bank runs in Taiwan since 1980

Year	Number of cases	Type of Institution	Reasons	Measures
1982	1 (Asia Trust)	Trust Company	Bad loans to related enterprises; sluggish real-estate market	ICBC (semi-official) asked by govt to invest and manage until 1988
1985	1 (Tenth Credit Co-operative of Taipei)	Credit Coop.	Bad loans to related enterprises	Govt forced it to close for 3 days, then ordered TCB (public) to take over management; in 1986, it was merged into TCB
1985	1 (Cathay Trust)	Trust Company	Spill-over from the bank run in the previous entry (owner was brother of the owner of Tenth Credit Coop. of Taipei); bad loans to related enterprises	Govt asked UWCCB (private) to invest and to take over management; in 1995 merged with UWCCB
	1 (Overseas Chinese Trust)	Trust Company	Bad loans and fraudulent behavior	Capital reduction, then adding capital by major 8 taking-over banks
1990	2	Credit Coop.	Rumors	Clarification by CDIC and authorities
1991	1	Subsidiary of foreign bank	Reports of problems at parent company	Same as above
1993	2	Credit depts of Farmers' & Fishermen's Assoc.	Factional disputes and rumors	Local govt, agriculture-related banks and CDIC assisted by sending people over to resolve disputes and by clarification

Table 6.3 Major bank runs in Taiwan since 1980 (Cont.)

Year	Number of cases	Type of Institution	Reasons	Measures
1994	3	Same as above plus credit coop.	Elections, factional disputes and rumors	Clarification by CDIC & authorities
1995	6	Same as above plus commercial banks	Loss from dealing in derivatives; bad loans to owner-related enterprises; bad (& illegal) loans to general manager of the assoc.; factional disputes; rumors	Clarification by CDIC & authorities; institutions asked by govt to give emergency loans; non-CDIC-insured institutions required/allowed to be insured
1996	9	Same as above	Personnel disputes; rumors; misconduct by employees	Emergency loans granted and CDIC sent staff over to resolve disputes; clarification by CDIC; non-CDIC-insured institutions required/allowed to be insured
1997	8	Same as in 1994	Misconduct by employees; low equities; bad (& illegal) loans to, and misconduct by, general manager of the assoc.	Clarification by CDIC and authorities; seizure by institutions designated by the govt

Notes:
1. CDIC, Central Deposit Insurance Corp., was established in 1985.
2. ICBC is International Commercial Bank of China.
3. TCB is Taiwan Cooperative Bank.
4. UWCCB is United World Chinese Commercial Bank.
5. The period of 1990–97 covers only cases involving the CDIC, representing over three-quarters of total.
6. This table does not include the recent bank runs on Taichung Business Bank.

Sources: Lin (1997 and 1998).

insurance from the ones without? Too often, they do not. On the owners' side, although they risk their position, prestige, personal wealth, and potential legal prosecution for fraud if their institutions fail, they still venture into perilous territories as a result of excessive risk-taking, poor judgement or illicit conduct (see Akerlof and Romer, 1993, for an interesting discussion on 'looting').

This question was resurrected in the 1998–99 episode of financial troubles. It was argued that if the government automatically bailed out or took over any financial institutions that were in trouble, then enterprises in the real sector could blackmail the government by holding a financial institution as 'hostage'. In the case of the bills financing company incidents, it was reported that the endorsement of commercial papers issued by related enterprises had been prevalent among many of these companies. Thus this practice could really create a hostage situation. The enterprises in the real sector could get fast cash from its related bills financing company, whose endorsement would ultimately be honored by the government.

So the indiscriminate bailouts, to the extent that the government can afford them, can indeed quench immediate fires, but they are not without costs. If the government is acting as an ultimate insurer of financial institutions, then tight supervision over routine procedures is very important — an effort equivalent to fire insurers trying to prevent fires. If supervision is poor, and the moral hazard problem is serious, indiscriminate bailouts can be self-defeating, as the cases of other Asian economies seem to indicate.

3.3 Financial Liberalization and Supervision[11]

The third issue is about the political economy of decision-making concerning the sequence, speed, and scope of financial liberalization and the related issue of adequacy of supervision. It is well known that McKinnon (1973, 1991) initiates the concept of financial deepening, and the idea that the sequence of financial liberalization is crucial for the economic development of less developed countries (LDCs) or formerly socialistic economies. 'Financial repression', the opposite of financial deepening, is characterized by the heavy hand of a government in controlling the financial side of an economy. In particular, domestic interest rates and foreign exchange rates are controlled by the government and are not necessarily in line with equilibrium market prices. As a result, the awkward financial system of an LDC distorts its resource allocation, and may cause its economy to be less competitive in the world market.

Traditionally, Taiwan's economy is characterized by the deep involvement of the government in all aspects of its economic activities. Following the global trend of liberalization and the success of its economic development on the industrial side, the government in Taiwan started a sequence of actions to liberalize its financial sector. But it seems that Taiwan did not exactly follow McKinnon's prescription to liberalize its financial markets. The master plan for financial liberalization, if any, was often compromised with market conditions or political pressure. There was of course an apparent trade-off here: faster liberalization could be expected to bring higher efficiency, while, at the same time, it would heighten risks. Finding a point of equilibrium would a difficult task.

An important example is the liberalization of the bills financing companies, which were the focus of the mini-crisis in Taiwan. Before 1995, there were only three bills financing companies in Taiwan. They were semi-official institutions set up to promote money market transactions. They have been conservative, as the rest of government-related or controlled institutions are. Profits were mediocre in the beginning, but later on, with the growth of the market and because of the oligopolistic structure, all three were earning high profits. Scholars and politicians alike called for opening up of the market.

The Ministry of Finance did not like the idea in the beginning. Taiwan's bills financing companies, the main business of which is to sell and endorse commercial papers, are unique in the world, as mentioned earlier. In most other countries such business belongs to the bank, and rightly so. The reasonable solution was for these bills companies to raise more capital and become banks, or for them to be absorbed into banks. However, as political pressure mounted, the Ministry of Finance agreed to open the market (*China Times*, 9 November 1998) before setting up an adequate supervisory framework. The threshold for paid-in capital was set at NT$2 billion, compared to NT$10 billion for commercial banks, and they were allowed to endorse commercial papers amounting to as much as 12.5 times their equity. Thirteen new bills financing companies were approved in all.

It could have been anticipated the new entrants would lead to fierce competition in the market, which would lead to trouble without greater oversight. But as indicated above, the government supervision was inadequate. There was an act to regulate the industry, which had, however, been described as rudimentary – for example, there was no provision for handling troubled bills financing companies.[12] Besides, the regulation of cross-holding of ownership among (related) companies in general has not been adequate in Taiwan. The combination of the two regulatory weaknesses proved to be lethal.

A typical scenario would develop in this fashion. First, an ambitious company would acquire a listed company through the large purchases of its stocks in the open market. Once that was done, wholly owned subsidiaries of the acquired company were established, and ordered to purchase stock in its parent company in the open market. The (new) owner of the acquired company could then sell most of his or her own stock, but retain control of the entire parent company through these subsidiaries. In addition, the new owner could create the appearance of good profits on paper by transferring part of the profits from related but unlisted companies, and then try to boost the stock price of the acquired listed companies to new highs, with help from all the subsidiaries. In the process, not only did the owner made a huge personal fortune, but was able to raise capital from the stock market at negligible cost, providing him with even more funds at his disposal.

If the owner also invested in a bills financing company, more easy credits would be forthcoming. The same method could be applied so that even with little actual paid-in capital, the control of the bills financing company could still be secured through numerous subsidiaries. Because the bills financing company was allowed to endorse commercial papers of up to 12.5 times the value of its equity, the multiplier effect could be very large.

The recently erupted Han Yang group incident is a case in point. The owner of the group, Hou Shi-Feng, rose among his ranks to become a wealthy businessman amidst the real-estate boom in the late 1980s. In 1995, he acquired Kuo Yang, a listed company, and from that point on expanded his business at a breath-taking speed, mostly likely along the path just described. He ventured into electronics (by acquiring another listed company), hotels, construction, cement, department stores and more real estate. In 1996, he and several of his fellow real-estate developers set up the Central Bills and Finance Corporation, which was referred to above, and more credit was forthcoming, permitting him to accelerate his expansion. One large real-estate land site purchase of NT$4.8 billion was made in 1998. Earlier in 1999, another land site was purchased at NT$2.0 billion. Many of these investments did not turn in the expected profits, and stock prices of the parent Kuo Yang Company began to fall. Since most of the stocks were used as collateral to raise debt amidst his efforts to retain control of the acquired companies through the subsidiaries and to gain additional funds, he tried very hard to maintain the stock prices. If the prices continued to fall, creditors would be spurred to sell the collateral stocks in the market, contributing to deeper fall in the prices (*United Daily News*, 6 November, and *Economic Daily News*, 10 and 28 November 1998).

His efforts at maintaining the prices met with a fatal blow on October

30, 1998, when the Central Bills and Finance Corporation, of which he is one of the major owners, was reported to be in trouble, also as indicated above. He resigned on 10 November from the chairmanship of all of the companies in his Han Yang group, 'in an effort not to let his personal financial crisis turn into a group-wide crisis' (quoted by *China Times*, 11 November 1998). But all of his efforts were in vain. He applied to the government for special financial assistance but was rejected. On 24 November 1998, he was detained by the prosecutor for the suspected last-minute embezzlement of funds from his enterprises, which owed banks an estimated total of NT$30 billion (*United Daily News*, 6 November 1998).

Such a case shows that there is much room for improvement in the supervision of the financial market, especially when it was rapidly liberalized. One would think a ratings system would be an important means of making the risk at the bills financing companies more transparent. In fact, according to the newly established Taiwan Ratings Corporation, which was created out of government efforts, only seven out of the existing 16 bills financing companies have applied for a rating, and only two of these seven belong to class A (*China Times*, 5 November 1998).

3.4 Rescue Operations

The fifth issue is about rescue operations in general (not confined to the financial sector), during economic downturns in Taiwan. The Five-Point Rescue Plan promulgated by the Premier referred to above is such an operation in nature. This is not the first time the government has done this. Table 6.4 reports the major rescue operations in the past ten years.

The apparent record, with the exception of the most recent episode, the outcome of which it is too early to tell, speaks favorably of these measures as Taiwan's economy recovered after each crisis. A real assessment, though, requires counterfactual simulations, which control other variables such as a general upturn in the global market. Suffice it to say that these measures might have had positive announcement effect on confidence building.

But, as in the case of bailouts of financial institutions, there could be a moral hazard problem, as mentioned earlier. If the enterprises knew that the government would bail them out if they encountered trouble, once they reached a sufficiently large size, they would have less incentive to contain risks. So bailout actions are better limited to cases of a crisis caused by an adverse environment facing the entire economy. Fortunately, all of the operations listed in table 6.4 are basically of this kind.[13]

More important, however, is the fact that none of the crises listed in

Table 6.4 Economy-wide rescue operations in Taiwan, 1987–98

Title	Contents	Background
1987 Prevention of chain bankruptcies of SMEs	Extension of maturity of loans for 6 months	NT dollar appreciation
1990 Boosting business	More loans to SMEs; encourage outward FDI; boost exports; strengthen retraining programs; extend grace period of check-bouncing; 1-yr extension of the Investment Encouragement Act; penalize banks that do not step up lending	Collapse of stock market
1993 Boosting economy	Release land for non-agricultural use; let in more foreign labor; 5-yr business income tax exemption for high-tech industry; allow enterprises to issue bonds overseas; allow setting up of new, private power-generating companies; more freedom to import PRC-made semi-finished products	Global slowdown and sluggish private investment
1996 Rescue operation	Help enterprises to get loans; write off check-bouncing records; extension of maturity of loans	PRC missile incidents and fall of stock prices
1998 Assist enterprises to acquire funding	Extension of maturity of debts for six months; Accept application for assistance by troubled enterprises	Check-bouncing and defaults in stock transactions by business groups and bills companies, and fall of stock prices amidst slower growth rates and Asian financial crisis.

Source: Economic Daily News, 5 and 9 November 1998.

table 6.4 were rooted in the overexpansion of government-implemented or encouraged industrial investments. As stated in Chu et al. (1998), this is because the Taiwanese government in recent years seldom carried out interventions methodically, persistently following well-developed master plans designed for industrial development at the initial stage. In most cases, it followed a learning-by-doing attitude. Additionally, most cases were tested by the market as the spontaneous follow-up investments by private enterprises were key to subsequent expansions.[14]

So compared to the Taiwan model of 'illustrative intervention', the South Korean model of 'directive intervention' has been much more intrusive in the economy, including the financial sector (Chu et al., 1998). As such it was more effective in rapidly producing the results, which is definitely a potential merit.[15] However, should the government make mistakes (ill judgement or bad luck) or lose its independence (corruption or influence from special interest groups), the result could be devastating.[16] Here, too, one sees a trade-off between high returns and risks, and the probabilities are functions of the competence and independence of government.

Competence and independence are called the 'supply factors' of government intervention in Chu et al. (1998). They are not invariant with respect to time and to regimes. Taiwan is an emerging democracy. As such, the 'by-products' of special interest groups influencing policies revealed in the history (and the present) of mature democracies are bound to arrive.[17] They no doubt have already, and the trend is for more to come. Actually, in the 1998–99 episode of rescuing operations, this problem was raised in the media (see, for example, *China Times*, 9 November 1998). If so, this is again a case against government intervention (on the supply side).[18] As for the demand side, it seems that for the real sectors the (socially legitimate) need for government intervention is becoming less, but for the financial sector, because of the increasing size of financial transactions, the demand seems to get greater. So here again, there is a trade-off.

4. CURRENT ACCOUNT BALANCES, THE SMES, AND THE MANUFACTURING SECTOR

In spite of the current round of financial turmoil and the lower-than-planned growth rates, it is often said that Taiwan has been more resilient to the Asian financial crisis than the other economies in the region. There are elements of truth in that assertion. While explanations can be found in the discussion above, here are some additional factors to consider.

4.1 Reliance on Domestic Savings for Investment Expenditure and Low Foreign Debt Exposure

When a bubble is bursting or about to burst, the ability of the authorities to manage a soft landing depends heavily on the exposure of that economy to foreign capital, particularly short-term capital. On this point, Taiwan is less vulnerable than the ASEAN economies, as it depends mainly on domestic savings rather than foreign capital for its investment expenditure.[19] Another way of saying this is that it has had a trade surplus, which means an excess of domestic savings over investment, given a small budget deficit, thus making Taiwan a net resource exporting rather than importing economy. Moreover, the absolute (rather than the net) foreign debt Taiwan owes has not been very large. According to Kawai (1998), in the period 1993–96, external debt as a percentage of GDP averaged 10.6 percent for Taiwan, whereas for those hardest hit by the crises – South Korea, Malaysia, Thailand and Indonesia – it averaged 17.3, 37.5, 37.6 and 53.3 percent, respectively, and for Singapore it averaged 11.2 percent.[20] As a result, during the October 1997 attacks on the NT dollar, Taiwan experienced some foreign capital flight, but the real sector suffered very little from the pullout, as foreign debt had constituted only a minuscule share of corporate borrowings.

Moreover, given that the trigger of the financial crises was large inflows followed by rapid outflows of short-term capital in the case of Malaysia, Thailand, and Indonesia, it is quite revealing that for the period of 1993–96, *short-term* debt flows as a percentage of GDP for these countries were around 24, 40 and 18 percent, respectively (Kawai, 1998; Bhattacharya et al., 1998). In comparison, at the end of 1996, Taiwan's foreign exchange reserves were US$88 billion, more than 75 percent of the combined reserves of Malaysia, Thailand, Indonesia and South Korea (Kawai, 1998).

This is perhaps one of the most important reasons why it is hard for these countries to manage a soft landing during a crisis. However, it would not be fair to regard any developing country that is running a trade deficit as doing something wrong. For some LDCs, overinvestment may be a problem, especially if they embark on a lot of white-elephant-type showcase projects that are not profitable. But if most investments are made prudently, there is little reason why these countries cannot borrow from abroad. In most developing countries, savings are often insufficient, and so it is natural to seek outside resources. They do not have to apologize for doing so. It is just that when they do rely on foreign capital for faster development, what they should attract is long-term direct investment, rather than short-term portfolio investment. To mismatch maturities — using short-term capital to finance long-term development projects — constitutes a major source of risk.

4.2 Taiwan's SMEs

Another oft-mentioned possible hypothesis explaining Taiwan's resilience is the flexibly interconnected structure of its manufacturing sector. Usually, it is the predominance of small and medium-sized enterprises (SMEs), with their flexibility and responsiveness to market signals, which is theorized to give Taiwan its resilience.

Another often-mentioned characteristic of the SMEs in Taiwan is their flexible relationship with the larger firms. Described as an 'amoebae', manufacturing in Taiwan consists of flexible horizontal and vertical linkages between large enterprises and SMEs (Chen, 1994); rather than being wed to one particular set of relationships, firms in Taiwan very often link up with different combinations of other firms to create interactive and changing networks of production, these linkages differing on a project-by-project basis.[21] Such a flexible network directly challenges the bounds of what comprises a 'firm'. This special characteristic of Taiwan's industrial structure would appear to go farther in explaining the resiliency of Taiwan's economy than simply the predominance of an SME sector. This feature also makes Taiwan's SMEs differ from those in most less-developed countries, which tend to be involved in more traditional industry and which tend to have fixed horizontal and vertical relationships.

Still, it would be premature to think the Taiwanese mode of industrial organization is necessarily the best in the world. In effect, the Asian crisis hit Taiwan at a time when the importance of Taiwan's SMEs in exports had already been declining for many years. Among manufacturers, SMEs' export share shrank from 71.8 to 55.5 percent between 1981 and 1994 (Hu and Schive, 1998). Moreover, long before the crises hit, many SMEs in Taiwan were in trouble due to the large appreciation of the New Taiwan dollar in 1987 and the consequent increase in domestic production costs. Many of them had to move their manufacturing overseas to prolong their survival (Chu, 1994a). Therefore, it is not clear at all that the SMEs in Taiwan have truly been the most resilient sector in heading off the strike by the Asian financial crisis. The hypothesis still needs to be tested.

It is of course true that the South Korean industrial structure is marked by a higher degree of concentration and vertical integration (Ahn and Kim, 1997). As the government often uses the business groups to forward its industrial development aims, these business groups enjoy privileges that sometimes become the excuse for corruption and overexpansion (see, for example, Chu et al., 1998; Chen et al., 1998; and Dobson, 1998, on the nature of government intervention in Taiwan and other East Asian countries). In Japan, even though there are numerous SMEs, it is said that a large share of the economy is controlled by keiretsu (family-based constellations of vertically and horizontally integrated businesses). Because the center–satellite relationship between the leading companies and their SME partners inside the business groups is more restrictive, the structure is more rigid than Taiwan's (Dobson, 1998).

These allegations may be true. But it is doubtful that there is a mode of industrial organization that is optimal for all economies at all times. Also, there are good (profitable, healthy and productive) business groups and bad business groups, just as there are good and bad SMEs in all economies, including Taiwan. The business groups in South Korea carried out government orders in the 1960s and 1970s to expand exports effectively, when that country experienced the highest growth rates in the world. The Japanese business groups were so competitive in the world market in the 1960s and 1970s that Western firms soon emulated their mode of production. How did this structure get demonized overnight?

4.3 The Importance of Manufacturing

Manufacturing has played and is still playing an important role in Taiwan's economy, unlike the situation in Japan, where it is much less important now than in the high-growth, earlier periods. During the stock market boom in Taiwan, the number of companies listed on the market increased rapidly, with many companies coming from high-technology (electric machinery, electronics and computer-related, and communications) industries. Companies already listed also adopted expansionary investment policies: these industries were able very effectively to tap into domestic savings and foreign 'hot money' by simply issuing more stocks (in essence, printing money) when their stock prices rose sharply during the boom.[22] This virtually negligible capital cost thus helped to fuel their massive expansion during the boom period.

Given these conditions, it has been these industries which allowed annual national growth rates to exceed 5 percent throughout the 1990s. They have been the lifeline of the economy, and currently make up over 50 percent of Taiwan's exports. At present, for example, Taiwan ranks first in the world in the export of motherboards, monitors, modems, mouses, hubs, keyboards, and notebook computers (*Forbes*, 1 June 1998).

Moreover, despite the fact that more traditional industries were crying for help in the late 1980s due to the NT dollar's appreciation, they were ultimately quite successful in upgrading their operations. Despite numerous predictions – on the heels of the successive waves of Taiwan's currency appreciation – that traditional SMEs were on the path to extinction, many of them were able to shift a large portion of their operations overseas, while others have launched new product lines on the island, thereby maintaining a competitive foothold. The overall effect of industrial upgrading has been impressive. It is clear from Chen and Chu (1994) that the shares of capital-intensive and human-capital-intensive industries in exports have both risen substantially from the mid-1980s to the early 1990s. Meanwhile, the share of high labor-intensive products in exports fell, and so did that of consumer non-durable goods. The latter's drop was surprisingly large: from 35.54 percent in 1985 to a mere 17.06 percent in 1993.

Given the share of manufacturing in Japan, it is doubtful that the growth of that sector, even if successful, would have been able to lift up the economy as it did in Taiwan. In line with the 'flying geese' paradigm, for many types of low-technology products, Japan has passed the stage of 'maturity' and is now entering the stage of 'reverse importing' (Lo, 1998). It would be hard for Japan to sustain a very large share of manufacturing in its total value-added in any case. The service sector has become dominant, and will probably be more so as the population ages rapidly. That sector, unfortunately, is not recognized as the foundation of Japan's comparative advantage.

5.   THE SOCIAL IMPACT OF THE MINI-CRISIS IN TAIWAN

Because the dip in Taiwan's economy did not occur until 1998, it is still too early to assess the impact of the 'mini-crisis' on the welfare of households. But it is worth noting that Taiwan's unemployment has been rising in recent years: from less than 1.8 percent in 1988–95 to 2.6 percent in 1996, 2.7 percent in 1997 and 1998. The mini-crisis probably did not cause rising unemployment, but there is little doubt that it exacerbated the problem.

Tables 6.5 and 6.6 below record the industry from which non-new-entrant, unemployed workers exited. The changes in industry classification are not very conspicuous, but the rises in the shares of manufacturing and construction are noticeable. The former share rose from 26 percent in 1995 to 28 percent in 1998; the latter rose from 15 percent to 18 percent. Among the private employees who are unemployed

Table 6.5 Taiwan's unemployment in 1998 (in '000s of persons)

Item	Grand total	Employers	Own-account workers	Unpaid family workers	Paid employees Private	Govern- ment
Total	2378	71	139	31	2051	86
	100%	100%	100%	100%	100%	100%
Agriculture, forestry, fishing and animal husbandry	48	1	12	4	31	0
	2%	1%	9%	13%	2%	0%
Mining and quarrying	5	0	0	0	5	0
	0%	0%	0%	0%	0%	0%
Manufacturing	656	11	11	3	624	7
	28%	15%	8%	10%	30%	8%
Electricity, gas and water	1	0	0	0	0	1
	0%	0%	0%	0%	0%	1%
Construction	434	13	11	1	406	3
	18%	18%	8%	3%	20%	3%
Trade and restaurant	590	34	68	18	469	1
	25%	48%	49%	58%	23%	1%
Transport, storage and communication	111	0	18	0	87	6
	5%	0%	13%	0%	4%	7%
Finance, insurance and real estate	79	0	0	0	79	0
	3%	0%	0%	0%	4%	0%
Business services	63	1	2	0	60	0
	3%	1%	1%	0%	3%	0%
Social, personal and related services	344	8	13	1	291	31
	14%	11%	9%	3%	14%	36%
Community service	0	0	0	0	0	0
	0%	0%	0%	0%	0%	0%
Public administration	32	0	0	0	0	32
	1%	0%	0%	0%	0%	37%

Source: DGBAS, *Monthly Bulletin of Manpower Statistics*, Taiwan, various issues.

Table 6.6 Taiwan's unemployment in 1995 (in '000s of persons)

Item	Grand total	Employers	Own-account workers	Unpaid family workers	Paid employees	
					Private	Govern-ment
Total	1418	48	74	21	1205	70
	100%	100%	100%	100%	100%	100%
Agriculture, forestry, fishing and animal husbandry	21	0	6	4	11	0
	1%	0%	8%	19%	1%	0%
Mining and quarrying	2	0	0	0	2	0
	0%	0%	0%	0%	0%	0%
Manufacturing	374	15	6	3	348	2
	26%	31%	8%	14%	29%	3%
Electricity, gas and water	0	0	0	0	0	0
	0%	0%	0%	0%	0%	0%
Construction	218	6	3	0	207	2
	15%	13%	4%	0%	17%	3%
Commerce	380	21	40	7	311	1
	27%	44%	54%	33%	26%	1%
Transport, storage and communication	49	0	8	0	39	2
	3%	0%	11%	0%	3%	3%
Finance, insurance and real estate	48	0	0	0	46	2
	3%	0%	0%	0%	4%	3%
Business services	0	0	0	0	0	0
	0%	0%	0%	0%	0%	0%
Social, personal and related services	46	0	0	0	46	0
	3%	0%	0%	0%	4%	0%
Community service	231	5	8	3	195	20
	16%	10%	11%	14%	16%	29%
Public administration	34	0	0	0	0	34
	2%	0%	0%	0%	0%	49%

Source: Same as for table 6.1.

but were previously working, the share of construction, which rose from 17 to 20 percent, is particularly large. This reflects the depression the nation's real-estate industry is in, that, as indicated earlier, is largely the result of the postponed bursting of the bubble.

In terms of age, the young cohort (15–24 years old), as before, suffers from the highest unemployment rate. It rose from 5.28 percent to 6.17 percent by March 1999. This is followed by the middle age group (25–49); its unemployment rate rose from 1.37 percent to 2.50 percent during the same period. Within the latter group, during and since the years of mini-crisis at the end of 1998, there have been some conspicuous rises in the unemployment rates of the 30–39 age group. In particular, the unemployment rate of the 30–34 (35–39) group rose from 1.82 (1.45) percent in July 1998 to 2.56 (2.12) in December of the same year, and changed to 2.50 (2.14) percent in March 1999.

Education-wise, it used to be the case that people with higher education were more likely to be unemployed. People with junior high school or lower education have had a lower unemployment rate than the other groups throughout the years. By the end of 1998, the situation remained the same, but the gap between unemployment rates of the different groups narrowed. In 1995, the unemployment rate for the lowest education group (junior high or lower), middle group (senior high and vocational) and highest education group (college or higher) was 1.18, 2.25 and 2.42 percent respectively; in December 1998 (March 1999), the rates became 2.71 (2.67), 2.98 (3.25) and 2.68 (2.54) percent respectively. Again, the depression of the real-estate and construction industry is probably at the heart of the problem, as young, low-educated workers employed in that sector lost their jobs. In comparison, the highest-educated workers seem to have suffered the least in terms of the small rise in their unemployment. This may have something to do with the booming computer-related manufacturing, which continued to grow rapidly, as indicated above.

The findings of a related panel study, which records the employment status of the same group of individuals over time, are also worth reporting here. This study is focused on a sample of 1,039 prime-age (born in 1953–57) working people, who were interviewed once before the mini-crisis (summer 1998) and once after (summer 1999). Tables 6.7 and 6.8 report the results of two multinomial logit models. The first model (Model One) analyzes the change in status from being employed to (i) still being employed but having changed jobs and (ii) becoming unemployed or having exited from the labor force. The second model (Model Two) is like the first one except that the status of being unemployed is separated from that of exit from the labor force.

Table 6.7 Results of a panel study: Model One

Variables/ Status	Changed jobs		Became unemployed or exited from labor force	
	Coefficient	t-value	Coefficient	t-value
Constant	−3.0354	−4.7170	−0.8810	−1.4630
GENDER	−0.4943	−2.1510*	−0.5941	−2.4830*
EDU1	0.2718	0.9020	−0.2483	−0.8400
EDU2	−0.2442	−0.7660	−0.8342	−2.4340*
EDU3	−0.8068	−1.9390	−1.7808	−3.2440*
SPOUSE	0.3506	0.8430	−0.1618	−0.4580
WKEXP	0.0487	1.7860	−0.0240	−0.7600
IND1	1.0706	3.0600*	−0.0624	−0.1450
IND2	−0.2076	−0.7990	−0.2296	−0.8780
IND3	0.4528	0.9960	1.1159	3.0460*

*Significant at the 5 percent level.
Notes: Number of observations = 1,039, Chi-squared = 85.1648, Degrees of freedom = 18.

Table 6.8 Results of a panel study: Model Two

Variables/ Status	Changed jobs		Became unemployed		Exited from labor force	
	Coefficient	t-value	Coefficient	t-value	Coefficient	t-value
Constant	−3.0374	−4.7160	−2.1572	−2.3730	−1.2581	−1.6850
GENDER	−0.4950	−2.1540*	−0.1144	−0.3070	−0.8773	−2.9090*
EDU1	0.2725	0.9040	−0.6001	−1.2080	−0.0702	−0.2010
EDU2	−0.2446	−0.7670	−0.8516	−1.6720	−0.8754	−1.9790*
EDU3	−0.8071	−1.9370	−2.7498	−2.4690*	−1.3633	−2.1650*
SPOUSE	0.3509	0.8440	−0.4883	−0.9550	0.0533	0.1160
WKEXP	0.0488	1.7840	0.0109	0.2290	−0.0426	−1.1000
IND1	1.0714	3.0620*	−0.5226	−0.6700	0.1436	0.2860
IND2	−0.2073	−0.7980	−0.4859	−1.1570	−0.0818	−0.2550
IND3	0.4517	0.9940	1.1378	2.2390*	1.0681	2.2900*

*Significant at the 5 percent level.
Notes: Number of observations = 1,039, Chi-squared = 92.6950, Degrees of freedom = 27.

The independent variables considered in the models are GENDER, which equals unity for males (mean = 0.5313); EDU1, which equals unity for people with 7–9 years of education (mean = 0.1790); EDU2, which equals unity for people with 10–12 years of education (mean = 0.2772); EDU3, which equals unity for people with 14 or more years of education (mean = 0.2320); SPOUSE, which equals unity for people with a spouse (mean = 0.8970); WKEXP, which is the number of years of working experience (mean = 18.3513); and IND1, IND2, IND3 are dummies for people working in the agriculture, services and construction sectors respectively (mean = 0.0741, 0.5255 and 0.0654 respectively; mining and manufacturing being the default).

It is clear from table 6.7 that four independent variables are significant at the 5 percent level: other things being equal, males and people with higher education (people working in the construction industry) are less (more) likely to become unemployed or exit from the labor force. The Chi-squared of the model is significant at 1 percent.

Model Two has a similarly significant Chi-squared. Two variables are significant in explaining the change from being employed to unemployed: EDU3 and IND3. This means that people with higher than high-school education (working in the construction sector), other things being equal, are less (more) likely to become unemployed. Four variables are significant in explaining the change from being employed to exit from the labor force: GENDER, EDU2, EDU3, and IND3. They generally mean that, other things being equal, males and higher-educated people (people working in the construction industry) are less (more) likely to exit from the labor force.

These results are in general consistent with the national figures reported earlier. The misery around the construction industry is particularly noteworthy: it gives solid evidence of the impact of the cyclical downturn in that sector, which was exacerbated by the mini-crisis.

6.   EFFORTS TO STRENGTHEN ASIAN MONETARY STABILIZATION

After two decades of growth, trade, and mutual investments, all East Asian countries are more closely linked to each other more than ever before. Kagami (1995)'s table 1-1 reports the trade matrix in 1970, 1980 and 1990. It is clear from the table that East Asia, including Japan, exported 40 percent of goods to itself in 1990. Among the economies in the region, Japan exported 29.4 percent of goods to other economies inside the region, the NIEs-4 (Taiwan, South Korea, Hong Kong and Singapore) exported 39.6 percent, and the ASEAN-4 (Thailand, Indonesia, Malaysia and the Philippines) exported 54.7 percent, while the PRC exported 58.7 percent. Such a high degree of trade interdependence also reflects the growing foreign direct investment inside the region.

Under such circumstances, it is very hard to imagine how these economies can be immune to the economic traumas in the other economies. The observed 'domino' phenomenon is very similar to the dynamic process of how an original shock in final demand triggers repeating rounds of adjustments in all sectors in a standard input–output analysis.

What should Taiwan and the other Asian economies do to ensure a swiftly recovery, and to install mechanisms to prevent similar crises from occurring again?

One thing that does need to be changed is the existing international monetary stabilization system. The wisdom, capability and sincerity of the existing monetary stabilization institutions are increasingly being questioned. As Bhattacharya et al. (1998) and numerous other authors have pointed out, the Asian crisis has had its origin in the mismanagement of the private, not the public, sector. And it was avoidable. When the economy experienced a credit crunch, the obvious policy reaction should have been to ease credits and to boost demand by fiscal expansion, as Taiwan did when it saw a slight drop in its growth rate at mid-1998, so there would be time to clean up the financial sector. This is also what the USA did recently in its effort to lighten the adverse effects of the collapse of LTCM (Long-Term Capital Management) on the rest of the financial sector and the real economy. The International Monetary Fund (IMF) team which came to the Southeast Asia's 'rescue' in 1997 recommended exactly the opposite measures. This has led Sachs to state that, 'Instead of dousing the fire, the IMF in effect screamed fire in the theater' (Sachs, 1988, p. 17). In August 1997, the IMF predicted Thailand's 1998 growth rate to be 3.5 percent, which in reality would almost definitely change sign. Stanley Fisher, first deputy managing director at the IMF, writes himself that 'Had we known, when the Thai programme was signed in August 1997, that Asia, including Japan, was heading for major economic slowdown, less fiscal contraction would have been recommended' (*The Economist*, 3 October 1998).

According to Sachs (1998), similar situations developed in the cases of Indonesia and South Korea in 1998, Bolivia in 1985, Poland in 1989, Estonia in 1992, Bulgaria in 1996, and Mexico and Argentina in 1995. He holds that the political economy of the working of existing international monetary stabilization mechanisms does not encourage institutions like the IMF to be as careful in its management of a crisis as it should be. It faces no competition, and is not really held accountable to any supervisory organizations.[23]

Japan was itself in big trouble when the Asian crisis hit. Given the importance of the Asian (particularly ASEAN) economies for its exports and investment, Japan was deeply disturbed and greatly affected by the crisis, which could not have come at a worse time. Soon after the outbreak of the crisis in Thailand and its subsequent contagion to Malaysia and Indonesia, and perhaps also after witnessing the sharp drop in the growth rate in Thailand after the IMF stepped in, Japan planned to spend US$30 billion on the problem by establishing an Asian Monetary Fund (Yamakage, 1998). In November, at the initiation of Japan, deputies of finance ministries and/or monetary authorities from most APEC members (Taiwan excluded) went to Manila to discuss the matter. Although the participants agreed to embark on a multilateral engagement in the Asian crisis, later becoming known as the 'Manila Framework', the proposal of an Asian Monetary Fund was rejected, mainly due to opposition by the IMF and the USA.

There could be multiple reasons why they rejected the idea. But the USA probably did not foresee at that time (i) that the crisis would spread to Russia, South America, and involve also the USA itself, (ii) the revelation and strong international criticism of the IMF management of the crisis, and (iii) the devastating effects of the crisis on the political, social and economic institutions in Asia and on its people.

Furthermore, South Korea was soon hit, and experienced a bankruptcy crisis in its financial market, even though it signed an agreement with the IMF on December 5, 1997. One of the main clauses of the agreement was to open the capital market to allow easier foreign takeovers of Korean enterprises. Then in 1998, the crisis spread to other parts of the world, and the USA itself was hit. The issue of reforming the existing international monetary stabilization mechanism finally became a global priority. In late 1998, at the G7 meeting, and at the meetings of the G24, which are supposed to supervise the operations of the IMF, the issue was raised by numerous countries. US President Clinton announced that he would convene a G22 (Taiwan again excluded) meeting to discuss the global financial crisis issue.

In November 1998, the APEC-21 Summit was held in Kuala Lumpur. The issue was hotly discussed and at the end of the meeting an announcement was made to the effect that (i) an early warning mechanism would be set up regarding the flow of international capital – specific measures to be further discussed at the G22 meeting, (ii) the Japanese proposal of spending US$30 billion to revitalize the Asian economy would be welcome, (iii) the multilateral efforts of revitalizing private sector growth in Asia by the USA, Japan, the Asian Development Bank and the World Bank, as well as other 'innovations', would also be welcome (*United Daily News*, 19 November 1998).

Taiwan, through its representatives at the ABAC (APEC Business Advisory Council), proposed the idea of Collateralized Bond Obligations or CBO. The arrangement is to first set up a Special Purpose Company (SPC) on the Cayman Islands or Labaun in Malaysia, with initial capital shared among Taiwan, the USA, Japan, Singapore, and Brunei. This SPC will then issue two tiers of bonds against the collateral and/or sovereign guarantees provided by the crisis-struck economies – the upper tier, which is investment-worthy and amounts to about US$7 billion, will be sold in the market; the lower tier amounting to about US$3 billion will be purchased by the authorities of the stronger Asian economies and by the Asian Development Bank. The idea was not formally endorsed by the Summit, but is said to be among the 'innovations' welcomed by the Summit and to be further studied in subsequent multilateral engagements.

So at least there have been some head starts. The idea of some kind of stabilization system is not yet dead, although the specific arrangements that will come out of the multilateral engagements are still unclear. Some Japanese officials call for the East Asian economies to peg their currencies not to the dollar but to a basket of currencies. In effect, if the central banks in the area had all looked at the real effective exchange rate rather than the simple nominal rate against the dollar, this would have been achieved. There is indication that after the lesson from the financial crisis has been learned, an increasing number of countries are already doing this. Where to go from here remains, however, unclear.

7. CONCLUSION

How do we lessen the effects of the Asian crisis that has already occurred? How do we prevent similar events from happening in the future? These are the questions the Asian countries must face.

An easy answer, sometimes given by prominent economists and by 'Asian specialists', is that a crisis like the Asian one is unavoidable, given the bad 'fundamentals' of the crisis-ridden economies. Interestingly, Taiwan is often used as an example of a 'model performer', given its allegedly open stock and foreign exchange markets, financial prudence, and the prevalence of SMEs.

But as discussed above, while there might have been mismanagement of financial institutions in some cases, and overdependence on short-term foreign debt in others, maybe the East Asian economies have not been all that unhealthy; just as Taiwan is actually far from being perfectly healthy. It is not always a bad idea to borrow from abroad. It is not always a good idea to have an overconservative financial sector. And SMEs are not necessarily more productive than larger ones in all cases for all economies and at all times.

In effect, if the Asian economies have been that unhealthy, how come the 1997 IMF annual report praises the Asian economies for good overall management (Sachs, 1998)? Why are government budgets in almost all developing Asian economies under control? Why were these same economies in the recent past described as economic 'miracles' by the World Bank, which specifically points to their good 'fundamentals', including macroeconomic management? Why is Asia recovering faster than most people had expected?

Taiwan is part of Asia and shares many characteristics that are also seen in other Asian countries. It would be right for these other economies to learn from their own experience as well as the experience of Taiwan, but it would not be wise for these economies to undertake dramatic surgical operations in order to fit the Taiwanese pattern. Each must find its own way. Taiwan should not be overconfident of its 'achievements', just as other economies should not completely lose confidence and try to undo everything, including the right things.

This said, there are important lessons to be learned from the Asian financial crisis in general, and from the Taiwanese experience in particular. These include the following.

(i) Bubbles, which were present in each and every one of the Asian economies that are directly or indirectly affected by the crisis, should be avoided. The larger the bubbles become, the harder it is to manage a soft landing.

(ii) The short-term movement of international capital should be watched. In the Southeast Asian economies, where bubble development coincided with the surge in the inflow of such capital, the authorities should have reacted earlier.

(iii) Risk management in general needs to be strengthened in all economies. Supervision must be strengthened when the financial sector is undergoing liberalization. It is of vital importance to regulate excessive risk-taking by financial institutions, to regulate the mismatch of maturities, to ensure transparency of accounts, and to make sure that internal risk management systems are installed.

(iv) Financial institutions should be independent of planning agencies and of industrial development policies, if financial risk is to be contained. If the state has control or strong influence over the financial institutions and if it imposes development projects, which do not have to undergo an honest review, another window of vulnerability is created, because the state may be wrong in its judgement of such projects. Such risks can be weighed against the benefits of fast results when the state is right.

(v) It is really time to consider the establishment of a regional monetary stabilization mechanism such as the Asian Monetary Fund. If successfully established, the Fund should provide a number of services to the region. It should assist the troubled economies in their revitalization, and install an early-warning system to detect financial risks. It should assist at the very early stages in a crisis to prevent financial institution failures from developing into economy-wide crisis. It should also recommend sensible policies, which will take into accounts the social impacts of the corrective measures.

If the East Asian countries can swallow all of these pills, many of which are very bitter, they will be able to pull themselves out of the current crisis sooner, and assure themselves of a brighter future.

NOTES

1. It also adopted restrictive measures in foreign exchange transactions, including the prohibition of domestic firms and financial institutions to engage in NDF trading in the foreign exchange market.

2. The government began accepting application for special loans by temporarily financially stranded enterprises 'that are otherwise healthy' (*United Evening News*, 10 November 1998) in early November 1998. It meanwhile asked all of the financial institutions to extend maturity of loans by six months, and declared that bad loans directly resulting from such extensions would not be 'counted' as such when the Ministry of Finance reviews their performances (for example, *China Times*, 8 November 1998).

3. In South Korea, the bubble was mainly related to overinvestment by the private sector, also fueled in part by inflows of foreign capital (Bhattacharya et al., 1998).

4. The non-performing loan ratio at mid-year 1998 in Japan was 14 percent, according to *Economic Daily News* (27 July 1998), Taiwan. The same papers report that the non-performing loan ratio was 10 percent for Singapore and Hong Kong, 12 percent for the Philippines, and 6 percent for Taiwan as a whole at mid-year, 1998.

5. This estimate is higher than the one given by Johnson (1998), namely a total of US$600 billion (or about 78 trillion yen at 130 yen per dollar).

6. The story is actually quite similar to what happened in the ASEAN countries in the late 1980s. It is worth noting that the channels through which foreign capital flows into Asian economies have been different. In Taiwan in the mid-1980s, the

inflow of funds came mainly from private enterprises, which borrowed from abroad and from banks, although the scope of their action was limited by foreign exchange exposure restrictions imposed by the government. Later, when residents were allowed to purchase and sell foreign currencies, funds also came from well-to-do individuals. Foreign short-term portfolio capital, such as mutual funds in the stock market, did not play a major role because of the then restrictive regulations. According to Bhattacharya et al. (1998), among the ASEAN countries struck by the crisis, in Indonesia, the channel of funds inflow was mainly through the corporate businesses, similar to Taiwan's situation in the mid-1980s. In South Korea and Thailand, non-bank financial institutions, that is, finance companies in the former and merchant banks in the latter, amassed funds from abroad. In Malaysia, both financial institutions and corporate businesses were restricted in their foreign debt exposure (a policy instituted due to large borrowings in the early 1980s), which explains why the inflow of foreign capital was less compared to GDP in that country during 1989–96 than in Thailand and Indonesia (see Bhattacharya et al., 1998, Figure IV.8).

7. Meaning that the purchased land site can be freely used as the required collateral.

8. Selective credit controls on the real-estate sector were lifted in September 1990 after 19 months of enforcement. One possible reason was that real-estate prices began to fall during the period.

9. See *Economic Daily News*, *China Times*, *United Daily News*, and *United Evening News*, issues of 31 October to 11 November, 1998. These also constitute the source of reports in the following discussion of recent incidents of crisis, and will not be repeated, although sources of specific figures will be referred to wherever deemed necessary. In addition, a more recent report in the *Economic Daily News* (22 May 1999) estimates the sum of non-performing loans related to the 17 business groups whose problems surfaced in the past year at NT$106.4 billion.

10. The terms are much softer than in the Central Bills and Finance Corporation case: (i) share price is tentatively set at NT$6.00 per share; (ii) third-party accountants will be invited to do a careful appraisal in three months; (iii) should the appraised price be lower than NT$6.00 per share, the current owner will pay the balance, which is guaranteed by a blank check Mr Chen has submitted to the Ministry of Finance; (iv) should the appraised price be higher, the institutions involved in the takeover have the option of paying the difference or sell all the shares back to Mr Chen at NT$6.00 plus interests (*United Daily News*, 10 November 1998). The deal is set amidst reports that about 20 percent of commercial papers guaranteed by Hong-Fu Bills Financing were issued by its related enterprises, that is, those belonging to the same Hong-Fu business group, so owners' equity may actually be negative (*China Times*, 10 November 1998).

11. Part of the material presented in this subsection comes from a paper presented at

the International Conference on Development of Contemporary Taiwan and Its Implications for Cross-Strait Relations, the Asia-Pacific Region and Europe, December 1998, organized by the Institute for National Policy Research and French Center for Research on Contemporary China. That paper is co-authored with Thomas Lee, to whom the current author is grateful.

12. The authorities' current action to take over troubled bills financing companies was said to be based on the Banking Act, which applies to financial institutions in general.

13. Although it should be pointed out that, because the last and most recent operation is very close to a major election, it was suspected by the media to have been partly politically motivated. It also seems that the recent round of crises is more related to wrongdoings by domestic businessmen than to the Asian economic crisis.

14. Take the man-made fiber industry as an example, Chu et al. (1998) note that in that industry rayon, the first product the government chose to develop as early as 1957, did not turn out to be the leading product. Rather, it was polyester, which the government finally chose to develop in 1964, that later dominated Taiwan's man-made fiber industry. It was a choice of the market, not government officials with perfect foresight in the late 1950s.

15. As pointed out in Chu et al. (1998), the Taiwanese government made numerous attempts at building up a large-scale automobile plant but constantly failed. So did the attempts to create large trading companies, which appeared to have been instrumental in promoting the exports for countries like Japan and South Korea. In the 1960s and 1970s, many people in Taiwan praised the South Korean system because it appeared to be faster in implementing development plans. Such praises were not completely groundless.

16. Unlimited access to the market is not, however, always risk-free. There could emerge a 'bandwagon' effect in voluntary private investment. In Taiwan, as stated in Chu et al. (1998), that phenomenon occurred in the early 1970s in the man-made fiber industry with the result that many enterprises suffered a great deal from the oil crisis in the mid-1970s. The government then intervened by proposing mergers, which were later successfully implemented.

17. See, for example, Olson (1982).

18. Kuo and Tsai (1998) argue that a more intimate relationship has been observed between politicians and business, particularly big business, and they assert that this is a general phenomenon among East Asian economies, and a major reason for the current financial crisis. See also Chu et al. (1998) and Chu (1998).

19. See, for example, Schive (1998).

20. Statistics for Hong Kong for 1996 are unavailable. For 1993–95, Hong Kong's average was 18.8 percent (Kawai, 1998).

21. See Ka (1993) and *Commonwealth Magazine* (1995).

22. At the end of 1997, the total market value of the capital market in Taiwan was

about the same size as total bank loans outstanding, which totaled NT$11.7 trillion (about 115 percent of GDP). See Chiu (1998).

23. As Sachs (1998) points out, when time and again the IMF's forecast of the economic growth rate in the economies it is trying to rescue is completely off the line, there have been no official explanations. Additionally, the officials that make the questionable decisions do not have to face formal and open interrogations. About the only economy that has considerable, although by no means comprehensive, influence over the IMF is the USA, which, unfortunately, did not seem to have foreseen the forthcoming sharp criticism of the IMF.

REFERENCES

Ahn, Choong Yong and Joo-Hoon Kim (1997), 'The Outward-Looking Trade Policy and the Industrial Development of South Korea', in Dong-se Cha, Kwang Suk Kim and Dwight H. Perkins (eds), *The Korean Economy 1945–1995: Performance and Vision for the 21st Century*. Seoul, Korea: Korea Development Institute.

Akerlof, George and Paul Romer (1993), 'Looting: The Economic Underworld of Bankruptcy for Profit', *Brookings Papers on Economic Activity*, pp. 1–75.

Bhattacharya, Amar, Stijn Claessens, Swati Ghosh, Leonardo Hernandeq, and Pedro Alba (1998), 'Volatility and Contagion in a Financially-Integrated World: Lessons from East Asia's Recent Experience', presented at the PAFTAD conference on Asia Pacific Financial Liberalization and Reform, May, Chiangmai, Thailand.

Chen, Chie-Shyuan (1994) (in Chinese), *Cooperative Networks and Livelihood Structures: A Socioeconomic Analysis of Taiwan's Small- and Medium-sized Industries*. Taipei, Taiwan: Taiwan Research Series.

Chen, Po-Chih and Yun-Peng Chu (1994), 'The Present State of the Taiwan Economy', presented at the 1994 Conference of the East Asian Economic Association, Taipei.

Chen, Tain-jy, Been-Lon Chen and Yun-Peng Chu (1998) (in Chinese), 'An Inquiry into Taiwan's Economic Development', presented at the Third Liang Kuo-Shu Memorial Conference on Review and Outlook of East Asian Development, organized by the Department of Economics at National Taiwan University, Taipei, Taiwan.

Chiu, Paul C.H. (1998), 'ROC's Experiences in Responding to the Asian Financial Crisis', *Economic Review*, ICBC, No. 304, pp. 1–7.

Chu, Yun-Peng (1994a), 'Taiwan's Investment Abroad and Its Implications for Regional Economic Interdependence', in Jaymin Lee and Young Sun Lee (eds), *Economic Cooperation in the Asia-Pacific*

Community. Seoul, Korea: Institute of East and West Studies, Yonsei University.

Chu, Yun-Peng (1994b), 'Taiwan's External Imbalance and Structural Adjustment: A General Equilibrium Analysis', *Asian Economic Journal*, 8, pp. 85–114.

Chu, Yun-Peng (1998), 'Taiwan and Asia: Towards the Establishment of an Asian Monetary Stabilization Mechanism', presented at the Workshop on Trends and Issues in East Asia, November 1998, Tokyo, organized by the Foundation for Advanced Studies in International Development, Japan.

Chu, Yun-Peng, Tain-Jy Chen, and Been-Lon Chen (1998), 'Rethinking the East Asian Paradigm: On Optimal Government Intervention', presented at the seminar on Rethinking the East Asian Paradigm, Singapore, November, sponsored by Sasakawa Foundation, Japan.

Chu, Yun-Peng and Thomas T.-H. Lee (1998), 'The Taiwanese Experience of Macroeconomic Risk Management', presented at the Seminar on International Finance, Tokyo, organized by the Asian Development Bank.

Commonwealth Magazine (1995) (in Chinese), The Amoebae Organizations: Invisible Advantages. Taipei: *Commonwealth Magazine*.

Dobson, Wendy (1998), 'Business Networks in East Asia: Diversity and Evolution', in Rong-I Wu and Yun-Peng Chu (eds), *Business, Markets and Government in the Asia Pacific*. New York: Routledge.

Henderson, Callum (1998), *Asia Falling? Making Sense of the Asian Currency Crisis and Its Aftermath*. Singapore: McGraw-Hill.

Hu, Ming-Wen and Chi Schive (1998), 'The Changing Competitiveness of Taiwan's Manufacturing SMEs', *Small Business Economics*, 1, pp.1–12.

Johnson, Lorne (1998), 'Economic Slowdown in Japan in the 1990s: A Summary', in Kar-yiu Wong (ed.), *The Asian Crisis: What Has Happened and Why*? Mimeograph.

Ka, Chih-ming (1993) (in Chinese), *Markets, Social Networks, and the Production Organization of Small-Scale Industry in Taiwan – The Garment Industries in Wufenpu*. Taipei: Institute of E Ethnology, Academia Sinica.

Kagami, Mitsuhiro (1995), *The Voice of East Asia: Development Implications for Latin America*, Tokyo: Institute of Developing Economies.

Kawai, Masahiro (1998), 'Evolving Patterns of Asia-Pacific Financial Flows', presented at the Pacific Trade and Development Conference on Financial Reform, Chiangmai, Thailand.

Lin, Guo-ching (1995) (in Chinese), 'Effects of Land Price on Economic Development', unpublished research report.

Lin, Wei-Yi (1997) (in Chinese), 'Financial Risk Management from Bank Runs' Point of View', *CDIC Information Journal*, Vol. 11, No. 2, pp. 1–24.

Lin, Wei-Yi (1998) (in Chinese), 'Risk Management of Taiwan's Financial Institutions', presented at the   Fifth Cross-Strait Financial Conference, Taipei, sponsored by Taipei Financial Development Foundation and Chung-hwa Institution for Economic Research.

Lo, Fu-chen (1998), 'Globalization and Transformation of Southeast Asian Economies', presented at the Third Liang Kuo-shu Memorial Conference on Review and Outlook of East Asian Development, organized by the Department of Economics at National Taiwan University, Taipei, Taiwan.

Medhi, Krongkaew (1998), 'Growth, Transformation and Crises in the Thai Economy, and Their Welfare Implications', presented at the Conference on Growth, Poverty and income Inequality in the Asia Pacific Region, organized by the School of Economics, University of New South Wales, Sydney.

McKinnon, R.I. (1973), *Money and Capital in Economic Development*, Washington DC: The Brookings Institution.

McKinnon, R.I. (1991), *The Order of Economic Liberalization: Financial Control in the Transition to a Market Economy*, Baltimore: Johns Hopkins University Press.

Olson, Mancur (1982), *The Rise and Decline of Nations*, New Haven, Connecticut: Yale University Press.

Sachs, Jeffrey (1998), 'The IMF and the Asian Flu', *The American Prospect*, March–April.

Schive, Chi (1998), 'Taiwan's Economic Role after the Financial Crisis', presented at the Third Liang Kuo-shu Memorial Conference on Review and Outlook of East Asian Development, organized by the Department of Economics at National Taiwan University, Taipei, Taiwan.

Werner, Richard (1997), 'Window Guidance and the Creation of the "Bubble" in Japan'. Mimeograph.

Yamakage, Susumu (1998), 'Crisis, Cooperation and Power Triangle in the Asia Pacific Region', presented at the Workshop on Trends and Issues in East Asia, Tokyo, November, organized by the Foundation for Advanced Studies in International Development, Japan.

7. Causes of the Korean financial crisis and its social impact: 1997–99

Suk Bum Yoon*

1. INTRODUCTION

The recent financial crisis in Korea, which started from November 1997, following similar crises in Thailand, Indonesia, and other Asian countries, has caused ineradicable sorrow and anger among the Korean people. Some believe that the pain and economic loss caused by the financial crisis are even greater than those of the Korean War, which erupted in 1950 and lasted three years until the middle of 1953. The International Monetary Fund's intervention at the beginning of the crisis further created very deep ignominy in the nation as the IMF's economic intervention has been conceived by the people as the *de facto* economic colonization of the country by the superpowers.

Young Sam Kim, then the president of the Republic, was thrown into deep disgrace. He was treated almost as a traitor who sold the country due to his ignorance, stupidity, and stubbornness. Korea's recent economic growth and development, perhaps the first successful experience in its long economic history, suddenly started to exhibit every sign of economic collapse with the beginning of the crisis. Banks collapsed and personal savings deposits evaporated. Stock prices fell and life-time savings in stock disappeared. Unemployment rose and no income was generated.

To most Korean people, this sort of phenomenon was only found in the economic history textbooks of advanced countries like the USA and the UK. Since the Korean economy had recently been industrialized, there was no such experience with economic downfall. A strong complacency

*An earlier version of this chapter was presented at the PROSEA workshop, Academia Sinica, Taipei, Taiwan, 14–15 June 1999. The author expresses his appreciation for creative discussion and comments at the workshop.

that banks never collapse and big firms never go bankrupt in Korea was present in the minds of most Korean people. The strong but hidden suspicions from a corner of academia that predicted the possibility of crisis in Korea after careful comparison with the case of the Mexican economy were ignored as unfounded allegations and even harshly criticized as a conspiracy to undermine the 'healthy' Korean economy by government officials. The mental rigidity and economic selfishness of high-ranking officials further exacerbated the situation.

This chapter intends to report comprehensively on the financial crisis in Korea, focusing on how it started, how it was connected to the overall economic crisis and its important social impact. As there are numerous studies concerning the economic impact, only the requisite aspects will be touched upon in this chapter. However, the social impact of the financial crisis is extensively illustrated in terms of income distribution, poverty incidence, and domestic migration.[1]

2.   BACKDROP

The retarded development and inefficient operation of the Korean banking sector are deep-rooted issues, having a long history in the state's political economy. The most salient features of the development of the Korean economy are exhibited in the manufacturing and industrial sectors. Expected parallel development could not substantially materialize in the banking sector, primarily due to the fact that the banking industry had not been provided with proper market motivation, particularly under the situation of excessive government protection and interference. This situation goes back to the earliest stages of development initiatives in Korea.

2.1 Government Dominance of the Banking Industry since 1961

After the successful *coup d'état* led by a small faction of forces within the army and marine corps in 1961, the military junta abolished the sole national legislative body, the National Congress, and replaced it with the so-called 'Supreme Council for National Reconstruction'. A number of new and drastic economic measures were implemented by the military junta, including strong monetary reform in 1962. Another draconian measure was the enactment and implementation of the so-called 'Law for the Retrieval of Illegally Accumulated Wealth', started in 1961 in order to enforce the sequestration of the so-called 'illegally accumulated wealth' mostly held by large business conglomerates.[2]

The sequestration of 'illegally' accumulated wealth held by business tycoons was implemented by the Commission for the Retrieval of Illegally Accumulated Wealth established under the law. The sequestration was extensively achieved in the form of the forced acquisition of stocks of commercial banks owned by the so-called 'illegal accumulator' target business groups. Through this process of sequestration, *de facto* nationalization of the banking industry was accomplished by the military junta. This was the beginning of a new phase for banking operations in Korea, which entailed an inevitable and unavoidable financial monopoly on a national scale, as the entire system was practically owned by the state.

The *de facto* nationalization of the banking industry was further strengthened by malignant revision of the Bank of Korea Law in 1962. The law virtually deprived the central bank of its independence and neutrality by weakening the role and functioning of the Monetary Board and diversifying the supervisory function of the Banking Supervisory Board. In particular, the revision of the central bank law negatively contributed to the weakening of open market operations and the rediscount policy of the central bank by substituting treasury bonds with so-called monetary stabilization bonds issued by the central bank and by politically determining rediscount rates without resorting to the market situation.

The official money market now became a degraded and inefficient money allocation mechanism, directly but inefficiently manipulated by the state and the ruling party. The official interest rate was arbitrarily set at an irrationally low level, which often did not even cover the rate of inflation.

Because of low official interest rates, the demand for and the supply of money, as expected, could not be equilibrated, and the excessive demand for money had to be channeled into the illegal underground money market. There was a wide difference between the official and the black market interest rates, which sometimes reached more than 15 percent. The illegal financial market played not only a positive role for matching demand and supply, but also a negative role for contributing to the further accumulation of wealth for those who had strong political connections, enabling them to borrow funds from the official banking system.

It was a natural consequence that unethical relations between politicians cum government officials and businessmen were established. Corruption, bribery, and interference in banking operations mushroomed. The banking industry could not develop healthily in its own way, but had to remain as an infantile and retarded industry forever under the disoriented guidance and protection of the government.

2.2 Excessive Dependence of Firms on Borrowing

When firms could enjoy low, sometimes negative, interest rates with rampant inflation and ever-increasing real-estate prices, it was 'rational' behavior for the firms to borrow as much as possible from the banking sector, particularly during the development process of the 1970s through 1980s. The domestic loans of private sector corporations reached approximately 600 trillion won, while accumulated foreign debt reached a level of 150 billion US dollars in 1997, both of which far exceeded the annual gross domestic product of the nation. Table 7.1 shows the debt ratio of the manufacturing sector by industry.

Table 7.1 Financial structure of manufacturing industries (%)

Industries	Equity ratio		Debt ratio	
	1996	1997	1996	1997
Manufacturing	24.0	20.2	317.1	396.3
Food & beverage products	16.9	15.2	492.5	558.4
Woven textiles	21.7	20.9	360.6	378.1
Apparel & fur articles	20.5	19.2	386.9	420.5
Leather & footwear	18.3	17.3	447.1	477.5
Wood & wood products	17.2	16.1	483.3	522.8
Pulp & paper	25.4	21.7	293.3	360.5
Publishing & printing	20.2	15.3	395.3	553.0
Refined petroleum products	20.3	15.7	392.9	538.6
Chemical products	28.1	26.7	255.5	274.7
Rubber & plastic products	23.1	16.4	333.5	509.3
Non-metallic mineral products	27.9	23.1	258.9	332.2
Basic metals	30.0	25.1	233.2	298.0
Fabricated metal products	24.5	22.4	308.4	346.4
Machinery & equipment	21.5	18.3	366.2	446.4
Office machinery	34.0	25.4	194.1	294.2
Electrical machinery	23.7	25.7	322.9	289.1
Radio, television & communication equipment apparatus	29.1	21.2	243.5	372.5
Medical & precision instruments	18.8	19.4	432.6	415.9
Motor vehicles	17.8	12.2	463.3	717.1
Other transport equipment	21.6	20.7	363.6	382.7
Manufacturing n.e.c.	14.6	7.2	583.1	1,292.1

Source: Bank of Korea, *Financial Statement Analysis for 1997*, 1998.

This phenomenon of excessive borrowing was more salient with the big corporations, called Jaebol, than with the numerous small- and medium-scale firms. Table 7.2 shows how much the biggest 30 corporations depended upon debt financing in the preceding two years of the crisis.

Table 7.2 Financial structure of Jaebols (%)

Group	1996		Group	1997	
	Equity ratio	Debt ratio		Equity ratio	Debt ratio
Hyundai	18.64	436.59	Hyundai	14.70	580.50
Samsung	26.88	271.98	Samsung	21.26	370.38
LG	21.97	355.18	Daewoo	17.49	471.81
Daewoo	22.87	337.27	LG	16.33	512.32
SK	20.99	376.32	SK	17.99	455.73
Ssangyong	19.70	407.50	Han Jin	9.84	916.49
Han Jin	15.20	557.90	Ssangyong	20.01	399.70
Kia	16.08	521.86	Han Wha	8.59	1,064.32
Han Wha	13.44	644.02	Kumho	9.52	950.96
Lotte	34.22	192.22	Dong-Ah	21.69	631.11
Kumho	17.34	476.76	Lotte	31.35	219.02
Halla	4.27	2,241.76	Halla	6.40	1,662.68
Dong-Ah	22.06	353.39	Daelim	16.44	508.41
Doosan	12.51	699.36	Doosan	14.23	602.51
Daelim	19.08	424.01	Hansol	20.01	399.82
Hansol	25.53	291.72	Hyosung	17.36	475.99
Hyosung	21.15	372.73	Kohap	17.43	473.61
Dong-Kuk Steel	31.30	219.51	Kolon	19.04	425.31
Jinro	5.89	1,599.17	Dong-Kuk Steel	23.33	328.55
Kolon	23.71	321.70	Dong Bu	22.29	348.59
Kohap	14.46	591.76	Anam	6.24	1,502.23
Dong Bu	31.64	216.03	Jinro	21.42	566.83
Dongyang	24.68	305.27	Dongyang	19.98	400.49
Haitai	13.22	656.44	Haitai	7.38	1,255.09
New Core	7.53	1,228.13	Shinho	10.90	829.30
Hanil	14.76	577.64	Daesang	13.57	637.11
			New Core	5.30	1,785.09
			Keo Pyung	21.09	433.79
1st–4th	22.44	345.57	1st–5th	17.47	472.45
5th–10th	19.28	418.79	6th–10th	13.53	639.17
11th–30th	17.73	464.16	11th–30th	13.90	621.48
Total	20.53	387.14	Total	16.10	521.53

Source: Financial Supervisory Board 1998.

As these two tables show, the debt/equity ratios of the manufacturing sector and private corporations in Korea were very much higher than international standards and increased up to 1997.

Once real-estate prices were stabilized and the interest rate reflected the market rates, the Jaebol encountered difficulties in paying back their principal and interest. The financial cost became too heavy for them to bear. Businessmen's clubs, like the Federation of Korean Industries, kept applying pressure on government officials, mostly on those in the economic and finance ministries, to arbitrarily lower interest rates, without paying much attention and effort to reducing their own debts. The big business groups also endeavored to expand their business excessively. Journalists sarcastically dubbed this behavior 'octopus-type expansion'. Duplications of industrial plants and excessive investment were the inevitable results, which brought inefficiency and less competitiveness in both the domestic and international markets. Heavy bribery and contributions to political funds by firms further aggravated firm competitiveness.

3.   PRELUDE

3.1 China Market

The newly emerging market in the People's Republic of China after the economic liberalization there played an important role in initially accelerating Korean exports. However, the gradual and steady industrialization in China has slowly encroached on overseas Korean markets with inexpensive Chinese export products. The unification and devaluation of the yuan in 1994 particularly affected Korean competitiveness in both overseas and domestic markets. China's cheap agricultural and fishery products invaded the Korean market, and Korea's dependency on Chinese products has been increasing, while Korean products are sold less and less in China. In comparison to the yuan, the won seems to be excessively overvalued. With strengthened labor unions in Korea maintaining relatively high wages, Korea lost its comparative advantage in the overseas market.

Frequent business failures in connection with Korea's investment in China were another important factor which negatively affected the Korean economic situation prior to the crisis.

3.2 Chronic Deficit in the Balance of Payments and the Decrease in the Foreign Exchange Reserve

Primarily due to the excessive optimism prevailing in Korea after the impressive economic growth, the marginal propensity to consume imported goods and services increased tremendously in Korea, particularly during the three years preceding the crisis. The Korean government also implemented erroneous policies of sudden and misguided globalization by liberalizing the domestic money market and joining the Organization for Economic Cooperation and Development, which further worsened the balance of payments situation and highly disturbed financial markets in Korea. Table 7.3 shows the recent trend in the current account balance of payments. Beginning in 1990, the deficit of the current account balance of payments basically showed a strong trend of increasing deficit, which reached a peak in 1996.

Table 7.3 Recent trends in the balance of payments (in million US$)

Year	Current balance	Year	Current balance
1988	14,505.4	1994	–3,866.9
1989	5,360.3	1995	–8,507.7
1990	–2,003.3	1996	–23,004.7
1991	–8,317.2	1997	–8,166.7
1992	–3,942.9	1998	40,039.4
1993	989.5		

Source: National Statistical Office, *Monthly Statistical of Korea*, May 1999, p. 220.

In addition, the basic government policy for foreign exchange borrowing was unfortunately focused on short-term lending, the maturity of which should be less than a year. There had never been an integrated monitoring mechanism to observe and advise the aggregated foreign debt situation of Korean firms and subsidiaries overseas. A large-scale influx and outflow of foreign exchange was made every day without being monitored and with minimal surveillance by the Korean government and the central bank, the results of which were easily agitated and highly unstable money and foreign exchange markets. Table 7.4 shows the foreign exchange reserve situation in Korea beginning in January 1997. As indicated in table 7.4, signs of a declining trend in the foreign exchange reserve started to appear in August 1997, three months before the actual crisis. The lowest point was eventually reached four months later in December 1997.

Table 7.4 Foreign exchange reserve (in million US$)

End of	Foreign exchange	End of	Foreign exchange
1997. 1	30,154.3	1998. 2	26,670.5
2	28,964.3	3	29,676.6
3	28,365.0	4	35,471.7
4	29,060.1	5	38,292.2
5	31,109.0	6	40,764.0
6	32,524.7	7	42,885.5
7	32,901.5	8	44,684.3
8	30,370.3	9	46,904.2
9	29,654.0	10	48,760.5
10	29,728.0	11	49,931.4
11	23,628.0	12	51,963.0
12	19,710.3	1999. 1	53,242.1
1998. 1	22,728.2	2	55,092.2

Source: Bank of Korea, *Monthly Bulletin*, March 1993, p. 119.

4.   THE CRISIS

It is not as simple as is usually 'assumed to pinpoint exactly the demarcating date for the financial crisis in Korea. The most conventional date is the day on which the Korean government decided to apply to the IMF for a series of emergency funds, and the Deputy Prime Minister for Economic Affairs was replaced. However, the crisis might have started far earlier than 21 November 1997.

4.1 Collapse of Big Firms

Excessively overlapping investment in the automobile industry in Korea had been extensively criticized by both academia and journalists when the Samsung Group planned and implemented a new automobile plant project. The Kia Automobile Corporation, which did not belong to any Jaebol, was highly indebted, and the management of the corporation was entrusted to professional managers by stockholders. Perhaps because Kia was not owned by any single Jaebol but by a large number of small and non-dominant stockholders, it became an easy target for an antagonistic merger and acquisition by other automobile companies owned by Jaebol.

The combination of these two factors plausibly caused the bankruptcy of the Kia Automobile Corporation. The main lending bank to Kia, the Cheil Bank, was the most severely hit when the insolvency situation developed with Kia. There was a long sequence of debates, diffidence, hesitancy, and sometimes vehement recalcitrance between the government and Kia in the process of attempting to resolve the situation. None of this contributed to resolving the problem, but did cause most of Kia's management and numerous high-ranking government officials, including the Deputy Prime Minister, to end up in jail with the fall of the Young Sam Kim regime.

The Hanbo Steel Corporation, which preceded the Kia case, is another good example of high debt dependence, unethical business–government ties, bribery and eventual collapse. It is also a typical case of excessive overlapping investment. When Hanbo collapsed, the main lending bank, this time Seoul Bank, was most heavily hit. When Jinro, the largest distillery in Korea, Haitai, the nation's largest bakery and soft drink supplier, and Sammi, one of the biggest alloy plants, also collapsed, the aggregate impact was inconceivably extensive and far-reaching. Thousands of firms related to these big corporations as suppliers or users of raw materials and parts, which had to maintain complicated networks of credit relations amongst themselves, were ultimately hit in a chain reaction to the initial Jaebol failure and collapsed.

4.2 Crisis in Banking System

The bankruptcies of the large firms were immediately connected to the banking system. The collapse of so many firms naturally led to the insolvency of other firms, which consecutively led to increased non-performing assets in the banking system. Because of the increasing scale of non-performing assets in the banking system, the liquidity position of the banks further deteriorated, and the credibility of the banking system as a whole started to fall. Large-scale deposit withdrawal was a natural consequence. As one of the most important indicators of this process, table 7.5 indicates the ratios of dishonored checks by province in Korea beginning from January 1997. As expected, the highest peak was realized in December 1997 in most of the provinces, and one or two months later in a couple of the other provinces, where the impact was inevitably delayed due to the industrial sublet structure.

As the dishonored check ratio increases, non-performing assets in the banking industry had to increase in similar proportion. Table 7.6 shows

Table 7.5 Dishonored ratio by province (%)

During	Total	Seoul	Pusan	Taegu	Incheon	Kwangju	Taejeon	Ulsan
1997.1	0.26	0.19	0.53	0.60	0.96	0.46	0.60	—
2	0.30	0.23	0.69	0.60	0.98	0.60	0.68	—
3	0.30	0.22	0.73	0.70	0.70	0.67	0.66	—
4	0.32	0.23	0.52	0.63	0.69	0.63	1.35	—
5	0.30	0.20	0.58	0.63	0.85	0.84	1.18	—
6	0.29	0.20	0.74	0.60	0.73	0.76	1.22	—
7	0.30	0.22	0.59	0.55	0.71	0.85	0.98	—
8	0.27	0.18	0.81	0.46	0.81	0.71	0.70	0.66
9	0.40	0.31	1.05	0.61	0.79	1.40	0.89	0.92
10	0.56	0.49	1.60	0.43	1.33	0.97	0.65	0.70
11	0.48	0.41	1.40	0.32	1.38	0.86	0.79	0.69
12	2.09	2.25	2.10	0.56	2.28	1.07	1.07	1.57
1998.1	0.72	0.58	2.17	0.61	2.38	1.07	1.64	1.17
2	0.83	0.69	2.99	0.49	2.95	1.72	1.56	2.05
3	0.62	0.49	2.70	0.39	2.18	1.90	1.43	1.64
4	0.57	0.38	3.19	0.52	1.84	1.65	1.51	1.70
5	0.62	0.49	2.29	0.86	1.43	1.02	1.08	0.98
6	0.58	0.47	1.69	0.90	1.10	2.18	2.16	1.25
7	0.69	0.60	1.64	1.86	1.60	1.27	0.87	0.84
8	0.55	0.48	1.48	1.59	1.24	0.92	0.48	0.87
9	0.42	0.35	1.95	0.90	1.29	1.05	0.52	0.97
10	0.28	0.18	1.41	1.65	1.81	0.44	0.48	0.59
11	0.26	0.20	0.83	1.10	1.30	0.55	0.51	0.52
12	0.17	0.13	0.74	0.53	0.72	0.35	0.30	0.60
1999.1	0.16	0.13	0.39	0.57	0.91	0.22	0.78	0.50

During	Kyonggi	Kangwon	Chungbuk	Chungnam	Chonbuk	Chonnan	Kyungbuk	Kyungnam	Cheju
1997.1	0.74	0.94	0.61	0.86	0.74	0.60	0.58	0.62	0.77
2	0.75	0.77	0.67	0.95	0.72	0.62	0.69	0.70	0.73
3	0.80	0.58	0.92	0.87	0.74	0.69	0.81	0.76	0.67
4	0.94	0.60	1.38	0.74	0.87	0.77	0.51	0.87	0.58
5	0.76	0.57	2.39	0.84	0.91	0.61	0.77	0.90	0.91
6	0.76	0.55	1.71	0.72	0.80	0.74	0.97	0.82	1.10
7	0.83	0.70	1.12	0.66	0.76	0.76	1.31	0.92	1.00
8	0.93	0.74	1.09	0.96	1.00	0.74	1.40	1.42	1.24
9	0.94	0.64	0.96	0.90	0.93	0.67	1.07	1.46	1.03
10	1.22	0.63	0.83	1.97	1.39	0.68	1.24	1.64	1.16
11	1.48	0.58	0.86	0.59	1.21	0.74	1.08	1.31	1.18
12	1.90	0.84	1.30	1.43	1.89	1.01	1.30	1.87	0.87
1998.1	1.68	1.13	1.84	1.46	1.60	1.10	1.64	2.71	0.84
2	2.65	1.41	3.32	2.64	1.97	1.76	2.39	2.60	1.15
3	1.99	1.28	1.47	1.66	1.93	1.69	1.64	2.29	1.33
4	2.24	1.58	1.83	2.05	1.86	0.74	1.37	3.46	1.03
5	1.47	1.24	1.42	3.43	1.71	1.20	1.15	2.63	1.30
6	1.43	1.30	1.85	1.30	1.45	1.37	1.29	1.80	1.42
7	1.18	0.97	1.25	1.09	1.13	0.95	1.04	1.32	1.00
8	0.98	1.12	3.62	0.94	1.11	1.00	0.74	1.27	0.69
9	1.00	0.63	1.82	1.10	0.49	0.85	1.10	1.18	0.59
10	1.26	0.99	2.14	0.73	0.47	0.61	0.57	1.21	1.10
11	0.97	0.55	0.83	1.27	0.43	0.71	0.41	0.84	0.38
12	0.41	0.46	0.57	0.63	0.48	0.47	0.52	0.57	0.34
1999.1	0.41	0.33	0.22	0.33	0.40	0.32	0.35	0.31	0.18

Source: Bank of Korea, *Monthly Bulletin*, March 1999, p. 119.

the highly worsened status of non-performing loan ratios of commercial banks. There have also been a number of closures of banking corporations. Out of 50 merchant banks, almost one half had to close their operations, and numerous commercial banks were merged.

Table 7.6 Non-performing loan (trillion won and %)

	Non-performing loan (A)	Total loan (B)	Ratio (A/B)	As percent of GDP
Commercial banks[1]	28.5	453.3	6.3	6.8
Merchant banks[2]	3.9	133.5	2.9	0.9
Total	32.4	586.8	5.5	7.7

[1] As of the end of Sept. 1997. [2] As of the end of October 1997.
Source: Ministry of Finance and Economy.

4.3 Foreign Exchange and Interest Rates

Foreign exchange rates had maintained a very stable level up to July 1997. However, a sign of slight change was observed starting in August 1997, and the dollar/won rate reached its lowest point in December 1997. As the foreign exchange reserves dwindled in December 1997, the exchange rate plummeted to its lowest level. This is shown in table 7.7.

Interest rates also skyrocketed during this period. Since credit tightening and bankruptcy cases were widespread and ever-increasing, commercial banks were reluctant to provide loans to the industrial sector. The credit crunch was everywhere, and liquidity was almost completely frozen, while interest rates soared. This phenomenon is also shown in table 7.8. High rates were also affected by the tight money supply recommended by the International Monetary Fund.

244 *The social impact of the Asian financial crisis*

Table 7.7 Major foreign exchange rates (in won per currency unit)

Year / month	US dollar	UK pound	DM	Japanese yen	French franc	HK dollar	Euro
1996.1	787.3	1,181.55	526.69	730.46	153.18	101.43	644.45
2	780.3	1,195.25	531.45	744.23	155.33	100.97	652.49
3	781.3	1,195.18	530.19	729.76	155.51	101.20	657.73
4	780.4	1,173.11	509.99	742.15	151.04	100.68	628.87
5	780.2	1,209.03	513.67	731.74	151.83	101.83	625.57
6	798.0	1,258.86	531.66	738.76	157.25	104.72	646.49
7	812.8	1,265.90	550.72	753.20	162.35	105.17	676.34
8	816.8	1,280.56	553.37	752.09	161.65	105.97	681.95
9	821.8	1,283.74	538.39	740.15	159.31	106.19	653.30
10	827.6	1,357.93	549.80	729.85	162.95	107.51	662.26
11	828.2	1,393.87	538.47	727.79	158.46	107.18	635.36
12	839.0	1,427.96	542.89	726.51	161.06	109.13	625.80
1997.1	849.9	1,388.80	525.82	705.69	155.95	111.66	604.74
2	866.9	1,404.74	511.80	715.30	151.76	111.56	586.29
3	879.4	1,463.17	534.53	723.18	158.55	115.77	617.20
4	893.6	1,454.44	517.01	702.72	153.32	115.16	607.28
5	892.1	1,461.21	525.73	765.49	155.53	115.11	632.17
6	889.5	1,478.46	510.26	775.29	151.35	114.60	610.38
7	890.5	1,456.77	486.17	755.93	144.08	115.18	589.67
8	895.9	1,461.69	498.62	746.69	148.21	116.39	604.36
9	909.5	1,474.02	519.40	756.28	154.64	118.21	629.57
10	921.9	1,611.23	562.82	803.25	167.61	125.00	692.08
11	1,025.6	1,965.66	659.83	910.11	197.10	150.55	815.99
12	1,484.1	2,345.69	790.95	1,087.82	236.38	182.63	973.65
1998.1	1,706.8	2,568.55	859.51	1,238.21	256.47	203.36	1,065.43
2	1,632.1	2,696.65	903.39	1,300.38	269.29	211.83	1,119.14
3	1,505.3	2,311.90	746.63	1,044.74	222.75	177.98	905.62
4	1,392.0	2,235.46	745.85	1,011.26	222.29	172.84	893.92
5	1,394.6	2,301.01	789.92	1,016.61	235.53	182.06	951.28
6	1,397.2	2,306.98	765.20	973.85	228.19	178.77	909.67
7	1,300.8	2,023.95	693.99	860.72	206.86	159.53	829.47
8	1,303.2	2,239.09	762.55	941.53	225.88	171.85	927.92
9	1,370.8	2,348.58	823.01	1,023.93	244.87	177.38	991.98
10	1,336.7	2,201.27	794.56	1,132.10	236.96	169.64	972.11
11	1,294.1	2,055.46	726.35	1,009.05	216.50	160.62	880.93
12	1,213.7	2,005.19	718.12	1,053.47	214.49	155.89	871.74

Source: Bank of Korea, *Monthly Bulletin*, March 1999, p. 117–18.

Table 7.8 Interest rates on loan (%)

End of	Interest rate	End of	Interest rate	End of	Interest rate
1996.1	9.0–12.5	1997.1	11.34	1998.1	17.53
2	9.0–12.5	2	11.33	2	17.12
3	9.0–15.0	3	11.47	3	17.18
4	8.75–14.75	4	11.49	4	17.14
5	8.75–14.75	5	11.36	5	17.05
6	8.75–14.75	6	11.38	6	16.59
7	11.17	7	11.38	7	15.42
8	11.03	8	11.60	8	14.88
9	11.05	9	11.83	9	14.24
10	11.12	10	11.71	10	12.90
11	10.92	11	12.31	11	11.79
12	11.10	12	15.32	12	11.11

Source: Bank of Korea, *Monthly Bulletin*, February 1997, 1998, p. 68, March, 1999, p. 65.

5. INTERVENTION

As the Korean economic situation was getting worse and the outflow of short-term investment accelerated, the Korean government finally decided to go to the International Monetary Fund in order to plead for emergency funds on November 21, 1997. After a close consultation with IMF officials, the Korean government submitted a memorandum on the economic program to the IMF asking for SDR 15.5 billion on December 3, 1997.

> The attached Memorandum on the Economic Program outlines the policies that Korea intends to implement over the next three years to address the fundamental causes of its current financial difficulties, thereby restoring and sustaining market confidence and returning the economy to a path of strong sustainable growth. In support of this program, Korea hereby requests a three year stand-by arrangement from the International Monetary Fund in an amount equivalent to SDR 15.5 billion.[3]

It is also interesting to observe how the Korean government evaluated the cause of the financial crisis, as stated in the memorandum.

> Since the beginning of the year, an unprecedented number of highly leveraged conglomerates (chaebols) have moved into bankruptcy. The high rate of

bankruptcies reflected a number of factors, including excessive investment in certain sectors, weakening export prices, and the government's greater willingness to allow troubled chaebols to fail. The bankruptcies spilled over into a sharp increase in non-performing loans (defined according to international standards) to 32 trillion Won (7 percent of GDP) by end-September, about double their level at end-1996.[4]

As the memorandum shows, the government pointed out three factors: excessive investment, weakening export prices, and the government's willingness to allow the jaebols to fail. The deeper behind-the-scenes problems are already mentioned in the earlier part of this chapter. Unfortunately, these factors are all closely related to corruption and unethical relations between businesses and politics.

The policy objectives the IMF wanted to accomplish were:

(i) a strong macroeconomic framework designed to continue the orderly adjustment in the external current account to contain inflationary pressures; (ii) a comprehensive strategy to restructure and recapitalize the financial sector and make it more transparent, market-oriented, better supervised, and free from political interference in business decisions: (iii) measures to improve corporate governance; (iv) the accelerated liberalization of capital account transactions: (v) further trade liberalization; and (vi) to improve the transparency and timely reporting of economic data.[5]

What the IMF desired from the Korean economy was already demonstrated in these aims. The IMF simply wanted to open the economy completely and at the same time improve the balance of payments. This gives one the strong impression that the IMF more or less represented the interests of the superpower economies rather than trying to revive the Korean economy. What the IMF prescribed for the Korean economy further supports this attitude.

5.1 Macroeconomic Policies

Basically monetary policies were recommended in this connection. In close consultation with IMF staffs stationed in Seoul, the IMF wanted to contain the inflationary rate within 5 percent by tightening supply of M3 from 16.4 percent at end-September to 15.4 percent end-December 1997 and consequently raising the market interest rate. As experienced, this prescription has not contributed to lightening the Jaebol's debt ratio, but contributed negatively in worsening business conditions in Korea. Moreover, there was virtually no policy for the foreign exchange rate, and only flexibility was emphasized.

5.2 Fiscal Policy

In the name of alleviating the burden on monetary policy, a tight fiscal policy was also prescribed. The expansion of fiscal expenditure necessarily entails increases in import demand, and this will definitely worsen the balance of payments. However, reduced fiscal expenditure also reduced the aggregate demand of the national economy, and this negatively affected business conditions in Korea and eventually caused more firms to be closed than anticipated. Measures to raise the corporation tax, the income tax, and the value-added tax were also erroneously recommended.

5.3 Financial Sector Restructuring

Since the financial sector in Korea had been under strong but misguided government protection and intervention, it was absolutely necessary to undertake strong measures to restructure this sector. In this connection, several measures were enacted, including the revision of the Bank of Korea Act, a consolidated financial supervision bill and a bill requiring corporate financial statements to be prepared on a consolidated basis and be certified by external auditors.

Financial institutions in distress were also to be restructured and recapitalized within a given time framework. Some institutions were to be merged, and others were to be suspended with protection of deposits. The participation of foreign firms in this procedure was also highly recommended. The adoption of international standards and greater transparency in operations were also prescribed.

5.4 Other Policies

Strong trade liberalization was prescribed, along with the liberalization of capital markets, including the domestic bond market, by eliminating restrictions on import diversification, equity shares, etc. All information concerning business operations was also to be openly released in order to maintain transparency.

The IMF released its statement concerning its approval of SDR 15.5 billion stand-by credit for Korea on December 4, 1997, the day after the Memorandum was signed by the Deputy Prime Minister and the Governor of the Bank of Korea and the second new IMF office was established in Seoul. As far as economic policy was concerned, Korea had lost its sovereignty. Ironically, the three running presidential candidates, then in the midst of the election campaign, were asked to endorse the memorandum and the IMF succeeded in acquiring their signatures of endorsement.

6.   IMPACT

6.1 Unemployment and Negative Growth

The tight money supply with high interest rates, drastic reduction of fiscal spending, structural adjustment of big business firms and banking institutions, and suspension and closure of marginal firms caused widespread unemployment and negative growth of GDP. Table 7.9 shows the unemployment status in Korea from January 1997 to the end of 1998.

As shown in table 7.9, unemployment started to increase from November 1997 and continued until July of 1998. The first nine months were the hardest time for workers. There were also large flocks of homeless people mostly spending nights in underground subway stations and quenching their hunger and thirst by begging. The historical record of an almost 8 percent unemployment rate was reached in 1998, and more than 1.6 million people lost their jobs.

The real wage also declined with less demand for labor and with a rise in the consumer price index. This somewhat improved the competitiveness of business firms since labor productivity increased with

Table 7.9 Unemployment rate (%)

	Unemployment rate		Unemployment rate
1997.1	2.6	1998. 1	4.5
2	3.2	2	5.9
3	3.4	3	6.5
4	2.8	4	6.7
5	2.5	5	6.9
6	2.3	6	7.0
7	2.2	7	7.6
8	2.1	8	7.4
9	2.2	9	7.3
10	2.1	10	7.1
11	2.6	11	7.3
12	3.1	12	7.9

Source: National Statistical Office, *Monthly Statistics of Korea*, May 1999, p. 100.

less employment and the real wage declined due to structural adjustment and inflation.

Growth rate of GDP in 1997 was 5.8 percent, while it declined to –5.3 percent in 1998. However, the growth rate is optimistically predicted around 6 percent for 1999.

Table 7.10 Real wage trend (in million won)

	1996	1997	1998	1998			
				1/4	2/4	3/4	4/4
Nominal wage	1.368	1.468	1.427	1.431	1.385	1.471	1.475
Nominal wage change (%)	11.9	7.0	2.5	0.1	–1.2	–8.1	–0.4
CPI (1995=100)	4.9	4.5	7.5	8.9	8.2	7.0	6.0
Real wage change (%)	6.7	2.4	–9.3	–8.1	–8.6	–14.2	–6.0

Source: Ministry of Labor, *Monthly Report on Labor Statistics Survey: 1998 issues.*

6.2 Changes in Saving Patterns

The national savings rate shows a slight decline from 33.4 percent in 1997 to 33.2 percent in 1998. The small decrease resulted from a negative growth rate of GDP and the further decline in consumption in 1998. While private sector savings rate showed a 2.5 percent increase due to a substantial reduction in consumption, the government savings rate decreased by 2.5 percent due to reduced fiscal revenue.

Because of the high interest rate policy prescribed by the IMF, the high income bracket enjoyed a higher positive savings rate, whereas those in the low income bracket suffered a negative growth of savings as shown in table 7.11.

Table 7.11 Savings, income and consumption changes in 1998 (%)

	Lowest 20%	Next lowest 20%	Middle 20%	Next highest 20%	Highest 20%	Average
Savings	–426.8	–16.1	–13.7	–9.4	13.0	–2.2
Disposable income	–19.3	–13.3	–11.8	–9.5	–1.2	–8.2
Consumption	–11.5	–12.5	–11.1	–9.5	–10.2	–10.7

6.3 Income Distribution and Poverty

Unemployment usually affected marginal workers most severely. The financial crisis, which led to a national economic crisis, also affected managerial class workers. However, the impact was greatest for those who belonged to the low income bracket and who were classified as unskilled marginal workers. The average savings of unemployed marginal workers could support their livelihood only up to approximately 11 months. This is perhaps the primary reason why the low income bracket suffered more in terms of savings loss.

The Gini coefficient, which was 0.2830 in 1997, increased to 0.3157 in 1998. This is a significant change in the trend of size-income distribution in Korea. The real situation could be even worse than it appears in statistics, since the increased interest income of the high income bracket in 1998 was not yet reported officially at the time the 1998 Gini coefficient was estimated.

According to a recent World Bank estimate, the urban poverty incidence in Korea increased from 8.6 percent in 1997 to 19.2 percent in 1998. The poverty threshold income used by the World Bank was estimated to be 4 US dollars per household per diem in the case of Korea.[6]

A local survey[7] also exhibited that due to the loss of jobs and income, 6 percent of those who felt they belonged to the middle class in 1997 felt that they no longer belonged to the middle class in 1998.

6.4 Migration Patterns

Annual inter-urban migration as captured by the National Statistics Office was substantially reduced primarily due to low mobility in job changes, whereas urban–rural migration increased due to the trend of unemployed urban workers to return to rural home towns. The impact of the crisis seemed to be less in the rural areas than the urban.

For the first time in the past 20 years, the Honam area, which is a dominantly agriculture-based region in Korea, experienced a net increase in immigration. This strongly indicates that urban–rural migration is a significant trend after the crisis.

7. CONCLUSION

Even though there are many ostensive symptoms of the recent financial crisis in Korea, the prime cause is undeniably corruption and unethical relations between business and politics. The state-dominated banking industry in Korea has always been under strong but misguided government control during the past half-century of its history. The Jaebol have always been the most favored clients of the banking system, and a portion of loans has always been used for bribes and political contributions. Therefore, the weakening and retardation of the banking industry along with the high reliance of Jaebol on bank advances are the natural consequence.

Strong but incompetent governments could not evaluate the real situation of the Korean economy, but consistently spent time and energy in publicizing what the regimes ostensibly accomplished in terms of expansions of various economic magnitudes. The internal debt of the Jaebols as well as the external debt of the nation has grown hand in hand and contributed decisively to the crisis.

As a result, the credibility of the nation plummeted and the people have to pay more interest to foreign creditors, low-skilled marginal workers are predominantly unemployed, and size-income distribution has worsened while the high income bracket enjoys more savings and becomes richer. The poverty incidence has increased and more homeless people are wandering, causing new social troubles, and the nation as a whole has fallen into deep disgrace. Korea has lost its economic sovereignty once again only 90 years after it lost its economic independence for the first time in its history.

NOTES

1. For example, refer to the recent conference, 'Economic Crisis in Asia' organized by the Korean Development Institute in March 1999.
2. The original law was enacted June 14, 1961 and the regulation concerning implementation of the law was promulgated July 12, 1961. Further procedural law and regulation were enacted October 26, 1961 and December 2, 1961, respectively. The final revision was made December 16, 1963.
3. The official letter to Mr Michael Camdessus, Managing Director, International Monetary Fund, Washington DC, dated 3 December 1997, written jointly by Kyung-shik Lee, Governor Bank of Korea and Chang-yuel Lim, Deputy Prime Minister and Minister of Finance and Economy.
4. Paragraph 4 of the Memorandum.
5. Paragraph 8 of the Memorandum.
6. *Chosun Ilbo* daily newspaper, 4 June 1999.
7. Hyundai Economic Research Institute survey, 1999.

REFERENCES

Ministry of Finance and Economy and the Bank of Korea (1997), *Korea: Memorandum on the Economic Program*.

Ministry of Labor, *Monthly Report on Labor Statistics Survey: 1998 issues*.

Ministry of Labor (1998), *Financial Statement Analysis for 1997*.

National Statistical Office (1999), *Monthly Statistics of Korea*, May.

Bank of Korea (1998), *Financial Statement Analysis for 1997*, Seoul.

Ministry of Labor (1997, 1998, 1999), *Monthly Bulletin*, various issues.

The Chosun Ilbo (1999), 4 June.

Index

Printed and bound by CPI Group (UK) Ltd, Croydon, CR0 4YY

23/04/2025

14660985-0002